How Technology Impacts Law

(And How Law Impacts Technology)

How Technology Impacts Law

(And How Law Impacts Technology)

Austin Mardon

Thomas Banks

Tim Chapman

Kelsey Godard

Mya E. George

Edited by Catherine Mardon

GM
★
PRESS

Cover Design by Clare Dalton
Typeset by Joshua Kramer

Print ISBN: 978-1-77369-818-2
eBook ISBN: 978-1-77369-819-9

Golden Meteorite Press
103 11919 82 St NW
Edmonton, AB T5B 2W3
www.goldenmeteoritepress.com

CONTENTS

CHAPTER 1 - INTRODUCTION

Throughout history, there have been multiple lenses used to gain specific insights into various subject matters. One of these lenses is known as a macro view. A macro view is a broad view of a subject over a large period of time, such as the bronze age. The bronze age ranges from 3300 BC to 1200 BC and affected different regions of the planet throughout it's 2100 year range (*Childs & Killick, 1993*). Transitioning from pre-modern to modern history, since the mid-20th century, society has found itself within the information age (*Manuel, 1996*).This transition is marked by a rapid shift from the reliance on traditional industry, which was first seen in the industrial revolution, to an economic system that relies on on information technology. Every aspect of life has been transformed by technology one way or another in the seven decades, an interesting example of this regards the use of cell phones. In the mid-'80s higher-end cars came equipped from the factory with car phones as a way to further the convenience of talking on the go.Now, take a second and think about the reliance that modern-day society places on smartphones. Think about the way that this reliance has changed over the last two decades from convenience to necessity. While technology has improved the everyday life of individuals, it has also had a marked impact on the functions of the justice system.The chapters below have been written from the perspective of four authors, covering different aspects of how specifically technology has impacted justice theory, law and the legal system.

Merriam-Webster defines technology as "the practical application of knowledge in a particular area," but when studying a subject as broad as technology, a more specific definition must be provided. For this book, our authors' definition of technology, while relatively inclusive, cannot account for all types of technological inventions that intersect with the legal system and is therefore non-exhaustive.

Digital technology: These include electronic devices that are involved in the generation, storing or processing of data. Their purposes include communication (email, phone calls, social media, online games, digital video conferencing, etc.), creating digital data (cameras or video cameras, audio recording devices, etc.), and storing or sorting data (electronic medical records, local drives for storing video footage, etc.), as well as the devices that host these digital activities (televisions, computers, cell phones, etc.). The internet, websites, and cloud storage are woven into our examinations of these kinds of technologies. These technologies consider both functions that would otherwise be impossible without them (such as recording video footage) and functions that are enhanced or streamlined with the help of technology (such as metal detectors).

Medical and biological technology: This definition of technology involves advancements in scientific processes to better understand, examine, and handle matters of biological sciences. This technology focuses on laboratories and methods of assessing the data gathered in laboratories, as well as establishing precedent within the courtroom. The efforts and progressions made concerning medical and biological technology within the justice system for example have resulted in the creation and maintenance of multiple DNA related databases. DNA has been crucial in solving decades-old cold cases in the United States and abroad as well as being used as an everyday resource for new investigations. It has also created several options to aid families looking to conceive as well as people looking to end their lives with dignity.

With an understanding of the definition of technology and the way it applies to this book, let's begin to learn about the ways in which technology has impacted the justice system. Technology has allowed legal researchers to transition from an analog or print based system, which got its start in the United States by John B. West, to a digital system which can be accessed either locally, state-wide, nationally or, in some cases, internationally. The transition from a paper system to a digital system struggled due to lack of network infrastructure, moving from organized notes to computer programs revolutionized the way legal research is performed. Despite the advancements made through the use of technology, outside factors such as a global health crisis can create a situation that forces society to lean even more on tech.

The COVID-19 pandemic began in March of 2020 with the world quickly shutting its borders. Masks became the norm while the world awaited vaccines. The justice system endured the same fate as the rest of the world, being forced to work from home or under strict medical policies if working around other people. Court systems in Canada had contingency plans in place prior to the pandemic but quickly found out that under pressure their pre-existing policies were not sufficient.Technological advancements in digital communication, such as Zoom and microsoft TEAMS, provided a logistic solution to the challenges faced by working from home, and quickly became common office spaces during the COVID-19 pandemic Despite the hardships introduced by the COVID-19 pandemic several critical cases were conducted such as Washington v. Top Auto Express Inc (*Florida Jury Delivers $411M Dollar Personal Injury Verdict by Zoom - Sawan & Sawan, n.d.*)

Everyone who uses technology on a daily basis has a basic understanding of how important technology can be for the justice system regarding communication and research but technology has created a new form of evidence that needs to be collected. In the early days of the internet, it was thought that what was put on the internet was completely anonymous but that is not true. One form of digital evidence is cell phone records. As technology has evolved, the advancements in cell phone technology have allowed law-enforcement agents to accurately pinpoint an individual's location An additional aspect of digital evidence is the monitoring of individuals online activity. If necessary, law enforcement agents are able to track visited webpages and any purchased products. Despite the ease of access to information that comes with the increase in technology use, law enforcement is still required to get court permission before gaining access to someone's cell phone records for example. In the same way that technology has created new types of evidence, it has allowed for the advancement in the collection, analysis and storage of traditional DNA evidence.

Just as digital evidence is used to track individual's online activities, DNA evidence can be used to track a persons physical whereabouts. The discovery of DNA fingerprinting in the 1980's revolutionized the way that DNA evidence was processed by investigators and the court system. DNA fingerprinting was first successfully used in a courtroom, i to prove that Andrew Sabarth actually was who he was claiming to be. Arguably the most important aspect of DNA technology was the creation of DNA databases that could be used as a central bank of knowledge. If unknown DNA is found at a crime scene it can be entered into a number of different databases, hosted by different countries, to seek a match. As technology has advanced the ways in which investigators can collect evidence or the ways in which that evidence can be used in court, it has also impacted the way private law functions.

The private legal system works similarly to the criminal justice system but handles the business of natural and corporate clients. Industries all over the globe has increased production and reduced costs by implementing automation into their production lines. An everyday example of this is self checkout machines, think of the last time you went to the grocery store did you get checked out by a cashier or did you simply do it yourself? This concept can also be applied to the private law sector with an estimated

23 per cent of a lawyers workload potentially becoming automated (*Automation, 2017*). Two main areas where automation is already being utilized within the private law sector are digital signatures and automated contracted reviews. These may seem simple and mundane but when you think about all the legal documents that require signatures and witnesses you can start to understand how critical it is to have these types of automations. The private law sector is not alone in taking advantage of the advancements in technology, governments have also joined in.

Technology allows governments to track the activities of their citizens. In early 2022, following the protests against the COVID-19 mandates in Ottawa, the Canadian government utilized the Emergencies Act to authorize the monitoring and freezing of private bank accounts in an attempt to quash the protests. Technological advancements in the private sector also bring forth benefits to the public sector. While within the consumer market facial recognition software is used as a handy way to unlock personal devices, western governments can utilize the technology as a tool for catching child sex abusers. Authoritarian governments, such as China, use facial recognition as a tool to track their citizens in large cities such as Beijing thanks to their extensive network of CCTV cameras. Technology is used by all aspects of the justice system from criminal courts to the private law sector as well as a tool to help rehabilitate those who are convicted of a crime and are sentenced to serve time in prison.

Technology has made it easier than ever to collect and produce evidence in a court of law. This improves the rate and quality of the number of convictions each year. It has been over twenty years since the devastating attacks that occurred on September 11, 2001 effectively changing the way the world conducts security checks for flights and more. In a post 9/11 world, airport security has seen a drastic change, the backbone of which is the metal detector. Over the past two decades, metal detectors have advanced to include body image scanners that allow for law enforcement agents to see if an individual is hiding objects within themselves. Another beneficial advancement that prisons have adopted is the use of CCTV and facial recognition software to efficiently track inmates. So far we have introduced ways in which advancements in technology have impacted the work completed by legal researchers, the court systems, governments and prisons. While technology offers immense benefits and opportunities, technology that is not directly regulated to the justice system can find itself dealing heavily with the justice system.

When growing up it is very common to imagine what life will be like in the future. Planning what one may study in school, what job, and how your family will start is a highlight of many life plans. It can be devastating for a young family to learn that they are not able to get pregnant for a number of medical reasons but with the advancements made in the field of assistive reproduction some of these families have been able to accomplish their goal of starting a family. Technologies such as in-vitro fertilization, artificial insemination and advancements in medication are all options available for families who are struggling to conceive. For same-sex couples as well as those who struggle to conceive technology now allows for effective cryptopresversation of sperm cells and eggs that have been donated. With these life changing advancements in reproductive technology, governments, such as Canada's, have introduced legislation that protects the well-being, privacy and ensures the ethical treatment of clients accessing these specialised services. The justice system has fundamentally aided in the creation of the legislation that allows for the safe delivery of the benefits that the advancements made to assistive reproductive technology but also the legislation regarding personhood, abortion and medical assistance in death.

If asked what the most controversial debate topic was, what would come to mind? One may say the current political situation, but arguably the most controversial topic surrounds abortion. The debate between pro-life and pro-choice has been ongoing for decades, with precedent-setting cases such as Roe V. Wade currently under review. In Canada, abortions became widely available in the 1960s before they became concrete with the Charter of Rights and Freedoms in 1982. The center of the abortion debate is the legal definition of personhood. To define when an individual can or cannot have an abortion, there must first be a legal definition of personhood. For example, in Canada, you are legally considered a person once you have been "completely proceeded" from your mother's body. At the other end of a person's life span, technology has given the medical field the ability to assist people in dying on their terms. Known in Canada as Medical Assistance in Dying (MAiD), MAiD gives doctors the option to aid an adult patient in making decisions to end their life through the use of regulated prescription drugs. Technology has created an environment where the individual citizen has access to life-altering medical treatments and the justice system is used to regulate the use of these advancements.

So far, we have scratched the surface of how technology has impacted several aspects of the justice system. From the conduction of legal research, the practicing of criminal and private law, and the development of medical legislation, the impact of technology is felt across the justice system. Each topic is designed, researched and written to provide a better understanding of the impacts associated with the introduction of technology into the justice system by providing simplified breakdowns of complicated terminology in combination with a discussion of relevant case studies. The topics discussed in this book are not the only ways that technology has impacted the justice system but serve as a starting point that covers several key areas of the topic. From the authors, we hope the chapters below provide an insightful look into the world of technology and the justice system.

REFERENCES

Automation Replaces About 23 Percent of Lawyer's Work. (2017, March 27). FindLaw. https://www.findlaw.com/legalblogs/technologist/automation-replaces-about-23-percent-of-lawyers-work/

Childs, S. Terry., & Killick, D.(1993). Indigenous African Metallurgy: *Nature and Culture. Annual Review of Anthropology, 22,* 317–337. doi:10.1146/annurev.anthro.22.1.317.

Manuel, C. (1996). *The information age : economy, society and culture.* Oxford.

Merriam-Webster. (n.d.). Technology. In *Merriam-Webster.com dictionary.* Retrieved June 2, 2022, from https://www.merriam-webster.com/dictionary/technology

Top Auto Express hit with historic $412M jury verdict in crash lawsuit. (n.d.). Retrieved June 9, 2022, from https://landline.media/top-auto-express-hit-with-historic-412m-jury-verdict-in-crash-lawsuit/

CHAPTER 2 - WHAT IS LEGAL RESEARCH?

"In a general sense, the legal profession cannot do without research and findings, because law is not static but dynamic subject to the changes of the society. Therefore, a lawyer must always engage in research to know the current law that will favour him."

- Umar Ishaq Katsinawa

An Introduction

Legal research has been defined in Black's law dictionary as "the finding and assembling of authorities that bear on a question of law", essentially meaning that it is the process by which one finds laws (in whatever form they may take, whether that be a statute, regulation, court order or court opinion/case law) to support one's argument in their specific case (*"Legal Research", n.d.; "The Basics of Legal Research in 3 Steps", n.d*). This type of research is carried out by a variety of persons involved in legal matters, from lawyers to law librarians and others in the legal field. The typical process of legal research involves first consulting primary sources of law in a specific jurisdiction, before looking at secondary authority (any relevant background information to the law provided by an unofficial source with no authority to set any laws, only to influence through writings such as law review articles) (*"Legal Research", n.d.; "Secondary Authority", n.d.*). Lastly, non-legal information can add further insight to the case at hand.

Timeline of Legal Research

Analog or Print-based Era

While the beginning of legal research is not exactly known, it has been traced back to the 1765 publication of Commentaries on the Laws of England by Sir William Blackstone, an English jurist (*"From Dusty Tomes to Artificial Intelligence: The History and Future of Legal Research", n.d.; "Sir William Blackstone", n.d.*). Advances in printing press technology and the ability to distribute printed scripts in the second half of the 19th century allowed for an increase in shared legal materials (*"From Dusty Tomes to Artificial Intelligence: The History and Future of Legal Research", n.d*). In 1843, the first lithographic rotary printing press was built by Richard March Hoe (*"A Brief History of Lithographic Printing", n.d.*). The mechanics of how the press worked, placing the image to be copied on a revolving metal cylinder rather than a flat surface, allowed printing to be accomplished much quicker. By the 1870s, hand-operated lithographic presses had become more common, and by the end of the century the offset lithographic printing press had also been invented. The first legal texts to be made and widely distributed were judicial decisions (*"From Dusty Tomes to Artificial Intelligence: The History and Future of Legal Research", n.d*). Following the accumulation of primary and secondary legal resources, systems of case organization and finding tools were also developed to manage the quantity of written information.

In the United States, modern legal research was heavily influenced by the work of John B. West, a lawbook salesman and founder of the West Publishing Company. Early on in his career, West produced common legal forms, reprinted hard-to-find legal documents, produced an index to Minnesota statutes, and had legal matters translated into Swedish for the use of many immigrant lawyers in the area (*Jarvis, 2010*). In collaboration with his brother Horatio, West wrote an eight page weekly publication which covered the Minnesota Supreme Court rulings dubbed "The Syllabi". The publication became so successful in its first 6 months that West Publishing Company expanded its coverage to other states (*"From Dusty Tomes to Artificial Intelligence: The History and Future of Legal Research", n.d.*). In 1879, West Publishing Company launched the National Reporter System (NRS), the first national reporting system for judicial decisions and rulings that provided lawyers with complete access to information to utilize case law in their legal research.

Digital Era

Before legal information came to be stored and accessed digitally, organizational systems and finding aids were used to manage physical information and documents. By the 1960s, there was some commercial success with making case law into a machine-readable format (*"From Dusty Tomes to Artificial Intelligence: The History and Future of Legal Research", n.d.*). A working group gathered by the Ohio Bar Association in 1964 explored possibilities of furthering computer capabilities in the legal field and they ultimately developed a system that was improved upon by Mead Data Central and released in 1973 under the name Lexus (which is now NexusLexus). The transition from paper to computer-based systems completely revolutionized legal research, making it possible to search large texts using keywords and access full copies of legal documents. West Publishing launched their own computer-system equivalent two years later, called Westlaw, and the two companies became the biggest competitors of the digital era. Widespread access to databases came later due to both logistical and technical constraints, including premature network infrastructure being unable to support the use of databases (thought they could support accessing full text files and conducting certain word searches), and the associated cost (*"From Dusty Tomes to Artificial Intelligence: The History and Future of Legal Research", n.d.*).

The Free Access to Law Movement

Since the advent of the internet and the resulting ability to share information to a large audience, there has been interest in making legal information easily accessible. In years previous to this, paper copies of legal research were largely inefficient tools and governments and private sector legal publishers could charge for individuals accessing their materials (*"Legal Information Institutes and the Free Access to Law Movement", n.d.*). The web enabled free public access because of its ability to serve as a low cost distribution system, as it did not place large costs on the publisher that they would need to recuperate in charging consumers.

In 1992, Thomas Bruce and Peter Martin founded an institution that was a first of its kind, the Legal Information Institute (LII) at Cornell Law School (*Meyers, 2020*). The LII has and continues to provide a vast amount of legal information primarily (but not exclusively) pertaining to American federal law to industry professionals, including by the persons working on this very book, and has been edited by students of the Cornell Law School. Other institutes going by the Legal Information Institute name with some additional identifiers based on association and location or other names, have been created with the goal of providing free access to legal information (*"Legal Information Institutes and the Free Access to Law Movement", n.d.*). These institutes provide information from multiple sources, not solely their own information, and collaborate through the Free Access to Law Movement.

The Australaisan Legal Information Institute (AusLII) is the result of a collaboration between the University of Technology Sydney and the University of New South Wales' faculties of law, starting in 1995 (*"Legal Information Institutes and the Free Access to Law Movement", n.d.; "Who We Are & What We Do", n.d.*). AusLII provides a variety of primary and secondary materials through its many databases, and it is important in this context for being the first LII to attempt to create a comprehensive national free access system to compete with commercial publishers. The institution has also helped in the creation of servers and databases for multiple other LIIs. The Canadian equivalent, the Canadian Legal Information Institute (CanLII) was created by the Federation of Law Societies of Canada in 2001 (*"Canadian Legal Information Institute (CanLII)* Acquires Lexum, a Montreal Technology Firm"*, n.d.). Like AuSLII, CANLII comprehensively covers Canada's federal system, and has since introduced a publication and discussion platform for case law (*CanLII Connects*), a commentary program and a guest writer program (*"More Commentary!", n.d.; "CanLII Connects", n.d.*).

The Free Access to Law Movement (FALM) is an association with more than 60 member organizations around the globe (*"Free Access to Law Movement (FALM)"*, n.d.). These organizations typically meet on an annual basis with the Law Via Internet conference, the first of which was held in Montreal in 2002 (*"Legal Information Institutes and the Free Access to Law Movement"*, n.d.). Membership in the FALM occurs via an invite from an existing member organization.

The Use of Artificial Intelligence in Research

Artificial intelligence (AI) describes computer systems which are able to perform functions and tasks that are considered to be in the realm of human ability (*Donahue, 2018*). These tasks can include recognizing speech, translating languages, and coming to a decision based on select data. A way in which AI is employed in the legal sector is through an application called machine learning. In this, a computer employs algorithms in software to learn and consequently adapt their functioning. AI can learn to recognize patterns and rules through a trial-and-error system or through training by humans providing specific data. In the legal sector, AI is currently employed in document review, analyzing contracts, predicting judicial outcomes, and legal research to save time and to do tasks more effectively than a single person could.

The IBM Watson software system, an AI system employed in many aspects of different businesses, can be used in the legal sector to find answers to questions that arise in legal research (*"Innovation and the Disruptive Impact of Technology on the Legal Sector", 2019.*). It can respond to questions in plain English and one company, Ross Intelligence, uses IBM Watson to find similar case law (*Donahue, 2018*). Using the IBM Watson analytics, Ross Intelligence's program for conducting legal research can read 40 million documents in only 15 seconds and the accuracy of such systems has been shown to outperform "expert lawyers" time and time again (*"Artificial Intelligence Beats Out Lawyers Again", 2018*). By integrating the use of AI systems into the legal research process, persons employed in the legal system can spend more time on other duties and tasks than spending long hours searching for data and can use more accurate analytics derived from AI.

REFERENCES

Artificial Intelligence Beats Out Lawyers Again | Law People. (2018). Retrieved June 7, 2022, from https://www.lawpeopleblog.com/2018/04/artificial-intelligence-beats-out-lawyers-again/

A brief history of lithographic printing | Better Printing. (n.d.). Retrieved June 7, 2022, from https://www.betterprinting.co.uk/blog/a-brief-history-of-lithographic-printing/

Canadian Legal Information Institute (CanLII) acquires Lexum, a Montreal technology firm | The CanLII Blog. (n.d.). Retrieved June 6, 2022, from https://blog.canlii.org/2018/02/28/canadian-legal information-institute-canlii-acquires-montreal-technology-firm-2/

CanLII Connects. (n.d.). Retrieved June 6, 2022, from https://canliiconnects.org/en/

Donahue, L. (2018). *A Primer on Using Artificial Intelligence in the Legal Profession - Harvard Journal of Law & Technology.* Retrieved June 7, 2022, from https://jolt.law.harvard.edu/digest/a-primer-on-using-artificial-intelligence-in-the-legal-profession

Free Access to Law Movement (FALM). (n.d.). Retrieved June 6, 2022, from http://www.fatlm.org/

From Dusty Tomes to Artificial Intelligence: The History and Future of Legal Research - Blue J Legal. (n.d.). Retrieved June 6, 2022, from https://www.bluej.com/ca/from-dusty-tomes-to-artificial-intelligence-the-history-and-future-of-legal-research/

Innovation and the disruptive impact of technology on the legal sector | Womble Bond Dickinson. (2019). Retrieved May 3, 2022, from https://www.womblebonddickinson.com/uk/insights/articles-and-briefings/innovation-and-disruptive-impact-technology-legal-sector

John B. West: Founder of the West Publishing Company on JSTOR. (n.d.). Retrieved June 6, 2022, from https://www-jstor-org.libaccess.lib.mcmaster.ca/stable/25664481

Legal Information Institutes and the Free Access to Law Movement - GlobaLex. (n.d.). Retrieved June 6, 2022, from https://www.nyulawglobal.org/globalex/Legal_Information_Institutes.html

Legal research | Wex | US Law | LII / Legal Information Institute. (n.d.). Retrieved June 6, 2022, from https://www.law.cornell.edu/wex/legal_research

Meyers, L. (2000). *CU Law institute web site has latest legal information, from Miranda to Elian | Cornell Chronicle.* Retrieved June 6, 2022, from https://news.cornell.edu/stories/2000/04/cu-law-institute-web-site-has-latest-legal-information

More commentary! | The CanLII Blog. (n.d.). Retrieved June 6, 2022, from https://blog.canlii.org/2018/04/20/more-commentary/

Secondary authority | Wex | US Law | LII / Legal Information Institute. (n.d.). Retrieved June 6, 2022, from https://www.law.cornell.edu/wex/secondary_authority

Sir William Blackstone | English jurist | Britannica. (n.d.). Retrieved June 6, 2022, from https://www.britannica.com/biography/William-Blackstone

The basics of legal research in 3 steps | Thomson Reuters. (n.d.). Retrieved June 6, 2022, from https://legal.thomsonreuters.com/en/insights/articles/basics-of-legal-research-steps-to-follow

Who We Are & What We Do. (n.d.). Retrieved June 6, 2022, from http://www.austlii.edu.au/about.html

CHAPTER 3 - THE IMPACT OF THE COVID-19 PANDEMIC ON THE PRACTICE OF LAW

"There is no precedent in living memory for the challenge that COVID-19 now poses to communities and world leaders"

- Ban Ki-Moon

The COVID-19 Pandemic

In December 2019, cases of a novel pneumonia-like illness were first reported in Wuhan, Hubei Province, China (*Janiaud et al., 2020*). By January 30th, 2020, coronavirus disease 2019 (COVID-19) was declared a public health emergency by the World Health Organization (WHO), being upgraded to the term pandemic shortly after on March 11th. In response to public health concerns over the pandemic, countries around the world quickly adopted measures such as quarantine for the sick or travellers, social distancing, and closures of populated institutions such as schools and "non-essential" workplaces to limit virus transmission. While immediate research efforts focused on the virus itself, the efficacy of therapeutics in treating persons with severe COVID-19, and looking at developing vaccine technologies for protection against the virus, at this point in the pandemic many are looking at the long-term impacts that the pandemic has had on the functioning of various systems in society from the hit that certain businesses took to how education has been shaped in online formats (*Ciotti et al., 2020*). The impact of the pandemic on the legal sector in Canada and other nations is an interesting and concerning area of research, with pandemic-related delays worsening an already slow court-based system and exacerbating the digital divide for some persons wishing to exercise their legal rights.

The Transition to Remote Practice

As is the responsibility of all public institutions and organizations, the Canadian courts had business contingency plans in place before the start of the COVID-19 outbreak (*Preston, 2021*). However, these plans were not comprehensive enough and banked on in-person access to the Courts being suspended for a maximum of three weeks in any national emergency. Despite concerns coming from the scientific community for some time about the likelihood of a pandemic, governmental pandemic plans never extended into developing plans for the maintenance of the justice system.

The United States is home to the National Association for Court Management (NACM), which was one of the first organizations to take action and develop a handbook for disaster plans and preparedness (4). This included four key steps. First, a risk assessment must be completed for each court to evaluate potential impacts of a specific disaster on the court, its functioning, and its members (*Preston, 2021*). Next, the primary functions and objectives of the court must be identified and prioritized in sustaining the court until the end of the disaster. Third, if possible, the court must secure another location in which to conduct business. Finally, leaders in the court and its administration must ensure that all personnel working in the court setting are kept aware of the disaster plans and know which role they must fulfill in the event of such an emergency. While one can recognize some pieces in this plan that could extend to a pandemic, it was clearly not designed with such an event in mind, but rather something like a natural disaster or event that would only temporarily immobilize judicial action.

The Attorney General of Ontario reflected aspects of the NACM disaster handbook in the creation of its business contingency plan (*Preston, 2021*). In addition, many provinces (including Alberta, Manitoba, Ontario, Quebec, New Brunswick, and Newfoundland and Labrador) had published guides directing contingency plans in the event of an influenza pandemic–excluding directions for court administration in the strict planning for public health measures. The Provincial Court of Alberta released a pandemic plan in response to COVID-19 and for future use in situations where the Provincial Court must restrict its operations. This plan was published with seven specific goals in mind: to maintain and preserve the rule of law, protect the health and wellbeing of court staff and the public, identify and maintain the court's essential functions, facilitate decision-making processes and develop a protocol for communications, minimize disruptions to the Court and its docket, and resume regular activity when it is safe to do so (*Preston, 2021*). While the Ontario Court of Justice implemented a protocol in May 2020 to halt criminal trials and preliminary inquiries, extend some filing deadlines, and deal with other matters such as the use of electronic signatures, it was not a comprehensive pandemic plan. At the same time, the Ontario Court of Justice also issued a call for "reasonable" steps to be taken to allow bail hearings to proceed without persons being taken into custody. Bail hearings during the height of the COVID-19 pandemic were largely conducted by audio and video conferences. The Ontario Court of Justice protocol stipulated that if private conversations are difficult to be had in a remote setting, then accommodations should be provided to correct the issue.

Even with aspects of disaster preparedness and quickly developed pandemic plans, governments and judicial courts did not prepare for the role that technology would play in filling service gaps and facilitating the remote practice of law. Courts have required integrated and secure systems, and any court staff working remotely needed to be connected virtually (*Preston, 2021*). With the switch to remote access, systems must also be accessible from prisons which was likely an additional hurdle for the institutions already facing extreme challenges in managing inmates under pandemic guidelines for public health and safety. Even if courts were in a privileged position to have had conferencing video conferencing tools before the start of the pandemic, the forced closure of public buildings prevented their use until later in the pandemic with a return to limited in-person activities. Bridging the digital divide and general issues in accessing technology was a huge challenge at the height of the pandemic, with the need to outfit staff working from home rather than in usual court or office spaces, the need to procure devices and a way to distribute them in a timely manner, sufficient training and use of new devices, and the necessary bandwidth for devices to connect properly and serve their intended function without significant hiccups. The learning curve in adapting to the use of technology in court settings has been commonly reported as a difficulty experienced by staff early on in the pandemic (*Preston, 2021*). Furthermore, the steep reliance on technology in the judicial system, as with other areas of life during the pandemic, has exacerbated socioeconomic divisions between persons and will continue to have an impact on the functioning of the courts in years to come.

The Use of Zoom Video Conferencing

Zoom Meetings, the video communications software program developed by Zoom Video Communications, was founded in 2011 with its beta version being launched in late summer of 2012 (*Kent, n.d.*). An improved iteration was launched in 2013 but it was not until the COVID-19 outbreak that Zoom truly catapulted in popularity, with 300 million daily meeting participants by April 2020. Although the market is home to many alternative video conferencing services such as Skype and Webex, Zoom had the advantage by quickly becoming the go-to option for online meetings early in the pandemic and users became accustomed to its features and how to use it (*Villasenor, 2020*). Many companies and universities signed with Zoom to be their primary provider for hosting online meetings, events, and classes, further solidifying the choice of many people to primarily use Zoom over other platforms.

However, Zoom is not without serious concerns and flaws in security and privacy. In March 2020, the company faced backlash over its self-proclaimed support of end-to-end encryption for video calls (*Villasenor, 2020*). End-to-end encryption means that it is converted into a code on the caller's end and is only decrypted once it reaches the other person's device (*Innes, 2022*). However, Zoom was using transport encryption at the time–allowing the company to access content of the video and audio calls. Zoom corrected its use of end-to-end encryption in the fall of 2020, protecting users' data with a conference encryption key that developers did not have access to, preventing the company from gaining access to video and audio content (*Aver, 2021*).

Another concern with the use of Zoom was the potential for interruptions, such as interference from so-called Zoom-bombers who were known to join calls and cause disruptions with profanity and in some cases, pornography and graphic images (*Sebenius and Mehrotra, 2020*). The Federal Bureau of Investigation released a public warning about "Zoom bombing" on March 30th, 2020, and urged users to avoid sharing links or meeting IDs online and from making Zoom meetings publicly available. To prevent unwanted guests in Zoom meetings, the platform has options such as requiring a password to enter the meeting, having the meeting organizer operate a waiting room and select persons to join the call, and a lock meeting feature to prevent anyone else from joining, even if they have the meeting ID and password (*Aver, 2021*).

The Impact of Remote Work in the Judicial System

The regular mishaps of using Zoom and other online conferencing software became part of popular culture jokes, but in the setting of a virtual courtroom there can be serious complications from small mistakes. Unmuted microphones at the wrong time can cause serious disruptions and can affect the ability of Court transcriptionists to do their job recording what was said (*Hasham, 2021*). Additionally, the easy mistake of being unmuted unintentionally has led to some issues in various courts when people have revealed information unintentionally (*Burkell et al., 2021*). Additionally, virtual Courts held over Zoom remain subject to the risk of Zoom bombers like any other meeting on the platform. A virtual Brampton Court was interrupted in February, 2021, by persons who posted both pornographic images and swastikas, which local police ended up getting involved in after the incident had occured (*Duhatschek, 2021*). Furthermore, with individuals being able to attend Court sessions from anywhere with internet access there have been abuses of this allowance that threaten the "smooth functioning and solemnity of the Court" (*Burkell et al., 2021*).

Another significant concern with the reliance on video conferencing centers on the inability of platforms like Zoom to be on the same level as face-to-face communication. Human connection is an important aspect of court proceedings, with decisions having to be made based on understanding of a person's intentions and/or innocence. Translating the court environment online does not allow for the same extent of human connection and the reading of facial expressions and emotions. After all, when one joins a Zoom meeting they are likely only showing their face and so a lot of non-verbal body expressions are out-of-frame and consequently missed. Empathy is less likely to be had, and some sources have observed trends in judges being more lenient to defendants and offering lower bail when seeing them face-to-face (*Scigliano, 2021*). Furthermore, long hours spent listening to testimonies online can contribute to so-called "Zoom fatigue" for participants and especially jurors who are new to court settings (*Jingnan, 2022*). When spending long hours sitting and staring at a screen, it can become challenging for anyone to focus on what is happening and be able to critically consider what is being said. While it may seem more accessible to have jurors join in online, as taking significant time off work and transportation are two of the largest barriers for participation, the experience remains radically different.

Critical Case Law to Come Out of Remote Practice

The largest compensatory reward to date was awarded following a completely virtual trial in the case of Washington v. Top Auto Express Inc. (*"Florida Jury Delivers $411M Dollar Personal Injury Verdict by Zoom", n.d.*). Former American Army Sergeant Duane Washington faced partial paralysis and extreme injuries after his involvement in a 45 car pile up on a major Florida highway in July 2018 after an 18-wheel semi truck lost control in bad weather (which has since also been associated with the truck speeding). Washington, who had been riding a motorcycle at the time, swerved to avoid the out-of-control semi and hit a stopped vehicle that did not have emergency lights on. After spending six months in hospital with critical injuries, Washington was left with chronic pain and metal rods throughout his body. Three children were also plaintiffs in the case, with one count of loss of cortium being filed for each child in connection to the loss of their father in the accident (*Fisher, 2020*). The Zoom trial was shorter than expected due to a lack of cooperation of the defendant, Top Auto Express Inc., with discovery requests although they did reject an early offered settlement totaling $1 million dollars (*"Florida Jury Delivers $411M Dollar Personal Injury Verdict by Zoom", n.d.; Fisher, 2020*). Lawyers spent their limited time speaking in the case on the damages caused during the accident and in the time afterwards. In October 2020 the jury favoured Mr. Washington, delivering a $411 million dollar personal injury verdict.

During 2020, in addition to the global pandemic, highly publicized racially-motivated attacks and injustices made headlines alongside widespread frustration and public protest both in the United States and internationally. The inclusion of the cases of the murders of George Floyd, Breonna Taylor, and many others in this section is relevant because of how the COVID-19 pandemic shaped the social environment of protests and consequential criminal trials. Increasing concerns and frustrations with financial hardships and incidences of racial discrimination and the disproportionate effect of the pandemic on racialized communities during the pandemic motivated many to join in protests (*"COVID-19 and the Black Lives Matter Movement: Managing Academic Realities", 2020*). Changes in working environments also enabled many to participate in protests when they likely would not have been able to otherwise. George Floyd was handcuffed by policemen in Minneapolis after a shop owner accused him of using a counterfeit bill, and after resisting arrest, police officer Derek Chauvin pinned him face down to the ground with his knee pressed against his neck. On videos that circulated around the internet, Floyd repeatedly said that he could not breathe, but the officers did not change how they were restraining him (*Hill et al., 2020*). Floyd died shortly thereafter in hospital. Social media platforms and posts shared on them helped to mobilize protestors and led more to see what had happened to George Floyd (*Ortutay and Seitz, 2020*). Apps with specialized features relating to mass communication and navigating encounters with police were also commonly used during these protests. An example of this is the app Citizen which allows users to post videos of protests and crime scenes. The trial, referred to as the state of Minnesota v. Derek Michael Chauvin, started at the end of March 2021 (*"COVID-19 and the Black Lives Matter Movement: Managing Academic Realities", 2020*). It was held in-person despite the pandemic and was the first criminal case in the state to be televised and broadcast live. A 12-person jury viewed videos and heard from 45 witnesses, but not from Chauvin himself. He chose to not testify which he had a right to do under the 5th Amendment. Chauvin was ultimately charged with second and third degree murder and manslaughter; he was the first white police officer in the state to be charged with the murder of a Black man.

Breonna Taylor was fatally shot in March 2020 after police entered her apartment uninvited as part of searching related to a suspected drug dealing operation (*Richer, 2020*). Taylor's boyfriend began firing in response to the allegedly unannounced forced entry, fearing that they were being robbed or targeted by someone. Multiple officers fired into the apartment, with some bullets entering neighbouring apartment units. The only person charged related to the incident was the police officer Brett Hankison and his charges were wanton endangerment for the bullets that strayed into a next-door apartment where a family was sleeping (*Guariglia, 2022*). Hankison was fired from policing following internal investigations but he was later acquitted of any charges. The city of Louisville has paid a $12 million settlement to the family of Breonna Taylor for her wrongful death, but members of the public have remained angry over the lack of justice received for her death.

COVID-19 and the Criminal Justice System

With social distancing measures and stay-at-home orders in place across Canadian provinces in the early months of the pandemic, concerns arose over the inability to distance individuals serving time in provincial jails and federal prisons. The distinction between the two types of correctional facilities is that persons with sentences under 2 years are placed in jails while for any longer and more serious offenses persons serve the time in a federal prison (*Correctional Service Canada, n.d.*).

However, conditions in both jails and prisons pre-pandemic did not offer much separation between individuals and poor ventilation systems (*Rodriguez, 2021.*). Individuals in both types of institution can be housed in cells with two or three beds in a small area, making distancing impossible, and visitations with family and loved ones allowed pre-COVID were largely halted to mitigate opportunities for the virus to spread from visiting persons to staff and prisoners. On the other hand, subjecting people to solitary conditions in prison settings as a way to uphold social distancing has been called tortuous in reports, subjecting an already vulnerable population to extreme isolation (*Sprott et al., 2021*).

Many members of the public called for the release of non-violent prisoners facing short sentences to be released early for the sake of their safety and others working and living in correctional facilities. The public safety minister during the start of the pandemic, Bill Blair, asked the heads of the prison system and parole board to seriously consider releasing some individuals early to limit the negative consequences (*Harris, 2020*). Between February and April 2020, approximately 6,000 inmates were leased from custody–though most came from provincial jails (experiencing a population drop of 25% overall) rather than federal prisons (which had a loss of 1% overall in the same time frame) (*Cousins, 2020*). While cases in prisons were not extremely high early on in the pandemic, there were large outbreaks at some institutions including the Mission Institution in British Columbia and the Multi-level Federal Training Centre in Quebec (*Ricciardelli and Buceris, 2020*).

COVID-19 Vaccine Technologies and Mandates

Vaccine technology has the potential to decrease rates and severity of illness, and consequently to lessen the economic burden of such illnesses. When it came to the SARS-CoV-19 pandemic, the largest event of its kind to affect modern society, the advent of vaccines were a key strategy in mitigating the health and social effects of the virus. Vaccination uptake, which is critical for the technology to provide adequate protection to a population, has been affected by many factors from personal beliefs to a distrust in science and government. Governmental response and forced measures in the name of public health is a critical consideration of the impact of the COVID-19 pandemic on legal action, and in light of medical advancements, includes a unique consideration of what technology is.

In order to understand the strategy behind the frontrunner vaccines which were first approved and distributed, one needs to have a basic understanding of the structure of the virus. This coronavirus is comprised of several key proteins: the S or spike protein, the membrane protein, an envelope protein, and the nucleocapsid protein (*Yan et al., 2021*). The virus is able to enter human cells through a receptor binding domain on the S protein and so the most successful vaccines have targeted this protein to prevent viral entry into host cells, thereby preventing infection. The vaccines developed by both Pfizer/BioNTech (now marketed under the name Comirnaty) and Moderna (marketed under the name Spikevax) utilized mRNA-based vaccine technology to achieve high efficacy against the virus. The altered mRNA provided in the vaccine essentially provides host cells with instructions for producing the viral S protein, enabling one's immune system to recognize the pathogen and develop a response against viral particles (*Verbeke et al., 2021*). Other vaccine candidates developed by AstraZeneca (called Vaxzevria) and Janssen or Johnson and Johnson (Ad26.COV2.S) used a vector-based delivery system where material from the virus were placed inside a modified form of another vaccine, in this case from an adenovirus, that does not cause illness (*Francis et al., 2022*).

Health Canada authorized the Pfizer-BioNTech as the first COVID-19 vaccine to be used in Canada on December 9th, 2020 (*"Health Canada Authorizes First COVID-19 Vaccine"*, *n.d.*). This authorization also required that the vaccine manufacturer continue providing Health Canada with information on the safety and efficacy of its doses. Moderna's vaccine was authorized later on December 23rd, while AstraZeneca and Janssen's vector vaccines were not approved until February and March of 2021 (*"Drug and Vaccine Authorizations for COVID-19: Applications Received"*, *n.d.*). The two mRNA vaccines remain the most widely administered COVID-19 vaccines in Canada, and has since approved the use of the Pfizer-BioNTech Comirnatry vaccine in children as young as five years old and the Moderna Spikevax vaccine for children age six and older (*"Vaccines for Children: COVID-19"*, *n.d.*).

Canada first began distributing vaccines to essential healthcare workers and long-term care and assisted living patients in December, 2020 (*Tang et al., 2021*). Vaccines were prioritized for persons with critical risk factors for having severe COVID-19 such as advanced age and comorbidities, while some provinces further focussed efforts on persons with such conditions living in areas with high numbers of cases. As with healthcare generally, provinces and territorial governments are responsible for determining vaccination eligibility and managing distribution instead of the federal government–a fact that was credited as limiting the speed and scope of initial vaccination efforts (*Felter, 2021*). Alberta gave its first doses of the Pfizer-BioNTech vaccine to intensive care unit (ICU) staff, respiratory therapists, and staff in long-term care homes but the extreme temperature storage meant doses could only be stored and used at specific Alberta Health Services sites to begin with (*"Here's the COVID-19 Vaccine Rollout Plan, Province by Province"*, *2020*). Vaccines were then made available to seniors (over the age of 75), long term care and assisted living staff and residents, and First Nations persons living on reserve over the age of 65. Ontario also allocated its first vaccines to healthcare workers in long-term care homes and other high risk settings. A reserve of the first doses were set aside for healthcare workers to be fully inoculated, but the province followed similar practices to Alberta in giving vaccines to First Nations persons, long-term care residents, and recipients of some types of home care (*Tsekouras, 2020*). Saskatchewan's first doses were designated for staff working directly (*"Here's the COVID-19 Vaccine Rollout Plan, Province by Province", 2020*). The province's first phase also specifically targeted vaccine uptake in remote northern communities in addition to populations already mentioned in the Alberta and Ontario plans, in an effort to prevent devastation in remote areas where people are farther away from emergency care. British Columbia followed similar priority trends as well, but including underhoused individuals and persons in remote communities in the first phase of vaccine delivery. The province then chose to provide vaccines specifically to "front-line workers" including grocery store workers, school staff and teachers, and people working in close quarters in food processing plants.

Canada, despite having access to a large vaccine supply, had difficulty in ensuring widespread vaccination coverage across all the provinces in territories. Once the initial phases were carried out, many provincial governments looked to enforce vaccination mandates to encourage persons who could receive the vaccine to do so. While there were many strong public reactions to restrictions and proposed enforcements, vaccine passports are not a new phenomenon. Public elementary schools have required children to receive necessary vaccinations, including Ontario requiring school children to receive 9 different inoculations, although parents have always had the opportunity to have their child exempted from the mandate for conscience, religious, or medical reasons (*Walkinshaw, 2011*). Ultimately, provinces and territories are in control of their policies and requirements, and although people are entitled to bodily autonomy and medical decision-making control under the Canadian Charter of Rights and Freedoms, Charter rights can be limited in cases of the security of the person when the government has a significant reason (such as a public health concern as serious as the COVID-19 pandemic) (*Dawson, 2022*).

The way in which vaccine restrictions were most readily applied across the country was by limiting access to non-essential, private services such as cafes and restaurants, and gyms. Alberta's provincial vaccine mandate was made optional for businesses, having places of business check for vaccine status or for a negative COVID test of customers before their entry or be subject to reduced capacity limits (*Bennett, 2021*). The province also resorted to offering prepaid debit cards to hesitant persons who got their vaccine after vaccine uptake proved to be an issue, spending around $15 million in direct compensation to vaccine hesitant Albertans. The city of Calgary made it mandatory for businesses to be a part of the provincial restrictions exemption program while it was in effect (*MacVicar, 2022*). Alberta's vaccine passport requirement was ended in February, 2022, after it was seen to improve vaccination rates and was deemed to be no longer necessary (*Heidenreich, 2022*). Public space capacity limits and indoor masking were lifted the following month. The Government of Ontario introduced its vaccine passport system in September 2021, requiring persons to show their vaccine record and valid photo identification to eat at restaurants or go to the gym (*"Ontario Vaccine Bookings up after Passport Announcement, Province Sees 865 New COVID-19 Cases", 2021*). Bookings of vaccination appointments were said to "double" by the day after the passport system was announced in the province. Ontario ultimately ended its vaccine passport shortly after Alberta on March 1st, 2022, citing a decline in hospitalizations as the primary justification for changes, but the province retained its indoor masking mandate (*Jabakhanji, 2022*).

The "Freedom" Trucker Convoy and Protests in Ottawa

A series of protests and border crossing blockades in response to COVID-19 restrictions and vaccine mandates were held in early 2022, by persons who described their movement as a "freedom" convoy. Hundreds of participants mobilized and drove in different groups together across Canada to reach the capital city of Ottawa. Protestors rallied together at Parliament Hill and occupied the core downtown area, and were known to create a lot of noise using vehicle horns and other devices. Ontario premier, Doug Ford, declared a state of emergency in the province to introduce legal sanctions on the blockages of key highways and trade routes. Over the first weekend of the Ottawa protests, seven people were arrested (five of which were charged with mischief) and a second two people were charged with driving while prohibited and mischief related to property business, respectively (*Lord, 2022*). All in all, there were over 60 investigations against protestors initially and more than 450 tickets issued (excluding additional fines for excessive noises). A 9.8 million class-action lawsuit was also raised against core organizers of the convoy and protests (*McGregor and Aiello, 2022*). The lawsuit sought $4.8 million for private nuisance and an additional $5 million in punitive damages as the actions of the convoy protestors were said to cause mental distress and torment to persons living in downtown Ottawa. A key argument on their side is that the noise made by semi trucks, in a range of 100 to 150 decibels is a dangerous sound level that can cause hearing damage and the truck horns are consequently not meant to be sounded for longer than a few seconds. A 21 year old public servant affected by the disruptions and noise, Zexi Li, was named as the lead plaintiff and Chris Barber, Benjamin Ditcher, Tamara Lich, and Patrick King were named as the key organizers. The Member of Provincial Parliament (MPP) for the Lanark–Frontenac–Kingston riding, Randy Hillier, was criminally charged for his participation in the protest convoy in late March 2022

(*Woods, 2022*). Hillier has faced 9 criminal charges, and was specifically charged for assaulting a police officer. Though he has been released from custody, Hillier was ordered to not post online about the convoy or mask mandate and had a $35,000 bond.

Invoking the Emergencies Act

The Emergencies Act was invoked for the first time since it was passed in 1988 on February 14th, 2022 to end the convoy-related disruptions and border blockades (*"Prime Minister Announces Public Order Emergency Commission Following the Invocation of the Emergencies Act", 2022*). The declaration was made by the Minister of Justice and Attorney General of Canada, David Lametti, with the support of both the Minister of Public Safety (Marco E.L. Mendicino) and the Minister of Emergency Preparedness (Bill Blair). The emergency declaration was then revoked by February 23rd and the Prime Minister established a Public Order Emergency Commission to evaluate this invocation of the Emergencies Act. Although the official reports from this commission will not be delivered until February 2023, there has been significant coverage of the inquiry in various news publications. Conservative politicians have called for the resignation of Mendicino from his role as the Public Safety Minister and have questioned Trudeau's response to questions asked in the initial inquiries of the commission (MacCharles, 2022). The outcome of this commission and how the Emergency Act is or is not used in the future to combat complicated governmental situations remains to be seen, but for now it remains highly controversial.

REFERENCES

Aver, H. (2021). *How end-to-end encryption works in Zoom | Kaspersky official blog.* Retrieved June 8, 2022, from https://www.kaspersky.com/blog/rsa2021-zoom-end-to-end-encryption/40562/

Bennet, D. (2021). *Premier Kenney says Alberta will keep COVID-19 vaccine passport into at least early 2022 | Globalnews.ca.* Retrieved June 14, 2022, from https://globalnews.ca/news/8261613/kenney-alberta-health-covid-19-vaccine-passport-2022/

Burkell, J., Eades, D., Lee, J., and Troyer, S. (2021). *Western News - Expert insights: The perils of Zoom courts.* Retrieved June 8, 2022, from https://news.westernu.ca/2021/04/expert-insights-the-perils-of-zoom-courts/

Ciotti, M., Ciccozzi, M., Terrinoni, A., Jiang, W.-C., Wang, C.-B., & Bernardini, S. (2020). *The COVID-19 pandemic. Critical Reviews in Clinical Laboratory Sciences, 57*(6), 365–388. https://doi.org/10.1080/10408363.2020.1783198

Correctional Service Canada. (n.d.). Retrieved June 7, 2022, from https://www.csc-scc.gc.ca/index-en.shtml

Cousins, B. (2020). *Provincial jails released thousands of inmates amid calls to slow the spread of COVID-19 | CTV News.* Retrieved June 8, 2022, from https://www.ctvnews.ca/canada/provincial-jails-released-thousands-of-inmates-amid-calls-to-slow-the-spread-of-covid-19-1.5061829?cache=gszlebujvvuylyge%3FclipId%3D68597%3FautoPlay%3Dtrue%3FcontactForm%3Dtrue

COVID-19 and the Black Lives Matter Movement: Managing Academic Realities. (2020). Retrieved June 10, 2022, from https://asm.org/Articles/2020/July/COVID-19-and-the-Black-Lives-Matter-Movement-Manag

Dawson, T. (2022). *Is mandatory COVID vaccination legal? Here's what Canada's charter says | National Post.* Retrieved June 14, 2022, from https://nationalpost.com/news/canada/is-mandatory-covid-19-vaccination-constitutional

Drug and vaccine authorizations for COVID-19: Applications received - Canada.ca. (n.d.). Retrieved June 17, 2022, from https://www.canada.ca/en/health-canada/services/drugs-health-products/covid19-industry/drugs-vaccines-treatments/authorization/applications.html

Duhastchuk, P. (2021). *Zoom bombers interrupt virtual court hearing with porn, swastikas | CBC News.* Retrieved June 8, 2022, from https://www.cbc.ca/news/canada/kitchener-waterloo/wrps-zoom-court-hearing-1.5924875

Felter, C. (2021). *What to Know About the Global COVID-19 Vaccine Rollout So Far on JSTOR.* (n.d.). Retrieved June 14, 2022, from https://www.jstor.org/stable/resrep29866

Florida Jury Delivers $411M Dollar Personal Injury Verdict by Zoom - Sawan & Sawan. (n.d.). Retrieved June 9, 2022, from https://sawanandsawan.com/florida-jury-411-million-dollar-injury-verdict-zoom/

Francis, A. I., Ghany, S., Gilkes, T., & Umakanthan, S. (2022). *Review of COVID-19 vaccine subtypes, efficacy and geographical distributions. Postgraduate Medical Journal, 98*(1159), 389–394. https://doi.org/10.1136/postgradmedj-2021-140654

Guariglia, M. (2022). *Police in Breonna Taylor death acquitted in telling verdicts.* Retrieved June 10, 2022, from https://www.nbcnews.com/think/opinion/police-breonna-taylor-death-acquitted-telling-verdicts-ncna1291105

Harris, K. (2020). *Bill Blair asks prison, parole heads to consider releasing some inmates to stop spread of COVID-19 | CBC News.* Retrieved June 8, 2022, from https://www.cbc.ca/news/politics/prison-covid19-csc-release-1.5516065

Hasham, A. (2021). *Ontario's court transcriptionists are struggling with 'horrible' audio quality at Zoom hearings | The Star.* Retrieved June 8, 2022, from https://www.thestar.com/news/gta/2021/02/04/ontarios-court-transcriptionists-struggle-to-deal-with-horrible-audio-quality-at-zoom-hearings.html

Health Canada authorizes first COVID-19 vaccine - Canada.ca. (n.d.). Retrieved June 17, 2022, from https://www.canada.ca/en/health-canada/news/2020/12/health-canada-authorizes-first-covid-19-vaccine0.html

Heinenreich, P. (2022). *COVID-19: Kenney announces Alberta vaccine passport program ending at midnight | Globalnews.ca.* Retrieved June 14, 2022, from https://globalnews.ca/news/8603220/alberta-covid-19-restrictions-lifted-update-february-8/

Here's the COVID-19 vaccine rollout plan, province by province | CBC News. (2020). Retrieved June 14, 2022, from https://www.cbc.ca/news/canada/covid19-vaccine-rollout-plans-canada-1.5836262

Hill, E., Tiefenthaler, A., Triebert, C., Jordan, D.,, Willis, H., and Stein, R. (2020). *How George Floyd Was Killed in Police Custody - The New York Times.* Retrieved June 10, 2022, from https://www.nytimes.com/2020/05/31/us/george-floyd-investigation.html

Innes, M. (2022). *What Are the Safest Video Calling Apps in 2022?* Retrieved June 8, 2022, from https://securitygladiators.com/security/software/video-calling/

Jabakhanji, S. (2022). *Ontario to remove vaccine passport system on March 1, masking requirements to remain in place | CBC News.* Retrieved June 15, 2022, from https://www.cbc.ca/news/canada/toronto/ontario-doug-ford-announcement-covid19-february-14-1.6350761

Jangnan, H. (2022). *Remote jury trials have pros and cons and an uncertain future post-pandemic: NPR.* Retrieved June 9, 2022, from https://www.npr.org/2022/03/18/1086711379/as-jury-trials-move-online-courts-see-pros-and-cons

Janiaud, P., Axfors, C., Van't Hooft, J., Saccilotto, R., Agarwal, A., Appenzeller-Herzog, C., Contopoulos-Ioannidis, D. G., Danchev, V., Dirnagl, U., Ewald, H., Gartlehner, G., Goodman, S. N., Haber, N. A., Ioannidis, A. D., Ioannidis, J. P. A., Lythgoe, M. P., Ma, W., Macleod, M., Malički, M., Hemkens, L. G. (2020). *The worldwide clinical trial research response to the COVID-19 pandemic - the first 100 days. F1000 Research, 9,* 1193. https://doi.org/10.12688/f1000research.26707.2

Kent, D. (n.d.) The History Of Eric Yuan's Zoom. Retrieved June 8, 2022, from https://dispatch.m.io/eric-yuan-zoom/

Lord, C. (2022). *Ottawa police, politicians seek swift end to trucker convoy | Globalnews.ca.* Retrieved June 16, 2022, from https://globalnews.ca/news/8599843/ottawa-class-action-lawsuit-court-residents-protesters/

MacCharles, T. (2022). *Justin Trudeau appears to contradict top minister | The Star.* Retrieved June 17, 2022, from https://www.thestar.com/politics/federal/2022/06/15/justin-trudeau-appears-to-contradict-top-minister-over-why-the-emergencies-act-was-used.html

MacVicar, A. (2022). *COVID-19: City of Calgary updates vaccine passport bylaw, including age and ID requirements - Calgary | Globalnews.ca.* Retrieved June 14, 2022, from https://globalnews.ca/news/8503078/calgary-covid-vaccine-passport-bylaw-changes/

McGregor, G. and Aiello, R. (2022). *Trucker convoy: Organizers facing lawsuit | CTV News.* Retrieved June 15, 2022, from https://www.ctvnews.ca/politics/lawsuit-filed-against-convoy-organizers-seeking-damages-on-behalf-of-downtown-ottawa-residents-1.5768731

National Association for Court Management – Strengthening Court Professionals. (n.d.). Retrieved June 8, 2022, from https://nacmnet.org/

Ontario vaccine bookings up after passport announcement, province sees 865 new COVID-19 cases | CBC News. (2021). Retrieved June 15, 2022, from https://www.cbc.ca/news/canada/toronto/covid-19-ontario-september-2-2021-update-1.6162245

Orutay, B., and Seitz, A. (2020). *How technology is helping George Floyd protesters organize, record police violence - National | Globalnews.ca.* Retrieved June 17, 2022, from https://globalnews.ca/news/7035160/technology-george-floyd-protesters/

Preston, B. (2021). *The Court System in a Time of Crisis: COVID-19 and Issues in Court Administration. Osgoode Hall Law Journal, 57*(3), 869–904.

Prime Minister announces Public Order Emergency Commission following the invocation of the Emergencies Act | Prime Minister of Canada. (2022). Retrieved June 17, 2022, from https://pm.gc.ca/en/news/news-releases/2022/04/25/prime-minister-announces-public-order-emergency-commission-following

Ricciardelli, R. and Bucerisi, S. (2020). *Canadian prisons in the time of COVID-19: Recommendations for the pandemic and beyond | The Royal Society of Canada*. Retrieved June 7, 2022, from https://rsc-src.ca/en/voices/canadian-prisons-in-time-covid-19-recommendations-for-pandemic-and-beyond

Richer, A. (2020). *Breonna Taylor death: Experts say case shows limits of law when police use deadly force - National | Globalnews.ca*. Retrieved June 10, 2022, from https://globalnews.ca/news/7355237/breonna-taylor-death-police-force-limits-of-law/

Rodriguez, J. (2021). *Coronavirus: Prison Transparency Project looks at Canada's prison conditions during pandemic | CTV News*. Retrieved June 7, 2022, from https://www.ctvnews.ca/health/coronavirus/public-health-crisis-canada-s-prison-conditions-during-pandemic-being-investigated-1.5375277

Scigliano, E. (2021). *Are Zoom Court Hearings Fair? - The Atlantic*. Retrieved June 9, 2022, from https://www.theatlantic.com/magazine/archive/2021/05/can-justice-be-served-on-zoom/618392/

Sebenius, A. and Mehrotra, K. (2020). *Zoom Struggles With Security Flaws as Demand for Videoconferencing Spikes | Time*. Retrieved June 8, 2022, from https://time.com/5814981/zoom-videoconferencing-security-flaws-coronavirus/

Sprott, J., Doob, A., and Iftene, A. (2021). *Do Independent External Decision Makers Ensure that "An Inmate's Confinement in a Structured Intervention Unit Is To End As Soon As Possible?"*. The John Howard Society of Canada. Retrieved June 7, 2022, from https://johnhoward.ca/drs-doob-sprott-report/

Tang, X., Gelband, H., Nagelkerke, N., Bogoch, I. I., Brown, P., Morawski, E., Lam, T., Jha, P., & Action to beat coronavirus/Action pour battre le coronavirus (Ab-C) Study Investigators. (2021). *COVID-19 vaccination intention during early vaccine rollout in Canada: a nationwide online survey. Lancet Regional Health. Americas, 2,* 100055. https://doi.org/10.1016/j.lana.2021.100055

Top Auto Express hit with historic $412M jury verdict in crash lawsuit. (n.d.). Retrieved June 9, 2022, from https://landline.media/top-auto-express-hit-with-historic-412m-jury-verdict-in-crash-lawsuit/

Tsekouras, P. (2020). *Ontario administers first doses of COVID-19 vaccine in Toronto | CTV News.* Retrieved June 14, 2022, from https://toronto.ctvnews.ca/ontario-administers-first-doses-of-covid-19-vaccine-in-toronto-1.5230004

Vaccines for children: COVID-19 - Canada.ca. (n.d.). Retrieved June 17, 2022, from https://www.canada.ca/en/public-health/services/vaccination-children/covid-19.html

Verbeke, R., Lentacker, I., De Smedt, S. C., & Dewitte, H. (2021). *The dawn of mRNA vaccines: The COVID-19 case. Journal of Controlled Release, 333,* 511–520. https://doi.org/10.1016/j.jconrel.2021.03.043

Villasenor, J. (2020). *Zoom is now critical infrastructure. That's a concern.* Retrieved June 8, 2022, from https://www.brookings.edu/blog/techtank/2020/08/27/zoom-is-now-critical-infrastructure-thats-a-concern/

Walkinshaw, E. (2011). *Mandatory vaccinations: The Canadian picture. Canadian Medical Association Journal, 183*(16), E1165-6. https://doi.org/10.1503/cmaj.109-3992

Woods, M. (2022). *Freedom Convoy: MPP Randy Hillier released after arrest | CTV News*. Retrieved June 15, 2022, from https://ottawa.ctvnews.ca/mpp-randy-hillier-surrenders-to-ottawa-police-to-face-freedom-convoy-related-charges-1.5837294

Yan, Y., Pang, Y., Lyu, Z., Wang, R., Wu, X., You, C., Zhao, H., Manickam, S., Lester, E., Wu, T., & Pang, C. H. (2021). *The COVID-19 Vaccines: Recent Development, Challenges and Prospects. Vaccines, 9*(4). https://doi.org/10.3390/vaccines9040349

CHAPTER 4 - DIGITAL TECHNOLOGY AS EVIDENCE

"There will come a time when it isn't 'They're spying on me through my phone' anymore. Eventually, it will be 'My phone is spying on me.'"

- Philip K. Dick

Introduction

Detectives pore over months of recorded phone calls between Scott Peterson, suspected of murdering his wife, and his former mistress, hoping to catch Peterson in a damning confession (*Pelletiere, 2017*). Investigators attempt to trace the last moments of Dutch hikers Lisanne Froon and Kris Kremers via the ninety photographs in their recovered cell phones (*Lyon, 2021*). A viral cell phone video of police brutality sparks months of protests and demands for justice for George Floyd and countless other Black Americans, becoming a key piece in the ensuing investigation and prosecution of the former police officer responsible (*Bogel-Burroughs & Arango, 2021; Green, 2020*). Digital technology captures many key elements of our lives, and therefore has also become a key part of our justice system.

Our correspondences are captured in text messages, phone call records, and emails; our memories are digitized in photographs and videos; our interests and curiosities are immortalized by social media posts and browser histories; and our movements throughout the days can be tracked by security cameras and cell phone towers. The most intricate of these digital footprints, such as those on computers, have been used in some form as evidence in court since the 1980's (*Pollitt, 2003*). The use of which have brought complex and contested policies, tensions with privacy laws, and ever-changing capabilities to convict or acquit defendants. In this day and age, it is nearly impossible to escape the surveillance of technology.

This chapter will discuss some types of digital evidence used in criminal cases, the admissibility of such evidence in court, the process surrounding acquiring and presenting such evidence, and the tensions between defendants' privacy and the details that digital evidence exposes about their lives.

Types of Digital Evidence

In its broadest definition, digital evidence is any digital data that can "establish that a crime has been committed or can provide a link between a crime and its victim or a crime and its perpetrator" (*Panchal, 2013, p. 964*). These can be the tools directly used in device-dependent crime, such as hacking sensitive internet servers, holding data hostage for ransom, or other felonies in the realm of cybercrime. Additionally, they can constitute evidence in a crime that only peripherally involves digital devices, such as security cameras catching a gas station robbery or the incriminating emails planning that robbery. They include but are not limited to files that are kept on computers or phones (photographs, text files, etc.), records of electronic communication (emails, text messages, IMs, etc.), and online activity (social media or website accounts, purchase or browsing history, etc.). As later sections will touch on, they also include data that is gathered by the idle activity of devices regardless of consent, such as cell-site location information that is recorded by cell phones communicating with cell towers.

Generally, digital data on computers and cell phones can be split into two categories: volatile data and non-volatile data. Non-volatile data is stored in the memory of a device and is preserved as-is even when the device is removed from power. This data can be stored on a CD or USB key, or preserved in a stable state within the file system (*Gustav, 2022; Sachowski, 2016*). This is data any typical user will recognise, such as all types of saved files from text files to music, installed programs, and the device's account information (including passwords). Read-Only Memory data and system and application events are also non-volatile, as are records of successful and failed authentication attempts, temporary and cache files, and registry data such as hardware components and applications. Non-volatile data is especially valuable during a forensic investigation and can provide a detailed portrait of the computer's and users' history (*Panchal, 2013; Sachowski, 2016*).

Volatile data, meanwhile, is within the stores of a device's memory that will vanish when the device is removed from power (*Gustav, 2022*). This includes records of processes or activities on the computer, such as when files were opened or when programs were closed (*Panchal, 2013*). RAM is often regarded to be volatile memory, but it has been proven that even after being removed from power or rebooted, some trace data remained for a brief amount of time (*Conrad et al., 2016*). Collecting this data during investigations is a significantly more sensitive process than collecting non-volatile data, and illustrates a reason why separating the suspect from their devices as soon as possible is believed to be crucial; a simple reboot could erase this evidence entirely (*Moore, 2005*).

Both these categories of data can be studied when the computer or other device is running in a process called a live analysis. In these cases, investigators do not search for files or at all manipulate the device, and instead observe the computer as it runs. A live analysis can be used to observe computers running sophisticated hacking program, for example. A dead analysis is the investigation of the physical drive after the system is shut down. Lastly, a post-mortem analysis can be issued if the system crashes and the investigators wish to discover what caused the crash and attempt to preserve what threatened to be lost (*Panchal, 2013*).

These methods of investigating digital data generally fit into the category of operating system forensics, meaning the process of investigating devices for the information within their files or metadata (*Javed et al., 2022*). Network forensics instead refers to "monitoring network traffic and investigating the attack source," such as in a large-scale hacking (*Javed et al., 2022, p. 11068*). Electronic images can be analyzed with digital image forensics, which assess the history of an image to discover whether it has been altered or entirely faked (*Javed et al., 2022*).

Cell phones can be scanned specifically for incriminating data using a variety of programs, with investigative guidelines, which will be noted in a later section, focusing on the preservation of accurate data as well as the acquisition (*Alief et al., 2020*). Some service providers in the United States sell access to their cell phone databases to law enforcement, allowing them to access user data and cell-site location information (*Kaelin, 2017*). A complication that is especially prevalent in cell phones is the ability for the user to remotely reset the phone to the factory state. This effectively erases the current data, or at the least makes it significantly harder to access. Investigators can protect the device by ensuring it does not connect to the remote network, often with as basica method as using airplane mode (*Alief et al., 2020*). Regardless of the analysis method and whether it is volatile or non-volatile data being searched, investigators must proceed with careful consideration. Devices, especially computers, can be dense with data and fortified with barriers such as password locks, so any onsite searches can take immense amounts of time (*Moore, 2005*).

Law enforcement can also create the circumstances with which to generate digital evidence against suspects. These methods include wire-tapping phone calls, installing photo radar, and surveilling with fixed security cameras or body-worn cameras. Websites can be created by law enforcement to lure perpetrators into interacting with the website (or "honey pot"), therefore incriminating themselves via their IP addresses or voluntarily-submitted information by signing up for the site. As early as the late 90's, this method was used to locate people distributing and receiving child pornography (*Moore, 2005*).

But what if a defendant wishes to argue that they never accessed that "honey pot" site, had never made an account on a site to sell illegal wares, or that they were not speaking with the victim in an online chatroom on a particular day? A browser history search may reveal the truth. In their 2020 conference Systematic Analysis of Browser History Evidence, Gros et al. studied Google Chrome, Mozilla Firefox, and Internet Explorer's browser histories and caches to see if the data these systems produced was completely accurate and therefore useful in court. Web browser history can be easily accessed or erased by any average user. The study found that a URL and the timestamp of when it was accessed were generally accurate and that tampering with that data beyond the browser's given options was difficult. The timestamp was rarely precisely accurate, but only by mere seconds. URLs recorded were almost entirely accurate, except for 3 out of 1767 data points recorded on Internet Explorer; these showed a URL that was never clicked on by the user. Google Chrome only created additional entries if there was a redirect from an http address to an https address. However, they concluded that background data or background processes while browsing websites do not generally create "false" entries in the browser history. Gros et al. also studied browser history that could be erased by any average user, and found that the "deleted" information remains in the cache, although with less reliable consistency. If a website was visited, regardless of if the browser history was deleted or not, that website would appear in the cache, and so they concluded that "URLs that are not contained in the cache can be used as strong evidence that they were not visited before" (*p. 10*).

Data other than browser history can be conveniently deleted off computers if an individual wishes to hide them from investigators, or as an unfortunate accident. However, this does not necessarily mean that the data is entirely lost. Even when files are deleted and unable to be seen or used, computers can store previously-deleted information in "free" or "slack" space while waiting for the file to be overwritten, allowing digital forensics investigators to recover the deleted files in whole or in part (*Panchal, 2013*). Alternatively, forensics can locate automatic back-up files, automatic temporary files, or Cloud files to find traces of what was deleted (*Feldman, 2006*).

To illustrate the intricate traces that digital evidence can leave behind, let us return briefly to the introduction of this chapter; specifically, the numerous pieces of digital evidence that made up the investigation of Kris Kremers and Lisanne Froon's disappearances. The two hikers vanished in the Panama jungle, but their devices were miraculously recovered intact. Investigators were able to not only examine the nearly 100 photographs the women took, but also deduce that an incorrect password was put into Kremers' phone 77 times, after approximately four days of attempted calls for help, then a subsequent power loss on Froon's cell phone. The first of these calls was at exactly 4:39 pm. Investigators noted that one random photo in the collection was deleted (*Lyon, 2021*). These minute details stitch together a vague picture of their disappearance. And yet, with all these details, captured with unbiased accuracy in the phones' data, the mystery of what happened to them has never been solved. The case of Froon and Kremers alerts us to the two sides of digital evidence: it can be intricate, honest, and hidden in the most unlikely of places, and yet can at times amount to nothing more than digital noise. Therefore, utmost care must be taken when isolating, acquiring, and examining digital data. Part of this care involves analytical guidelines to separate the wheat from the chaff, but also how to ensure that the ways it is acquired–and what, exactly, is acquired–is lawful and not at risk of being rejected from court.

Privacy Rights and Digital Evidence

Nowadays, someone does not need the keys to an individual's house to gain a detailed look at their personal life: they only need their cell phone, which, chances are, they carry in their pocket or purse at any given time. These little devices and all the data within them present unprecedented access to someone's history, relationships, financial information, interests, and affiliations, and therefore present new challenges when considering their admissibility as evidence in court and where exactly they stand under legal protections from unwarranted searches.

In Canada and the United States, two fundamental rights protect citizens from unwarranted searches upon their property or possessions: the Fourth Amendment in the Constitution, and the Canadian Charter of Rights' Protection Against Unreasonable Searches. These regulate the protection of one's digital devices (such as a laptop), and one's digitally-recorded history (such as a complete list of phone call records), but they have been forced to play catch-up with rapidly-evolving technology and how society operates with that technology. This section will mainly examine the Fourth Amendment in particular.

The 1980's saw computers becoming increasingly involved in crimes, and initially there were few international regulations regarding which officials could search devices and how those searches were administered. Searches could be done with in-house equipment by anyone within the investigation who knew their way around a computer rather than a digital forensics expert (*Pollitt, 2003*). The Federal Law Enforcement Training Center and the International Association of Computer Investigative Specialists stepped in to set up training programs, which were eventually supported by specialized units and digital evidence laboratories. The 1990's saw various discussions regarding the need for standards and attempting to put together guidelines for international corporations and other organizations. These included the International Organization on Computer Evidence, the Federal Forensic Laboratories in the United States, the United Kingdom's Association of Chief Police Officers, and the European Network of Forensic Science Institutes (*Pollitt, 2003*). However, many of the guidelines used today were created by the Scientific Working Group on Digital Evidence, the UK Association of Chief Police Officers, and the US National Institute of Justice (*Mountrakis & Ioannou, 2019*).

Above all else, evidence of any kind is only admissible in court if it is used to prove the facts of the case, and must have been obtained with authorization (*Mountrakis & Ioannou, 2019*). In most cases where law enforcement wish to search a premises or the belongings of a suspect, they require consent from the suspect themselves. However, if the suspect refuses to give consent or is not in a position to give consent, a search warrant may be issued by an authority, such as a judge or magistrate (*Cornell Law School, n.d.*). The search may be restricted or directed by the person who issued the warrant, but those conducting the search must also provide reasoning as to what they will search and why those specific objects may be of critical importance in the case: for example, they may prove that in previous cases of the sale of illegal goods, criminals used the internet on the computer to find buyers, and therefore the computer must be searched (*Cornell Law School, n.d.; Mountrakis & Ioannou, 2019*).

Much like physical evidence, such as entering a house or looking through a locked safe, digital evidence is beholden to the regulations of a search warrant or other physical warrantless searches. Suspects may provide consent for digital devices to be searched, as can particular third parties such as an employer if the crime was done on a work computer, or the co-owner of a shared computer in a private residence (*Cogar, 2003; Feldman, 2006*). However, the search can only cover what is plainly accessible and what belongs to the individual who consented; therefore, any files or accounts password-protected by the non-consenting individual (and not known by the consenting individual) cannot be searched (*Cogar, 2003*). All bets are off if the computer or device was stolen; all this information can be freely searched without these aforementioned barriers (*Feldman, 2006*).

This matter of shared computers ties into the expectation of the Fourth Amendment that all devices are protected from seizure and search if the device's owner had a reasonable expectation of privacy in regards to that device (*Cogar, 2003; Peters, 2014*). In Katz v. United States, law enforcement used listening devices to record the defendant's phone calls in a telephone booth, eventually using these recordings against him in court. The defense argued that when using a phone booth, one reasonably expects complete privacy regarding what they say. Notably, the listening devices were in the booth rather than tapping the phone, so the other side of the conversation was not recorded or used as evidence (*"Katz v. United States", n.d.*). Despite counterarguments that eavesdropping is always a risk when speaking in public, the case created the Katz principle: a person must prove a subjective expectation of privacy and this expectation of privacy must be recognised as reasonable by society (*"Katz v. United States", n.d.; Tokson, 2022*). Courts decide the exact parameters of this on a case-by-case basis, which has resulted in varied interpretations (*Tokson, 2022*).

Furthermore, not everyone in a given society agrees on what a reasonable expectation of privacy may entail, even when considering previous rulings and well-understood social norms (*Marshall et al., 2019*). A study by Marshall et al. (*2019*) as well as studies cited in their accompanying paper found that participants had expectations of privacy that differed from courts' rulings. For instance, they expected that information that revealed their physical location would be more protected by the Fourth Amendment than it is in actuality, especially cell-site location information (data that shows which nearby cell towers a cell phone sent data to). Participants said that they would be unlikely to allow searches of their cell-site location information and even less likely to allow searches of the cell phone itself. Generally, people were more protective over their cell phone data and related digital data than the courts had previously ruled.

Besides consent, another key requirement of lawful searches is that there must be reason to believe that the device is connected to a crime; why the device must therefore be searched should be explained to a magistrate (*Cogar, 2003; Mountrakis & Ioannou, 2019*). Law enforcement must clearly outline why they believe evidence is stored in the device and what specifically is being searched. This often connects to the officer's understanding of and previous experience with the crime they are investigating (*Cogar, 2003; Mountrakis & Ioannou, 2019*). If the suspect's possible crime is not directly related to technology, an officer may argue that their crime is indirectly involved and therefore still requires a search of the device. For example, the difference between a server hacker and a thief who scouts out affluent neighborhoods on Google Maps (*Mountrakis & Ioannou, 2019*). Officers can also retrieve evidence from anything in plain view, such as an open laptop screen, but they are unable to search and seize the entire computer for more evidence (or even click on any visible files) unless previous qualifications have been met (*Cogar, 2003*).

Another notable obstacle to an individual's privacy is the search-incident-to-arrest exception. This exception allows police officers to search an individual and their close surroundings upon arrest, with the purpose of locating any weapons or evidence at hand that could be destroyed if not seized immediately (*"Criminal Procedure — Fourth Amendment — Florida Supreme Court Holds that Cell Phone Data Is Not Subject to the Search-Incident-to-Arrest Exception. — Smallwood v. State, 113 So. 3d 724 (Fla. 2013)"*, 2014). For example, if police catch a hacker working on their laptop, they can claim the laptop so the hacker's roommate does not have the chance to uninstall any incriminating programs. A cell phone could be on a suspect's person and therefore be searched without a warrant, but there has been significant pushback on this because of the amount of information that can be held in a cell phone. More than a wallet or a purse, a cell phone could expose an extremely detailed summary of the suspect's recent history. Courts compared searching a cell phone with searching an entire home, like "an open door into the most private details of an arrestee's life" (*"Criminal Procedure — Fourth Amendment — Florida Supreme Court Holds that Cell Phone Data Is Not Subject to the Search-Incident-to-Arrest Exception. — Smallwood v. State, 113 So. 3d 724 (Fla. 2013)"*, 2014, p. 1063). This conflict backs many arguments that cell phone searches must be rigorously and uniquely protected under the Fourth Amendment and similar privacy protections.

Another related conflict is the third-party doctrine and how its scope has changed to accommodate digital devices, to the detriment of citizens' privacy. The third-party doctrine, presented by the Supreme Court in the 1970's, is an exception to the Fourth Amendment that renders evidence admissible in court even if the discovery or acquiring of that evidence violated the Amendment (*Tokson, 2022*). It qualifies the condition that a person must have a reasonable expectation of privacy for the Fourth Amendment to protect their activity: if the information was knowingly shared with a third party, then the person could not claim to expect their information to remain private (*Marshall et al., 2019*). An example in relation to physical evidence is that if someone lends their car to a friend for a week, they cannot claim that they reasonably expected that the friend would not see the unregistered firearm in the back seat. In relation to digital evidence, this can be as simple as posting a personal thought to a public forum or selling stolen items through a public site like eBay. Additionally, the Fourth Amendment does not protect someone from having the police investigate all the calls they made during a month's period, for they willingly dialed those numbers and had them routed through the phone company (*Tokson, 2022*).

The expanding realm of digital communications and digital data has made the third-party doctrine increasingly complex. With internet activity being filtered through internet service providers and countless amounts of data being logged in records or servers outside of the devices themselves, questions have been raised as to what the voluntary (and informed) disclosure of digital information truly means (*Nairn, 2021*). Someone may control what sites they interact with, what apps they download, and what messages they send online, but a layperson may not have a grasp on just how much data is transferred to their internet service provider and what that data can reveal about their activity. Critics of the third-party doctrine's broad reach also mention that using a cell phone is nearly unavoidable in daily life (*Tokson, 2022*). If using a cell phone and the internet every day is required for business and personal life, how much consent can individuals truly give?

An original stop-gap to this issue originates in 1986. Congress presented the Stored Communications Act, creating protections for "email and other digital communications stored on the Internet by [...] establishing a structure and criteria for voluntary and involuntary disclosure of information maintained by internet service providers about their customers" (*Marshall et al., 2019, p. 7*). Court orders were therefore required to have internet service providers disclose information to law enforcement, rather than have that information entirely and freely accessible by the third-party doctrine. Investigators must therefore acquire subpoenas to lawfully access names, addresses, telephone connection records, services used, means of payment, and other information, from internet service providers (*Cogar, 2003*).

2011 saw the arrest of four men who were suspected in a series of robberies. One of the men believed to be connected to the series was Timothy Carpenter, and the investigation team obtained his cell-site location information via his cell phone service provider. The information, illustrating the data his cell phone sent to nearby cell towers as he travelled with the phone on his person, was extremely detailed–12,898 location points to be precise–and gave the investigators a crystal-clear picture of his whereabouts over four months. This information placed him within proximity of the robberies, and he was eventually charged with twelve criminal charges for the robberies and other crimes (*Marshall et al., 2019; Nairn, 2021*). Under the third-party doctrine, Carpenter had no expectation of privacy regarding his cell-site location information since he voluntarily carried the cell phone that was transferring that information to his service provider, but the defense was adamant that Carpenter could not have ever consented to investigators to essentially stalking him for every moment across four months (*Tokson, 2022*). Even if Carpenter was in public, where he did not have a reasonable expectation of privacy regarding his location because of factors like traffic cameras or other people seeing him, he could not consent to every single moment of his day being recorded and subsequently examined. These moments detailed people he knew, places he visited, and, ultimately, crimes he committed (*Nairn, 2021*). While Carpenter could be assumed by society to know that his cell-site location information was being collected by his service provider, the degree to which he was being surveilled was not reasonably understood or assumed by society. In the discussion that arose from the court proceedings, a new unofficial test was created to allow more nuance in future rulings that pit the Fourth Amendment against the vast scope of digital data: the Carpenter test (*Nairn, 2021; Tokson, 2022*). The Carpenter test asks if the scope of location data collected via digital devices is too detailed and immense to truly be consented to (*Nairn, 2021; Tokson, 2022*).

An argument against the Carpenter test is that the gathering of data was not so unlike bank or business records in their scope and the amount of protections deserved. There are also those who critique the Carpenter test because it is too lenient, instead saying that the test does not provide additional useful nuance to the third-party doctrine, does not apply to concerns about the collection of IP addresses, and presents a new, very high threshold for the digital tracking of an individual's location to be considered inadmissible. Even "six months of recording every location where an individual connects to a network" will not be protected under the Fourth Amendment under the Carpenter test's standards (*Nairn, 2021, p. 1050*). Nairn's 2021 paper refers to a case where a defendant was surveilled by a camera installed in his backyard by law enforcement. His assertion that the camera violated the Fourth Amendment was disregarded, since the fact that it was a camera fixed in one place, filming only one part of his house, meant that it did not meet the threshold of surveillance which Carpenter would protect. In the end of the Carpenter case, the Court of Appeals for the Sixth Circuit stated that the defendant did not, after all, have a reasonable expectation of privacy regarding cell-site location information, so regardless, the Carpenter doctrine did not do many favours for Carpenter himself (*Nairn, 2021*).

While plenty of searches and seizures of digital data are protected under the Fourth Amendment and the comparable Protection Against Unreasonable Searches, nuances can often allow some digital searches to slip through the cracks. However, discussion and debate continues on how to better strengthen these protections, both to keep citizens safe and to better investigate serious crime. There are further standards that digital evidence is beholden to – mainly regarding how they are collected from devices and safely preserved during investigations.

Acquiring Digital Data as Evidence

Once law enforcement has been authorized to search digital devices according to the Fourth Amendment or other regulations against unlawful searches, there are further rules to follow regarding how that search is conducted. Alongside the aforementioned protections of the Fourth Amendment, digital evidence can be rendered inadmissible if courts decide that the techniques used to acquire it were improper (*Mountrakis & Ioannou, 2019*). While petitioning for a search warrant from the magistrate or judge, law enforcement must be very specific about which devices they wish to search and what information they will be searching for. The evidence they collect and present should align with those answers to avoid being challenged (*Moore, 2005*). Detailed documents must prove the authenticity of the evidence, record the transfer of the evidence, note the time of collection, and contain the "integrity documentation to compare the digital fingerprint of the evidence" (*Mountrakis & Ioannou, 2019, para. 23*). Investigators must create a detailed record of how they acquired the evidence, in order for a third party to later follow these instructions, replicate the results, and evaluate the employed methods of search and discovery. These recorded actions must prove that the evidence was obtained using the best method possible (*Moore, 2005; Mountrakis & Ioannou, 2019*).

After the evidence is gathered, additional criteria regulate how digital evidence is stored and handled. Evidence cannot be tampered with or altered, which in some cases describes as simple an action as an officer moving a computer file to a different folder or even turning on the computer in the first place (*Mountrakis & Ioannou, 2019*). The smallest alteration could contaminate a file and render it apt for scrutiny in court. Similarly, it is incredibly easy to create false evidence, either accidentally or on purpose. Consider a prosecution's argument that must prove that a file was last opened on a particular date by the suspect. If, without first copying the file and moving it off the computer, investigators accidentally open the file and change the date that records when it was last opened, their evidence is rendered inaccurate (*Moore, 2005*). Copies of digital files may be made, as long as the court can be reassured that the copy is entirely accurate and the original was never tampered with (*Mountrakis & Ioannou, 2019*).

Digital evidence is delicate and ephemeral, yet paradoxically it is equally hard to erase entirely or avoid creating in involuntary ways. The immense amount of information it may hold against an individual can help protect society or can provide too much opportunity for law enforcement to overstep.

REFERENCES

Alief, F., Rosselina, L., Suryanto, Y., & Hermawan, T. (2020). *Framework design for the retrieval of instant messaging in social media as electronic evidence [Paper presentation]*. 2020 7th International Conference on Electrical Engineering, Computer Sciences and Informatics, Yogyakarta, Indonesia. doi:10.23919/EECSI50503.2020.9251888

Bogel-Burroughs, N. & Arango, T. (2021, March 8.) *What to know about the trial of Derek Chauvin. The New York Times.* https://www.nytimes.com/live/2021/derek-chauvin-trial-explained

CNN. (2003, November 19). *Transcript Peterson, Frey phone call.* https://www.cnn.com/2003/LAW/11/19/peterson.frey.transcript/index.html

Cogar, S. W. (2003). *Obtaining admissible evidence from computers and internet service providers. FBI Law Enforcement Bulletin, 72*(7), 11-15. Retrieved from https://www.ojp.gov

Conrad, E., Misenar, S., & Feldman, J. (2016). *CISSP Study Guide* (3rd ed.). Syngress. doi:10.1016/B978-0-12-802437-9.00003-5

Cornell Law School. (n.d.). *Search warrant.* https://www.law.cornell.edu/wex/search_warrant

Criminal Procedure — Fourth Amendment — Florida Supreme Court Holds that Cell Phone Data Is Not Subject to the Search-Incident-to-Arrest Exception. — Smallwood v. State, 113 So. 3d 724 (Fla. 2013). (2014). *Harvard Law Review, 127*(3), 1059–1066. http://www.jstor.org/stable/23741392

Feldman, J. E. (2006). Lost? No. Found? Yes. Computer tapes and emails as evidence. *American Journal of Family Law, 19*(4), 245-249.

Green, B. P. (2020, June 5). *Smart phone video shows the facts about America's police.* Markkula Center for Applied Ethics. https://www.scu.edu/ethics-spotlight/systemic-racism-police-brutality-and-the-killing-of-george-floyd/smart-phone-video-shows-the-facts-about-americas-police/

Gros, T., Dirauf, R., & Freiling, F. (2020, May 1-12). *Systematic analysis of browser history evidence* [Paper presentation]. 13th International Conference on Systematic Approaches to Digital Forensic Engineering (SADFE), Erlangen, Germany.

Gustav, M. (2022). Significance of digital evidence in forensics. *Journal of Forensic Biomechanics, 13*(2), 9-10. doi:10.35248/2090-2697.22.13.391

Javed, A.R., Ahmed, W., Alazab, M., Jalil, Z., Kifayat, K., & Gadekallu, T. R. (2022). A comprehensive survey on computer forensics: State-of-the-art, tools, techniques, challenges, and future directions. *IEEE Access, 10.* 11065-11089. doi: 10.1109/ACCESS.2022.3142508

Kaelin, B. (2017, January 31). *Cell phone forensics - Extracting personal data from cell phones.* Forensic Science Degree. https://www.forensicsciencedegree.org/cell-phone-forensics-extracting-personal-data-from-cell-phones/

Katz v. United States. (n.d.). CaseBriefs. Retrieved May 25, 2022, from https://www.casebriefs.com/blog/law/criminal-procedure/criminal-procedure-keyed-to-israel/arrest-search-and-seizure/katz-v-united-states-2/

Lyon, R. (2021, February 11). *Lost girls: The unsettling fate of Kris Kremers and Lisanne Froon.* Medium. https://medium.com/the-mystery-box/lost-girls-the-unsettling-fate-of-kris-kremer-and-lisanne-froon-2cc065261f7b

Marshall, E. W., Groscup, J. L., Brank, E. M., Perez, A., & Hoetger, L. A. (2019). Police surveillance of cell phone location data: Supreme Court versus public opinion. *Behavioral Sciences & the Law, 37*(6), 751-775. doi:10.1002/bsl.2442

Mountrakis, P. & Ioannou, M. (2019). *Admissibility of digital evidence in court.* Mondaq Ltd. https://www.mondaq.co.uk/cyprus/trials-appeals-compensation/822096/admissibility-of-digital-evidence-in-court

Moore, R. (2005). *Search and seizure of digital evidence.* LFB Scholarly Publishing LLC.

Nairn, J. (2021). One small step, but no giant leap: How Carpenter v. United States failed to increase cell phone privacy. *Rutgers University Law Review, 73*(3), 1031-1055. Retrieved from https://rutgerslawreview.com

Panchal, E. P. (2013). Extraction of persistence and volatile forensics evidences from computer system. *International Journal of Computer Trends and Technology, 4*(5), 964-968. Retrieved from http://www.http://ijcttjournal.org/

Pelletiere, N. (2017, September 14). *Amber Frey remembers recorded calls with Scott Peterson: 'I was shaking.'* ABC News. https://abcnews.go.com/US/amber-frey-remembers-recorded-calls-scott-peterson-shaking/story?id=49763587

Peters, J. B. (2014). Criminal procedure - More protection for digital information? The Supreme Court holds warrantless cell phone searches do not fall under the search incident to arrest exception; Riley v. California, 134 S. Ct. 2473 (2014). *Wyoming Law Review, 15.* 571-591. Retrieved from https://scholarship.law.uwyo.edu/

Pollitt, M. M. (2003). The very brief history of digital evidence standards. In: Gertz, M. (eds), *Integrity and Internal Control in Information Systems V. IICIS 2002. IFIP — The International Federation for Information Processing* (vol 124 pp. 137-143). Springer. doi:10.1007/978-0-387-35693-8_8

Sachowski, J. (2016). Understanding digital forensics. *Implementing Digital Forensic Readiness.* Syngress. doi:10.1016/C2015-0-00701-8

Tokson, M. (2022.) The Carpenter test as a transformation of Fourth Amendment Law. *University of Illinois Law Review.* doi:10.2139/ssrn.4094166

CHAPTER 5 - DNA AS EVIDENCE

"I wondered whether Batie blamed DNA. She laughed. 'Oh, no, honey,' she said. 'DNA is science. You can't blame DNA. You can only blame the people who used it wrong.'"

- Matthew Shaer

Introduction

The previous chapter discussed the extent of information that technology can reveal about a person, but cell phones and location data are not all that technology has evolved to reveal about individuals and their personal lives. The mid 1980's introduced DNA fingerprinting: the process of examining a person's DNA to identify information such as an individual's genealogy, the viability of organ and blood transplants, their genetic predisposition to certain illnesses, and, in the case of legal investigation, if they are a match with any biological material discovered at a crime scene (*Rockowitz et al., 2008*).

DNA fingerprints, also known as DNA profiles, are so unique that the likelihood of one exactly matching two different people in a population is nearly impossible, except for in the case of identical twins. While this technology can be used to discover a multitude of information about a person, this chapter's concern is how DNA profiles in their many forms can be used as evidence in court to prosecute–or exonerate–criminals.

This chapter will cover the process of DNA fingerprinting, the history of DNA fingerprinting in laboratories and courts, how this information is stored in databases, and the ongoing controversies regarding how it can be misused.

DNA profiles

Deoxyribonucleic acid (DNA) resides in the nuclei of cells, which carry the genes of the body and regulate the activities of the cell (*Encyclopaedia Britannica, n.d.*). DNA is made up of two coiling threads, connected by ladder rung-like chemical bases called nucleotides. There are four different types of nucleotides (adenine, guanine, thymine, and cytosine), which connect in pairs to create the "rungs" of the DNA's characteristic double-helix. Adenine always connects with thymine, while cytosine connects with guanine. What makes each person's and animal's DNA unique is the order of these pairings within the double-helix. These variations in order are called "polymorphisms" (*Blair, 1990*).

DNA is notoriously resilient and can be analyzed from skeletal remains or ancient remains such as fossils or mummies. Some of the oldest recovered samples of DNA are estimated to be up to 800,000 years old (*Clark, 2014; Gannon, 2012*). An individual's specific DNA profile is exceedingly rare; even if 99 per cent of DNA is identical from human to human, that last 1 per cent is so rare that "the chances of two people having the same DNA profile are nearly impossible"—and that impossibility includes both people alive at the time of analysis and those who have lived across all time (*Clark, 2014, p. 205*). In this way, DNA analysis is not only useful to law enforcement, but to researchers of ancient societies and investigators attempting to identify deceased individuals. A DNA profile "refers to a numerical representation of thirteen specific points ('loci') on a person's inactive DNA" (*Clark, 2014, p. 204*). These thirteen points, also called variable number short tandem repeats (STRs), represent for most analysis methods that detailed 1 per cent of DNA information that sets each person apart (*Clark, 2014; National Institute of Justice, 2011*).

The process of creating a DNA profile begins with the crime scene itself. DNA is gathered from biological materials left behind, such as hair, nails, blood, or skin cells (*Clark, 2014*). If there are arrestees, law enforcement can collect DNA samples via a buccal swab inside the cheek that is sent to an accredited lab to be analyzed (*Ortyl, 2019*). The nucleus is assessed to see if DNA can be extracted to create a sufficient profile. If the DNA sample is corrupted or flawed in some way, such as if it is mixed with another person's DNA or if the DNA sample is too broken down to provide clear information, the results are inconclusive and unable to be used in an investigation. They may even appear to contain important distinguishing information, such as particular "rungs" and marks, where in actuality they do not (*Clark, 2014; Ortyl, 2019; Shaer, 2016*).

If two samples of DNA are the same, that produces an inclusion result, or a match. This means that there is an extremely low probability that the DNA of the person tested and the DNA at the crime scene belong to different people. However, if the two samples do not match, that produces an exclusion result or a nonmatch. This can still cut down on the amount of suspects or help a defendant be proven innocent (*Ortyl, 2019*).

Evolution of the Science

DNA fingerprinting was discovered in 1984 at Leicester University in Leicester, United Kingdom, by Dr. Alec John Jeffreys and his colleagues Dr. Peter Gill and Dr. Dave Werrett. The process's discovery was a happy accident (*Hansen et al., 2008; Rockowitz et al., 2008*). Earlier in Jeffreys' career, when searching with a colleague for a way to detect and clone a beta-globin gene in rabbits, he had developed a unique technique using enzymes to "cut double-stranded DNA into fragments whenever a specific short sequence of DNA bases occurred on the strands" (*Harbison, 2017, para. 5*). A record of a DNA sequence could then be produced. After publishing his and his colleagues' research,

Jeffreys noted that particular fragments in DNA vary from individual to individual and are related to their ancestors. He developed a simple version of the techniques used today to detect these different patterns. Harbison (2017) describes the method that he used in 1984:

> *Jeffreys placed fragments of DNA with varying numbers of repeating sequences into wells at one end of a gel electrophoresis container, and he connected the positive and negative charges to either end of the container and applied an electric current across the gel. The DNA fragments moved through the gel, toward the positively charged pole, at differing speeds based on the molecular weight or size of the fragment. [...] The X-rays produced a chart-like picture in which the various fragment lengths appeared as what Jeffreys called a smudgy, blurry mess of dark marks at various places along the length of the X-ray image. When he compared the three X-ray images from related individuals, he could clearly see a similar pattern, which identified the genetic pattern in related individuals. Jeffreys had stumbled upon a method to identify related individuals based upon the features of their DNA (paras. 12-13).*

In the 1990s the United States, the United Kingdom, and the European Union began to focus on using the Polymerase Chain Reaction (PCR) method (Lynch, 2003). The PCR method amplifies DNA samples, focusing on STRs, to create "billions of copies of certain loci" (*Clark, 2014, p. 207*). PCR allows even a sliver of a sample to create a usable DNA profile. This increases the amount of workable data in only hours, no matter how small or degraded it may be, and creates a DNA sample that can be analyzed within a couple days (*Clark, 2014; Rockowitz et al., 2008*). PCR is also popular in other molecular biology sciences (*Rockowitz et al., 2008*).

The DNA is then run through "capillary electrophoresis in order to label the strands of DNA at specific loci" (*Clark, 2014, p. 210*). This creates consistent and comparable graphics of the thirteen loci with which to compare different samples. Peter (2005) describes them as appearing akin to "bar codes that identify items for sale" (para. 6). However, this method can be risky if the DNA is contaminated and then incorrectly duplicated and enhanced; this may result in the focus redirecting to the DNA left by investigators or unrelated personnel who were involved in working the crime scene (*Peter, 2005*). This entire process is repeated with the DNA with which analysts wish to discover a match. The two profile "bar codes" from the suspect and from the crime scene are then compared to see if those thirteen specific loci match in any substantial way–either an exact match if they are looking for who exactly was at the scene, or a partial match if they are looking for a relative or genetic connection (*Clark, 2014*).

Mitochondrial DNA (mtDNA) is a unique facet of DNA found within the cytoplasm of cells and is mainly inherited through the maternal line. The mtDNA analysis method may not be as specific as the STR method, but it can provide results where no others can. If the evidence at the crime scene does not contain nuclei which can be used with another method of DNA profiling, mtDNA can usually step in, especially with extremely degraded or ancient samples (*Clark, 2014; Peter, 2005*). It being inherited through the mother means that it can "solve historical mysteries revolving around maternal lineage" (*Peter, 2005, para. 9*) and plays a main role in ancestry and genealogy tests (*Ortyl, 2019*). mtDNA was used alongside STR to identify victims after the World Trade Center disaster (*Peter, 2005*).

The partner to mtDNA is Y-Chromosome analysis, wherein the Y-Chromosome, passed down paternally, is searched for in the nucleus's DNA. Especially in cases of violent crime or sexual assault, the search for Y-Chromosome DNA "essentially blinds the machine to any female DNA," allowing laboratories to more easily isolate the culprit (*Clark, 2014, p. 209*).

Familial DNA (or genetic genealogy) is not necessarily a different scientific process, but instead a different way of assessing DNA profiles to investigate cases (*Chamary, 2020; Ortyl 2019*). DNA is gathered from the crime scene like in the other methods, but investigators search for both complete and partial matches (*Ortyl, 2019*). Partial matches can indicate a familial connection. As it is incredibly unlikely that two unrelated people have the exact same DNA profile, it is logical to assume that DNA profiles with significant similarities belong to people who are blood related. An individual's DNA is made up of approximately half of one parent's DNA and half of the other's; therefore, familial DNA searches can also locate siblings, grandparents, or cousins using other differently-sized slices of the genetic profile they already know (*Chamary, 2020*). If a match is found (whether the assumed family member is in the criminal database or in a public, voluntary database such as genealogy sites), investigators can locate these family members and pursue a new lead (*Ortyl, 2019*). In 2018, the familial DNA method came to fruition in the case of the Golden State Killer, a once-cold case of "12 homicides, 45 rapes, and 120 home invasions in the 1970's and '80s in California" (*Leahy, 2018, para. 1*). Investigators combined the DNA profiles with birth certificates and census data. This web of people was examined for potential suspects who could have plausibly committed the crime, such as those who were comparable to police sketches. Eventually, Joseph DeAngelo was arrested and pled guilty to the crimes (*Chamary, 2020*).

DNA Fingerprinting in the Courtroom

In 1985, Alec Jeffreys was invited to the UK courts to introduce DNA profiles to the judicial system through the case of Andrew Sarbah. Sarbah was born in London, but moved to Ghana with family when he was four years old. At 15, he returned to London with valid British and Ghanian passports, only to be accused by customs officers of being a cousin who was using a doctored passport to enter the country illegally. Jeffreys was contacted by the Sarbah family's legal counsel, who hoped that Jeffreys could prove Andrew Sarbah was the boy he and his papers claimed he was (*Aronson, 2005; Harbison, 2017*).

Jeffreys initially hesitated because while his technique could prove the existence of a familial relationship, it could not prove what that relationship exactly was (Harbison, 2017). If his test could not produce specific results, it would have little sway in a case where the prosecution argued that Sarbah was an impersonating cousin rather than a son. His test was also missing a key set of genes: Sarbah's father was not available to give a DNA sample (*Harbison, 2017; Jeffreys, n.d. a*).

Nevertheless, Jeffreys took on the case. To solve the matter of the missing father and to determine Sarbah's exact familial connection, Jeffreys used the DNA fingerprints of Sarbah's mother and siblings to construct the DNA profile of the father. He used this and Sarbah's mother's DNA to create a clear profile indicating that Sarbah's DNA came directly from both parents: all parts of his profile originated from either parent's profiles (*Jeffreys, n.d. a*). Jeffreys stated that this result was irrefutable proof of Sarbah's origin: the probability of this occurring coincidentally was less than 1 in 33 billion. The court, however, was unimpressed: Jeffreys' lab was the only one that could replicate his results since the process was so new and unique, which cast doubt on the process. No one could technically prove Jeffreys' results wrong (*Aronson, 2005*).

Despite this, the Home Office case against Andrew Sarbah was eventually dropped and Sarbah could return home to the UK (*Aronson, 2005*). Jeffreys stated that this case was "the first time that DNA, all this modern arcane science of molecular genetics, had actually been used to go out in a non-clinical context and actually directly help someone" (*Jeffreys, n.d. b, para. 1*). Jeffreys and his colleagues submitted a report about the Sarbah case (while it was still ongoing) to Nature, and despite a negative peer review about DNA evidence that prompted Jeffreys to contact the editor of the magazine to set the story straight, the press was excited about this new technology and its apparent fairy tale success in court (*Aronson, 2005*). Jeffreys and his colleagues found themselves being asked to help on "thousands and thousands and thousands" of immigration cases like Sarbah's (*Jeffreys, n.d. c, para. 1*).

Jeffreys' breakthrough and the UK courts would again intersect in 1986. The body of a teenage girl, Dawn Ashworth, was found in the village of Enderby (*Aronson, 2005*). The case resembled the unsolved murder of Lydia Mann in Leicestershire three years prior, and a search began for what investigators presumed was one culprit for both rapes and murders (*Peter, 2005*). Investigators called in Jeffreys for his expertise when they arrested Richard Buckland, a 17-year-old boy who worked near where Ashworth's body was discovered, and they wanted to compare the boy's DNA to the DNA on the bodies of the girls. While he had experience in immigration cases, Jeffreys' method had never been used in a murder trial (*Aronson, 2005; Peter, 2005*).

Jeffreys had to use a new method of DNA fingerprinting to assess the crime scene, especially that of Mann's, which was three years old at this point. He typically used multi-locus tests in his immigration cases, but the limited pieces of DNA at the aged crime scene required his developing single-locus method. Despite the fact that Buckland had confessed to Ashworth's murder, the analysis concluded that his DNA did not match the DNA found at the crime scene. However, investigators were correct in their suspicion that the murders were connected: the DNA of the murderer of both girls was the same. Though they had not found the perpetrator, the analysis regardless provided a key piece of the puzzle for investigators, and allowed the innocent boy they had arrested to walk free: the first innocent person exonerated thanks to DNA evidence (*Harbison, 2017; Hansen et al., 2008; Aronson, 2005*).

Investigators had noted the blood type of the perpetrator via the DNA left at the crime scene, and so they moved to attempting to find him in the area (*Harbison, 2017*). They requested blood or saliva samples from men with matching blood types in the three towns that surrounded the crime scene. Though sources vary on the exact age range of those sampled, it is believed that men in their teens to thirties or mid-thirties were asked to provide a sample; somewhere between 4500 and 5500 samples were tested (*Aronson, 2005; Peter, 2005; Tande, 1989*). None were a match. Although it seemed to be a dead end, a local man was overheard saying that his coworker, Colin Pitchfork, convinced him to provide a blood sample under Pitchfork's name as a favour. When investigators finally got a sample of Pitchfork's DNA, it turned out that this missing DNA matched that of the murderer. He pled guilty in 1988 and received a life sentence, in the first criminal case where DNA was a part of the evidence (*Aronson, 2005; Clark, 2014*).

Notably, Pitchfork confessed before his DNA was examined and compared to the crime scene at all, so the DNA profile never technically went to trial (*Hansen et al., 2008*). The first person who maintained their innocence but was convicted thanks to DNA profiles was Tommie Lee Andrews in 1988 in Florida (*Blair, 1990; Hansen et al., 2008*). While initially standing trial in 1987 for aggravated burglary and rape, the prosecutor initially failed to convince the jury that DNA technology was accurate and reliable enough to clinch the case against Andrews. It was in his retrial that he was convicted for over 100 years thanks to that DNA evidence (*Hansen et al., 2008*).

Cases using DNA evidence would then spread across the globe. At the time, many United States defense attorneys pushed back on DNA profiling's presence in courts, as it did not pass the Frye Test (which requires that scientific evidence used in court must have earned widespread acceptance in its field) nor did laboratories provide transparent and clear information on how they were creating these profiles. With little understanding of the science and techniques, it was difficult for some judges to believe the reliability of DNA profiles, and for both the defense and prosecution to accurately argue around them (*Shaer, 2016*).

1989 held another landmark case, also in the United States: Spencer v. Commonwealth was the first time a sentence of capital punishment was upheld by a State Supreme Court using DNA evidence (*Blair, 1990; Rockowitz et al., 2008*). Blood and semen samples at multiple rape and strangling crime scenes eventually led investigators to Timothy Wilson Spencer, and the case proceeded to the Virginia Supreme Court where the DNA was the sole basis upon which to convict Spencer. Therefore, the prosecution brought forth many experts in the fields of molecular biology, genetics, and population genetics, to strengthen the case of the DNA fingerprint (*Blair, 1990*). The prosecution asserted that an "improperly conducted test or inadequate DNA sample would result only in no match at all" rather than a false positive (*Blair, 1990, p. 865*). (This assertion will be touched on in the Controversies section of this chapter). Blair's 1990 report on the case describes that at least the court of Spencer v. Commonwealth had "unconcealed enthusiasm" for DNA fingerprinting (*p. 865-866*).

That same year, the second-degree murder case of Joseph Castro in New York would introduce the development of a three-prong test for DNA's admissibility in court, which Hansen et al.'s 2008 paper outlines as such: "(1) is there a generally accepted scientific theory arguing that

DNA sequences differ between individuals and that difference can be tested, (2) is there a reliable technology that can be performed to detect these DNA differences, [and] (3) was that DNA technology applied correctly in this particular case" (p. 38). The DNA evidence in the Castro case (blood on the defendant's watch the prosecution asserted was the victim's) was deemed inadmissible since the court did not trust that the testing laboratory in question used proper and reliable scientific techniques. As a result, universal standards for DNA testing within laboratories were put in place by the FBI's Technical Working Group on DNA Analysis Methods *(Hansen et al., 2008)*.

With DNA now being used in more and more cases, there became a need for databases to contain all that information. Country-wide–or even universal–databases could help link past offenders to current crimes with great efficiency. By the mid-1990s, the process to create these databases was underway.

DNA Fingerprinting in Databases

In England in 1995, the Forensic Science Service created the National DNA Database, a collection of DNA profiles that grew to hold 3 million profiles within just ten years of its creation (*Hansen et al., 2008*). Over in the United States, processes were underway at a similar time, with the DNA Identification Act of 1994 being passed to protect DNA data under privacy laws and allow the federal government to use DNA in cases thanks to national indexes (*FBI, n.d.; Ortyl, 2019*). The DNA Identification Act outlined requirements for quality assurance, privacy, and expungement that all laboratories must adhere to. The Act also specified whose DNA data can be collected in a database. This list includes but is not limited to: convicted offenders, arrestees and detainees, unidentified human remains (such as in large-scale disasters), missing persons, DNA recovered from crime scenes even if no perpetrators were found, and relatives of missing persons (*FBI, n.d.; Ortyl, 2019*).

Alongside the DNA Identification Act, the FBI formalized their own DNA database from 1990, called the Combined DNA Index System, or CODIS (*Clark, 2014; Ortyl, 2019*). CODIS (still in use today) allows law enforcement to search DNA they have collected against their state database of profiles for matches (*FBI, n.d.*). The DNA profiles stored in CODIS use thirteen STR loci (*Clark, 2014*). Through this system, law enforcement can see DNA profiles, the name of the agency that submitted the profile, and the laboratory that did the analysis. However, they cannot search outside their state collection, nor can they access any personal identifiers of the individuals such as name or address (with the occasional exception for missing persons records); therefore, both the agency who supplied the DNA to the CODIS system and the laboratory who examined this sample of DNA must communicate to confirm the match and access more information (*FBI, n.d.; Ortyl, 2019*)

Only individuals and criminal justice agencies authorized by the FBI can access CODIS (*FBI, n.d.*). They may access samples and records for one of four purposes: (1) law enforcement identification, (2) in judicial proceedings if proven to be admissible, (3) for defendants to defend themselves in their trial, and (4) non-crime related reasons such as population statistics, identification research, protocol development, or quality control, provided that personally identifiable information is removed from the DNA profile (*FBI, n.d.*).

The National DNA Index System (NDIS) is a connected system established by the FBI in 1998. It is the national level of the CODIS system, and similarly collects DNA profiles such as those described and regulated by the DNA Identification Act of 1994 (*Ortyl, 2019*). It allows law enforcement agencies at all levels in the United States to compare DNA profiles across the entire country, rather than only in their particular state (*Hansen, 2008*). NDIS accepts PCR, Y-chromosome, and mtDNA profiles, though Y-chromosome and mtDNA profiles are solely used for missing-person related cases, resulting in a database that contained 6,031,000 offender profiles and 225,400 forensic profiles after a decade of operation and had found matches or other key data in 71,800 investigations (*FBI, n.d.; Hansen, 2008*).

NDIS has strict regulations when it comes to the DNA that is submitted to their database. Laboratories must sign a Memorandum of Understanding regarding seven main standards, at risk of being barred from using the system. Ortyl describes these standards in a 2019 paper:

> *(1) the DNA data must be generated in accordance with the FBI Director's Quality Assurance Standards; (2) the DNA data must be generated by a laboratory that is accredited by an approved accrediting agency; (3) the DNA data must be generated by a laboratory that undergoes an external audit every two years to demonstrate compliance with the FBI Director's Quality Assurance Standards; (4) the DNA data must be one of the categories of data acceptable at NDIS, such as convicted offender, arrestee, detainee, legal, forensic (casework), unidentified human remains, missing person, or a relative of missing person; (5) the DNA data must meet minimum CODIS Core Loci requirements for the specimen category; (6) the DNA PCR data must be generated using PCR accepted kits; and (7) participating laboratories must have and follow expungement procedures in accordance with federal law (para. 15).*

CODIS allows law enforcement to search through NDIS databases; therefore, all the profiles accessed through both these systems are beholden to the aforementioned strict standards (*Ortyl, 2019*). Entries should be removed from the database entirely if a conviction is overturned or if a charge has been completely dismissed (*FBI, n.d.*) However, as will be discussed in the Controversies section, not all databases are associated with CODIS or NDIS, which introduces privacy concerns.

While it was once only the laboratory of Alec Jeffreys and his colleagues who had the required technology and expertise to create DNA profiles, now regular citizens can send DNA to laboratories and get access to genealogy information through services like 23andMe or Ancestry.com (*Ortyl, 2019*). These two websites' databases each contain from millions of entries sourced from around the globe. Both websites deliver up to 700,000 data points to users regarding their DNA profile and genealogy, and cover over 1,000 regions. These reports can be used to understand a user's extended family tree and family history, or help the user discover any genetic health risks (*McDermott, n.d.*).

Controversies and Challenges

DNA fingerprinting's accuracy appears to safeguard the method against doubt, corruption, or error, but it may actually be our modern trust in the process that renders it so ripe for risk.

Even decades after DNA fingerprinting first appeared in court, Alec Jeffreys maintained that his discovery and methods were not entirely foolproof. At a briefing on the 20th anniversary of his scientific breakthrough, Jeffreys said that false positives were possible in criminal cases, given that the "genetic profiles held by police" were "not sophisticated enough to prevent false identifications" (*Jha, 2004, para. 1*).

Sophisticated or otherwise, the way these profiles are held is also of concern. Though, as discussed, there are regulations in NDIS and

CODIS that control the expungement of DNA profiles in cases of charges being dismissed, United States law enforcement do not solely use NDIS and CODIS to collect and search for DNA matches. The amount of information in these official databases and their adjoining accredited laboratories can make retrieving relevant matches time-consuming, and so some law enforcement agencies opt to use private laboratories. These laboratories are not regulated by CODIS, and therefore may have lower-quality samples (such as partial DNA samples or samples that contain mixtures of multiple individuals' DNA), and, more concerningly, they are not required to ever eliminate DNA records (*Ortyl, 2019*). This could put more people at risk for false positives in criminal cases, and raises questions about the Fourth Amendment and people's right to their personal privacy as discussed in chapter 4. These databases are also, in some cases, restricted to a small area and populated by DNA samples collected by police; for example, the New York City Police Department's local database contains "over 82,000 DNA profiles" and "is separate from the state-operated database and is not subjects to the same rules and oversight" as those regulated by CODIS (*Ortyl, 2019, para. 23*). In Orange County, California, a 145,000-sample database has been collected thanks to an incentive that "allows certain non-violent offenders to give DNA samples in return for the dismissal of the charges against them" (*Ortyl, 2019, para. 24*).

The way DNA evidence is examined and handled by so many people risks a defendant's ability to cross-examine the reliability of that evidence. If something went wrong within the collection, transportation, or analysis process, who do they interrogate? Whose testimony is of interest? Different laboratories could use different processes to acquire or examine the DNA, some of which may be improper depending on the state of the scene and the training of those doing the collecting (*Clark, 2014; Lynch, 2003*).

The same qualities that make DNA an ingenious key in investigations are also what make it incredibly sensitive and difficult to work with. A criminal may be unable to control if one of their hairs or a scattering of skin cells pins them to a crime scene, but in the same way, every other person in the investigative process that handles the DNA in any capacity must be just as careful to not contaminate the microscopic evidence. Clark (2014) warns specifically that PCR testing may accidentally multiply traces of the incorrect DNA, leading all tests to focus on the wrong person.

The case of O.J. Simpson is an example of how DNA profiles may damage the investigation in the lab. Simpson was on trial for the murder of his ex-wife, Nicole Brown, and her friend, Ron Goldman, in Nicole's condo. Blood from all three people was scattered on Brown's condo walkway and driveway, in Simpson's car, in Simpson's house, and on Simpson's socks (not to mention the famous ill-fitting glove). Three laboratories confirmed that Simpson's blood was at the crime scene. The scene seems perfectly damning: the prosecution claimed Simpson cut his hand during the murders and spread both his and the victims' blood as he left Brown's home and drove to his own. But the defense argued that it was almost too perfect. In fact, the laboratory that tested the blood had made a series of gaffes that made them seem incompetent at best, manipulative at worst (*Hansen et al., 2008*).

These errors include but are not limited to: (1) samples were collected with damp swabs, put into plastic bags, and left in the heat for hours, creating conditions that are proven to degrade DNA, (2) a lab worker admitted to spilling a vial of Simpson's blood in the evidence-processing room, possibly resulting in sprinkles of blood getting on other evidence from the crime scene, and (3) blood collected from Simpson was never properly labelled and stored in an unmarked envelope, while other samples went missing. Simpson was ruled not guilty, though a later civil trial would eventually convict him (*Hansen et al., 2008*). Two of the lawyers who fought to prove that the laboratory mishandled the evidence, Barry Scheck and Peter Neufeld, went on to use DNA analysis to win 178 exonerations (mainly of wrongfully convicted Black Americans), showing that they trusted DNA's lack of bias if it was properly collected and handled (*Shaer, 2016*).

Any crime scene can be filled with DNA evidence that is entirely unrelated to the crime. If someone is murdered in their living room by a stranger, their friend's DNA will likely be on every surface if they often come by to visit: hair on the sofa, skin cells in the carpet, perhaps even fingerprints on the murder weapon if it was an object that belonged in the house. It was a circumstance like this which fuelled the prosecution against Amanda Knox, a young woman who was falsely convicted for the murder of her roommate, Meredith Kercher, in 2007. Knox's fingerprints were found on Kercher's bra clasp and a kitchen knife's handle in Knox's boyfriend's kitchen–both items that she would have had a reason to touch, such as when sorting laundry and cooking (*Hooper, 2011*). Kercher's DNA was found on the knife blade, but it was eventually ruled that this tiny amount was most likely contamination, since the knife was inspected after lab technicians handled 50 of Kercher's items. The bra clasp (which also contained scant traces of Knox's boyfriend's DNA) was also examined under unideal circumstances: six weeks after the murder and after spending those six weeks in a crime scene that was being crossed by countless people without protective gear or gloves (*Brayson, 2016*).

Media bias and a tangle of testimony made both of these cases more complex than any evidence tampering could manage, but both illustrate how easily DNA can be scattered around a scene or in a lab by accident. It takes a keen investigator and skillful lab technician to separate the true evidence from the natural presence of DNA, and to treat the DNA with care and utmost caution. Small, degraded, and especially mixed samples can be difficult to parse; in his 2016 article for The Atlantic on the downfalls of DNA fingerprinting, Shaer describes mixed samples as a stack of transparency films and an interpretive art. Shaer explains a case where, in Georgia, 2002, a teenage boy was found guilty on the basis of his DNA being a part of mixed DNA in a rape case. However, around a decade later, 17 lab technicians were asked by a pair of professors who were interested in the case to determine if the teenage boy was definitively a contributor to the DNA mix. Four said it was inconclusive and the remaining twelve said the defendant's DNA was not a part of the mix. Only one agreed with the court that had judged him guilty. Shaer also describes a case in Europe where one person's DNA was tracedto more than 40 crime scenes…but it was from the worker who made the testing swabs for the DNA. Additionally, Shaer notes how in 2012 case, a man was arrested for murder because the victim's DNA was under his fingernails, but this was only because they had been treated at the same hospital that day and given the same oxygen-monitoring device on their hands.

While DNA evidence was once doubted because of risks like faulty laboratories or juries plainly not understanding what they were being told or not trusting the science, there are also risks when opinion swings the other way entirely. A DNA match presented as a headline to a court case could mean that people become entirely convinced of the culprit, regardless of accuracy. Even a decade later, Knox, especially, is the target of countless online conspiracies about her guilt, many of them hinging on DNA. This was occasionally called the "CSI effect"—DNA profiling had been sold as a perfect, unbiased, unquestionable proof, and people began to treat it as such (*Shaer, 2016*). Hearing that someone's DNA has been found on the murder weapon or under the victim's fingernails sounds like–and often is–a clear conclusion. However, skepticism (and the understanding of the processes and sciences behind it in order to level that skepticism rationally and accurately) must be maintained.

Conclusion

Advancements in DNA forensics have revolutionized crime investigations by giving law enforcement what appears to be a direct, unbiased link between crime scenes and their perpetrators. It can reveal the truth in both Supreme Court cases of violent crime, or be delivered right to the home of a private resident to provide information on their distant ancestors or any genetic health concerns. However, as with many technological advancements, it isn't the technology itself, but the people implementing and analysing it that give it its true power, for better or for worse.

REFERENCES

Aronson, J. D. (2005). Dna fingerprinting on trial: The dramatic early history of a new forensic technique. *Endeavour, 29*(3), 126-131. doi:10.1016/j.endeavour.2005.04.006

Blair, C. T. (1990). Spencer v. Commonwealth and recent developments in the admissibility of DNA fingerprint evidence. *Virginia Law Review, 76*(4), 853-876. doi:10.2307/1073213

Brayson, J. (2016, September 30). *Why the DNA evidence against Amanda Knox failed*. Bustle. https://www.bustle.com/articles/186393-what-was-the-dna-evidence-in-the-amanda-knox-case-crime-scene-findings-raised-many-questions

Clark, C. (2014). DNA analysis and the confrontation clause: "Special needs" category for DNA testimonial evidence. *Golden Gate University Law Review, 44,* 195-220.

Chamary, J. V. (2020, June 20). *How genetic genealogy helped catch the Golden State Killer.* Forbes. https://www.forbes.com/sites/jvchamary/2020/06/30/genetic-genealogy-golden-state-killer/?sh=25bb45675a6d

Encyclopædia Britannica, inc. (n.d.). *Nucleus.* Encyclopædia Britannica. Retrieved May 27, 2022, from https://www.britannica.com/science/nucleus-biology

FBI. (n.d.). *Frequently asked questions on CODIS and NDIS.* FBI. https://www.fbi.gov/services/laboratory/biometric-analysis/codis/codis-and-ndis-fact-sheet

Gannon, M. (2012, October 10). *How long can DNA last? A million years, maybe more.* NBC News. https://www.nbcnews.com/id/wbna49366487

Hansen, A. J., Perry, A. H., &a Anderson, W. E. (2008). *DNA fingerprinting an interacting qualifying project report.* Worcester Polytechnic Institute.

Harbison, C. (2017, June 17.) *Alec John Jeffreys (1950–).* The Embryo Project Encyclopedia. https://embryo.asu.edu/pages/alec-john-jeffreys-1950

Hooper. J. (2011, October 4). *Amanda Knox: Police under fire over botched investigation.* The Guardian. https://www.theguardian.com/world/2011/oct/04/amanda-knox-meredithkercher

Jeffreys, A. (n.d. a). *The Ghana Immigration case* [Interview transcript]. Cold Spring Harbor Laboratory. https://dnalc.cshl.edu/view/15107-The-Ghana-Immigration-case-Alec-Jeffreys.html

Jeffreys, A. (n.d. b). *After the Ghana Immigration case* [Interview transcript]. Cold Spring Harbor Laboratory. https://dnalc.cshl.edu/view/15109-After-the-Ghana-immigration-case-Alec-Jeffreys.html

Jeffreys, A. (n.d. c). *Results of the Ghana Immigration case* [Interview transcript]. Cold Spring Harbor Laboratory. https://dnalc.cshl.edu/view/15108-Results-of-the-Ghana-Immigration-case-Alec-Jeffreys.html

Jha, A. (2004). *DNA fingerprinting 'no longer foolproof.'* The Guardian. https://www.theguardian.com/science/2004/sep/09/sciencenews.crime

Leahy, S. (2018, April 25). *Alleged Golden State Killer busted by DNA. But are tests '100%' accurate?* National Geographic. https://www. nationalgeographic.com/science/article/dna-testing-accuracy-golden-state-killer-science-spd#:~:text=DNA%20testing%20and%20a%20 genealogy%20database%20reportedly%20provided,by%20the%20Sa-cramento%20Sheriff%20on%20charges%20of%20murder.

Lynch, M. (2003). God's signature: DNA profiling, the new gold standard in forensic science. *Endeavour. 27*(2), 93-97. doi:10.1016/S0160-9327(03)00068-1

McDermott, M. (n.d.). *23andMe vs Ancestry DNA.* Genealogy Explained. https://genealogyexplained.org/dna-testing/23andme-vs-ancestrydna/ index.html#:~:text=23andMe%20and%20AncestryDNA%20 both%20offer%20the%20savvy%2C%20adventurous,the%20 unabridged%2C%20raw%20data%20of%20your%20DNA%20test.

National Institute of Justice. (2011, March 2). *What is STR analysis?* National Institute of Justice. https://nij.ojp.gov/topics/articles/what-str-analysis

Ortyl, E. (2019). DNA and the Fourth Amendment: Would a defendant succeed on a challenge to a familial DNA search? *American Journal of Law & Medicine, 45*(4), 421-442. doi:10.1177/0098858819892746

Peter, G. (2005). DNA as evidence - the technology of identification. *New England Journal of Medicine, 352*(26), 2669-2671.

Rockowitz, S., Dufour, N., Skowran, R., & Landry, E. (2008). *DNA fingerprinting.* Worcester Polytechnic Institute.

Shaer, M. (2016). A reasonable doubt. *The Atlantic, 317*(5), 46-55.

Tande, C. M. (1989). DNA Typing: A New Investigatory Tool. *Duke Law Journal, 1989*(2), 474–494. https://doi.org/10.2307/1372621 Automation Replaces About 23 Percent of Lawyer's Work. (2017, March 27). FindLaw.

CHAPTER 6 - TECHNOLOGY IN LEGAL PRACTICE

"Technology will be the main driver of change. And, in the long run, we will neither need nor want professionals to work in the way that they did in the twentieth century and before."

— *Richard Susskind*

In this book, we have reviewed the relationship between technology on public law and evidence. However, the value and impact of technology in private law—relationships between natural and corporate persons—cannot be overstated. Legal practice is continuously developing and responding to pressures created by technology in several respects. First, technology is transforming practice with legal automation. Mckinsey & Company, a leading consulting firm, suggested in 2017 that legal technology could replace 23 per cent of a lawyers' work if embraced by law firms (*Automation, 2017*). The use cases for legal technology are driving market investment. In 2021, venture capitalists poured more into the research and development of legal technology than ever before with investment topping over 1 billion USD (*Metinko, 2021*). Technology is creating greater pressure on law firms to deliver more value at less cost. American states and Canadian provinces and territories are loosening practice restrictions in order to enable persons without formal legal training to take on a greater volume of legal work with the assistance of legal technology (*Skolnik, 2021*). In Great Britain, the consulting firm Deloitte projects that 114,000 legal jobs, a sizeable portion of the overall market, are likely to be automated within the next twenty years (*Deloitte, 2017*). In this context of change and disruption, lawyers need to find efficiencies to cut down on routine, low-value work and maximize the time they have to solve clients' greatest challenges. To surmount this task, lawyers and law firms have taken to adopting and independently developing legal technology. The purpose of this chapter is to address the impact of technology in the private practice of law. This chapter will identify, describe, and analyze the leading legal technologies that lawyers and law firms are using or developing. In particular, this chapter will review the current technologies supporting law firms in transaction management, contract design, due diligence, and discovery and, moreover, address the emergence of smart contracts.

Practice Tools & Technologies

In Canada and around the world, leading law firms have embraced a variety of technologies to transform the practice of law, reduce costs, and drive business growth. These firms have taken aim at the 23 per cent of work that can be automated or supplemented by legal technology. In order to appreciate the current state of the legal technology market, it is fruitful to review the suite of technologies at issue. These technologies bear on lawyers' work drafting, closing, and reviewing contracts and written content and supply support in transaction management, signature collection, and contract review.

Legal transaction management technologies are one suite of products popular in private practice. Closing Folders, a leading platform, is a technology used in transactional law that leverages digital documents to improve process efficiency and security. Transactional lawyers have the role of overseeing financial dealing to ensure their client's best interests are represented and legally safeguarded. These lawyers primarily deal with mergers and acquisitions of corporate entities such as in standard private transactions, takeover bids of traded companies wherein one company offers to buy another, and the purchase and financing of securities and assets. These lawyers' projects may involve considerable complexity because they are changing the ownership of assets and performing due diligence to ensure there are no hidden liabilities and business risks. Any given legal deal could involve hundreds of documents the content of which contains terms that bind a client's ability to act or effect the transfer of money or assets. The traditional method of conducting the business of law in rooms full of paper documents is problematic because it places greater administrative and organizational pressures on lawyers for which clients are uninterested in paying. Relying on human organization involves a greater risk for error and can have costly delays. Enterprise has developed technology to assist lawyers in solving this problem. Transaction management software like Closing Folders tracks all the documents at issue in a transaction, automatically identifies where signatures are required on the documents, compiles relevant documents in PDF, and enables lawyers and their clients to review the progress of the deal in respect of what documents have received signatures. Transaction management legal technology has improved the speed at which commerce can occur by simplifying the legal progress underpinning commercial financial transactions.

Technologies enabling digital signatures are relied on by products like Closing Folders. Law firms use legal software like DocuSign to email and monitor files that are to be digitally signed by clients at their convenience. Digital signatures have become commonplace, such as clicking the "I accept" on an online terms of service page. In Canada, the use of digital signatures is regulated by the provincial and federal governments in acts such as Alberta's Electronic Transactions Act or the Canada Business Corporations Act and Personal Information Protection and Electronic Documents Act. This government legislation specifies in what circumstances it is permissible to use legal technology to capture signatures for legal purposes. In general, Canada's electronic signature regulatory regime is highly permissive. but there are a variety of exclusions within legislation, the extent of which is not relevant for the purposes of this chapter. In the context of using electronic signatures, consent and jurisdiction must be considered. As a general rule, it is required that both parties signing a document consent to the use of electronic assistance. Moreover, parties signing an electronic document must consider the jurisdiction in which a contract is accepted via signature. The adoption of legal technologies can create legal risk and uncertainty. For example, a party to an agreement could claim that they did not consent to the digitalisation of the contracts process if they later decided the agreement was disadvantageous to their interest. Likewise, a disaffected party could claim that a contract was formalized in a jurisdiction other than the one intended in order to secure a legal or procedural advantage because, from a legal perspective, a contract crystallizes upon acceptance in whatever jurisdiction the acceptor is situated. For these reasons, it is essential that everyone from lawyers to laypersons engaging in legal relations responds to the pressures and impacts of legal technology by considering the whole of their contract. Issues such as digitalisation consent and contract jurisdiction can be easily rectified by adding provisions into the written contract to state that digital signatures are mutually accepted and to state the jurisdiction in which disputes over the contract will be heard. In this manner, digital signature technology is representative of the pros and cons of legal technology in general: it saves time and comes with some legal risk which, while dramatic, can be remedied through planning and proper contract construction. Overall, digital signatures are well accepted and are an essential part of the modern practice of law.

Automated contract review is another disruptive legal technology in private practice. These technologies, such as Litera Contract Companion, aim to reduce the cost and amount of time spent on reviewing or amending legal agreements. They function by analyzing the contract text and identifying the important clauses for human review. These technologies can read and identify the purpose of contract provisions, cross-reference provisions that cite one another, check defined terms, and flag errors with dates, dollar values, or party names and locations. Similarly, Thomson Reuters offers Contracts Express, a document automation system aimed at simplifying the drafting of new contracts, which functions by filling out existing contract templates with information based on a questionnaire a lawyer completes. Automated contract review relies on machine learning technology. Machine learning is the process of using computer algorithms to draw predictions from large datasets with minimal or no human oversight. Automated contract review leverages large data sets to train computers to recognise patterns in contract design and predict errors and omissions (*Catterwell, 2020, p. 91*). These technologies are aimed at proofreading and perfecting contracts which lawyers have already drafted. They do not actively assist in the application of the law behind the drafting of contracts. However, the most sophisticated contract review softwares, like Luminance, aim to actively assist lawyers in contract design by leveraging databases of "100 million documents in over 80 languages across hugely diverse fields of law" in their contract drafting (Luminance). These technologies have the ability to form a conceptual understanding of a document and match it to all others within the database in an effort to identify anomalies and support regulatory compliance. As an example of the power of contract review, a small team working on a project at the world's largest law firm, Dentons, in Dubai was able to review 180,000 documents in 2 weeks as opposed to 60 working days, thus releasing a time savings of 80 per cent. Another legal innovation comes from JPMorgan Chase, the largest bank in the United States, that developed a machine learning program to undertake automatic analysis of loan agreements. The bank developed an algorithm that can autonomously classify and sort clauses into one hundred and fifty different attributes of credit contracts more accurately than human reviewers and claims to have reduced the amount of paid lawyer hours by 360,000 hours or 41 calendar years (*JP Morgan, 2013*). These technologies work effectively because many contracts follow a predictable architecture and structure (*Gerding, 2013, p. 1339*). In contradistinction, it is unlikely that machine learning will enable automated argument generation for the litigation as this process requires complex thought, an appreciation for subjectivity, a capacity for interpreting ambiguity, and a deep understanding of the words, context, and purposes of the dispute or contract at issue (*Catterwell, 2020, p. 95*). However, at the very least, automated contract review tools are becoming increasingly adept at recognising ambiguity. A recent study showed that machine learning paired with natural language processing (the ability for computers to understand human text) could detect ambiguity in contracts with "80 per cent accuracy, 100 per cent precision, and 85 per cent recall scores" (*Candas, 2022, p. 12*). In addition to contract review assistance, there are technologies specifically tailored to due diligence and discovery. Due diligence is the process of reviewing documents to confirm the underlying facts involved in a corporate legal situation (for example the sale of a property or the filing for a loan). Discovery is the process of submitting all relevant prior to a trial to secure the relevant evidence and question the opposing side. These legal tasks can involve hundreds of documents that need to be mined for key facts, names, and patterns. Overall, automated contract and text review is accurate and can enable huge time savings. However, there are minimal threats to law as a profession about the adoption and use of new legal technologies as it was reported that AI would reduce lawyers' billing hours by only 13 over the next five years (*Marchant, 2017, p. 24*). Overall, automated contract review is already used in the practice law to tremendous effect and, in future, will likely continue to grow in adoption and effectiveness.

Smart Contracts

In this chapter, we so far discussed how a variety of technologies simplified and expedited tasks in the private practice of law. However, we have not addressed one of the greatest emergent technologies that could transform legal practice, smart contracts. Before describing smart contracts, it is important to understand the blockchain system on which they exist. At its heart, blockchain is a digital ledger that records transactions (*Monrat, 2019*). Similar to how companies and banks record transactions in a central private ledger, blockchain records events in a public decentralized ledger that is held in stored in computer network systems around the world. The advantage of this technology compared to standard ledgers is that it is near impossible for one bad-actor to fraudulently alter the blockchain record because all records are confirmed by the whole network which is distributed and controlled by a large number of different parties with different interests. Verification of contracts or transactions occurs on a network of thousands of computers that spans the world over. This means that contractual dealings can occur without a trusted intermediary like a bank, payment processor, or law firm. This technology is known as blockchain in that it operates on a series of mathematical calculations which lock into place single events such as a change in ownership (known as blocks) and add them to a traceable history of past events (the chain). The importance of blockchain technology from a legal perspective is that it enables the use of smart contracts. Smart contracts are contracts governed by and expressed in computer code. Smart contracts operate on the Ethereum blockchain. The code in these contracts automate the fulfillment of the provisions within the contract, for example by executing a task or imposing penalties. From a client perspective, the draw of smart contracts is that the fulfillment of the contract is immediate and so reduces the cost and uncertainty involved in pursuing claims through traditional legal channels.

It is helpful to refer to examples to appreciate the use of smart contracts in practice. While the technology is relatively new, smart contracts have been tested in real-scale commercial environments. Axa Insurance, a multi-billion dollar French multinational company, launched a flight-delay insurance product based on smart-contracts in 2017 (*ArtificialLawyer, 2020*). When a consumer purchased a flight protected with the insurance, the transaction would be entered into the blockchain and became uneditable and irrevocable. The code and provisions of the smart contract was integrated with global air traffic reporting databases. If a flight was delayed more than 2 hours, the smart contract would automatically be triggered and pay out to the consumer: no claim submission, no interpretation, no hassle. This product was axed in 2020 due to insufficient demand from consumers for flight protection, following significant decreases in travel due to the ongoing COVID-19 pandemic. However, Axa's product showcases the core value proposition for smart contracting: payment is immediate and automatic, the contract's conditions are custom to the person on the other side of the contract, and, lastly, smart contracts can be cost efficient as there are no lawyers or specialists involved in the appraisal and payout of the claim. Another example of the application of smart contacts is the major international law firm Hogan Lovells that created a proof of concept with smart contracts concerning earthquake insurance in New York City in 2017 (*Norton, 2017*). In contract law, the method for preserving the immutability of an agreement would be preserved with an anti modification clause preventing the parties from varying the terms of the agreement at a later date. In smart contracts, no such clause is needed as the computer code operating the contract itself provides for this function.

For further clarity, another use case for smart contracts are contingent agreements. For example, in the sale of a house or property wherein one party has a contract which specifies that the sale will only come to fulfillment on the condition that the other party sells their house. Traditionally, a failure to follow a provision such as this would require costly litigation in order to secure a judgment to secure costs or an order requiring that the party sell. However, utilizing smart contracts the sale could be automated and immediate under the pre-authorised smart contract. Indeed, the automatic enforcement of smart contracts is contemplated to go so far as to having an apartment door lock automatically when a tenant fails to meet their payment obligations or having a leased car disable its ignition capacity itself when payments are in default (*Woebbeking, 2019, p. 110*). There is great promise for the future of smart contracts especially as the world we interact with on a daily basis becomes increasingly more connected on the internet and there are an increasing large number of autonomous or sensor based-products like Tesla cars (*Dahlqvist, 2019*). Besides providing greater certainty for consumers, smart contracts will impact lawyers. In particular, it is predicted that smart contracts will impact lawyers by reducing the scope of their work "registering and transferring assets, verifying the completion of certain conditions precedent, monitoring covenant compliance, registering and discharging security" in addition to any other task that has a binary result which can be mediated by computer code (*Middleton, 2018*). Smart contracts, by these means, have the potential to replace a large portion of the tasks assigned to corporate and commercial lawyers.

On the other hand, smart contracts will also create new work for lawyers. In particular, the commercial use of smart contracts extends well beyond these limits. In particular, the leading potential uses for Ethereum smart contract applications include "financial derivatives, identity and reputation systems, file storage, insurance, cloud computing, prediction markets" (*Vujicic et al., 2018, p. 4*). There is a strong use case in a variety of Ethereum applications. To be clear, smart contracts are digital and computer-code expressions on the provisions established in human contracts and so can be unintuitive. Therefore, it is probable that smart contracts will predominantly continue as a tool utilized by lawyers as opposed to a tool that draws work away from lawyers to laypersons. Smart contracts may have large use in low value online transactions for which it would be cost-prohibitive to seek legal redress in conventional channels (*Ortolani, 2015, p. 595*). It is imagined that smart contracts could underlie a system of commercial arbitration, replacing the charge-back model or escrow protection that exist today, wherein transactions would be concluded in a stateless currency such that which Facebook attempted to create wherein online dispute resolution providers control the flow of money to safeguard the transaction (p. 620). Contracts have advantages when immutable including in that they prevent parties from bluffing and renegotiating the contract after its conclusion under the threat of having to pursue a lengthy litigation process (*Davis, 2006, p. 496*). However, it can be economically inefficient to operate under immutable contracts. In particular, parties may wish to have flexibility in the operations of their contracts to suit commercial realities and, moreover, requiring a contract to be immutable may make some parties less likely to want to engage in a deal (p. 496).

Despite the uses of smart contracts, there are limitations to their functionality as a legal technology. One limitation is that smart contracts require events to be binary (true or false) in order to self-execute provisions or apply penalties. Smart contracts will not function in circumstances such as where a contract provision requires interpretation. This limitation is significant because legal contracts often have clauses that require interpretation, such as whether one party is making best efforts to bring the contract to fulfillment or whether a certain action is reasonable. Smart contracts can assist with fact-based provisions to trigger automatic relief. Standard legal contracts will set out the ambiguous terms that will remain the preserve of human interpreters.

Another challenge (or benefit depending on one's perspective) is that smart contracts are built on the blockchain with the purpose of being immutable and unchangeable. In other words, once the parties sign and establish a smart contract it cannot be revoked or altered even if both parties want to change the agreement. This contrasts with traditional legal contracts where the parties generally have flexibility to adjust the terms of a contract to their preference. To the extent that smart contracts depend on real-world data inputs (referred to as oracles), they can be changed through one's altering of the data on which their provisions depend. Smart contracts may also include terms that depend on and refer to the outcomes of other smart contracts. In general, smart contracts persist even if there is an error in the construction of the contract, a change in law occurs, or one of the parties ceases to exist. Smart contracts can even be used to enforce illegal or immoral terms of an agreement that a standard court of law would not condone or uphold (*Woebbeking, 2019, p. 112*). Another limitation of smart contracts is that they are not a legally recognised document. Merely because individuals have entered into a smart contract does not mean that there was a legally recognised and enforceable contract in the Alberta courts of justice nor does it mean that any lawyer or client relationship was created. Another business limitation of smart contracts is that they operate on the public, distributed blockchain. For this reason, the terms and provisions of a smart contract will necessarily be public.

While there are some means by which to disguise or hide transactions occurring on the blockchain, such as by using pseudonyms or mixing the assets that are being transferred between cru-currency accounts, this presents a challenge and threat to business privacy and an impediment to the widespread use of smart contracts (*Bitmix, 2021*). Lastly, another challenge in the use of smart contracts is the technical capacity of the Ethereum blockchain in terms of the volume of transactions (triggered contracts) that the system can handle. Currently, the Ether Network can handle only 30 transactions in a second resulting in delay and increased costs for conducting business on the platform. There are plans to increase the functionality of the system to 100,000 per second in the next several years (*Millman, 2020*). Comparatively, Visa and Mastercard process about 5,000 transactions per second as of recent years (*Vlastelica, 2017*). Overall, there are serious limitations to the use of smart contracts that will limit their widespread adoption for commercial purposes.

Corporate governance is another area of business law that could be impacted by the use of smart contracts. The Canada Business Corporations Act sets out a legal regime for the operation of corporations including in respect of shareholder rights, reporting requirements, and quorum requirements. It moreover imposes duties in the law of fiduciaries and negligence which requires board-members to adhere to certain standards of conduct and ethics. As a result of this regulation and liability, lawyers serve in corporate governance positions in order to assist the boards to operate, sit on committees for audits, handle regulatory compliance, and assist with investigations or inquiries. However, smart contracts have given rise to a novel form of corporate entity, the decentralized autonomous organization or DAO. The first DAO, which was termed "TheDAO", raised $150 million for the purposes of investment management (*Kolber, 2018, p. 212*). The idea behind TheDAO was that the decentralized organization was to act autonomously pursuant to smart contracts and that investment proposals were to be decided by the will of the majority of fund-investors. The idea of a DAO governed by smart contracts is an expansion of the idea that algorithms can form the basis of contractual relations, such as the computer models that are tasked with independently trading in financial products or goods, and thus can act as agents for corporations (*Scholz, 2019, p. 17*). Infamously, TheDAO collapsed as a decentralized organization when a flaw in its smart contract design was exploited in order to withdraw 55 million from the fund. The fact that this exploit occurred exposes a key risk to the use of smart contracts: their strict construction. Smart contracts are strictly construed and extremely literal given their digital format. They run on the same code on which computer programs operate. When there is an error in their design, there are no safeguards that prevent an individual from leveraging that error to their own benefit. In future, DAO could operate to execute a large number of tasks traditionally handled by lawyers supporting an organization in a board position. Indeed, a DAO itself can take legal actions autonomously based on its smart contract underpinnings. Moreover, the advent of novel legal technologies such as a smart contract based DAO raises questions about legal responsibility. In the case of the 55 million dollar exploit, it is unclear who bears legal responsibility for the loss as there are no named directors of the organization and furthermore the shareholders themselves may be anonymous (*Hinkes, 2016*). This lack of responsibility may create legal and regulatory challenges for the DAO to interact with other organizations in the process of business contracting as would a government-recognised cooperation. This challenge may be overcome by specifying some person or organization as the acting authority or spokesperson for the DAO despite the fact that its decisions are not under their control but rather directed by the shareholders. By these means, lawyers on the cutting edge of technology and law may consider creating, supporting, and engaging in the operation of DAO.

Last, financial services and lending are large practice areas for lawyers. Finance lawyers work on behalf of banks and lenders on projects such as syndicated loans, preparing commitment letters, and setting up legal frameworks for the security interest (the asset backing the loan that can be retrieved by the bank) in asset based lending and debt finance arrangements. Smart contracts are relevant in this context given that they underpin decentralized finance or DeFi. DeFi emerged in 2017 with a purpose of enabling persons to engage in traditional activities of finance like lending, borrowing, trading, insuring, and earning interest without involvement from banks or exchanges and instead using technology (cryptocurrency and smart contracts). One of the leading examples of smart finance is Aave, a smart contract product, which offers borrowing assets and interest on staked assets (*Meegan, 2021, p. 7*). Loans on the Aave platform are given out from a shared pool of assets that earn interest and are granted to borrowers who must stake collateral worth more than the amount they are withdrawing. In these financing arrangements, there is no need for the involvement of lawyers because security assets are governed by the smart contract as are other binary elements to financial contracts such as "if the Borrower receives a certain credit rating from one of the major credit rating agencies, the Borrower's loan pricing will move to a certain level." (*Middleton, 2018*). By means of disintermediation and automation, DeFi has the potential to reduce the scope of the work of banks and financial lawyers and thus drive down costs of purchasing financial products and services (*OECD, 2021, p. 39*). And, similarly, has the potential to reduce the silosation of the financial sector and, in so doing, promote innovation and build more dynamic financial ecosystems. The benefit of DeFi is that it could disrupt the closed legal model of financial services and promote inclusion and accessibility on the public blockchain. However, the law must evolve to accommodate DeFi. Given its novelty, DeFi is largely unregulated and thus there are risks to investors in situations such as "loss of capital, manipulation, technical bugs, exploits, thefts, hacking, and loss of funds through user or protocol error" (p. 60). Moreover, there are a lack of rules binding how investing occurs which could open up DeFi to a serious financial disaster akin to that occurring in 2008 or a similar scenario. DeFi, like any other, is a technology to which law and regulation will catch-up in time. Overall, in these respects, technology will supplant or complement the work of lawyers and bankers working in a highly regulated space. The application of these technologies will change the ways in which legal markets operate.

It is highly likely they will reduce the fees and market dominance law firms have in routine legal projects like drafting wills, basic contracts for the sale of goods, or in due diligence searching. On the other hand, lawyers in highly specialized fields of law and in areas of law in which there is little evidence for computers to interpret will be in a stronger position to avoid market displacement (*McGinnis, 2019, p. 3057*).

The Metaverse is a locus for the development of law and technology. The Metaverse, in short, is a virtual version of the internet as a whole. Futurists anticipate that it will be the online world in which we spend significant amounts of time, playing, working, and learning. The Metaverse is a novel technology and idea. For this reason, there is no uniform agreement in the literature as to what it contains or how precisely it is defined. Nevertheless, examples of business within the Metaverse include virtual art galleries, virtual live concerts, simulated reality environments, online worlds/games wherein one uses a virtual avatar, and virtual landscapes in which to purchase digital real estate, and the sale/acquisition of digital objects. In the Metaverse, law and technology collide given the fast pace of investment and economic development occurring in the sector. Indeed, it is forecasted that the market for products, services, and assets based in the Metaverse will reach $800 billion by the year 2024 as major technology companies such as Apple, Google, Amazon, Facebook, and Microsoft rush to establish themselves within the space (*Joshi, 2022*). A fundamental part of the operation of law and legal regimes is jurisdiction. In the Metaverse, the operation of law is uncertain and as the internet operates in a semi-regulated manner with multiple overlapping jurisdictions and interests ranging from democratic societies to totalitarian regimes such as China which strictly control access to information. For this reason, the Metaverse is likely to be "an international, partially interoperable array of metaverses, each subject to a different mix of state authority, corporate oversight, and participatory governance" more than a truly decentralized, libertarian, and non-state global commons (*Garon, 2022, p. 7*).

In Canada, law and legislation will likely enable a free and uncensored Metaverse. Canada has no single state administrative organization tasked with regulating the internet and the Metaverse developing within it. The Canadian Government cannot use its criminal or regulatory powers to apply censorship directly as part of the internet infrastructure, such as banning the use of certain consumer applications. However, the government still has some influence over the web. The Canadian state controls the internet via two bodies. First, the Radio-television and Telecommunications Commission which is charged with regulating internet access but not content. Second, the Office of the Privacy Commissioner of Canada holds jurisdiction over internet use and works to ensure that privacy is maintained and protected. Western Governments will likely limit their involvement online to protecting abuses of privacy law, a key area of risk within the Metaverse such as when "Facebook [now Meta] paid one of the largest privacy settlements in US history, $650 million, for violating an Illinois state law regarding the storage of users' biometric data" (facial scan) (*Wieshofer, 2022, p. 4*). Moreover, non biometric data can be captured and understood by social media sites that can predict sexuality, ethnicity, personality, intelligence, drug use, parental separation, age, and gender" with near perfect accuracy (*Kosinski, 2013, p. 4*). The Government's jurisdiction of power extends only to those internet activities that have a "real and substantial connection to Canada" per the Supreme Court in Society of Composers, Authors and Music Publishers of Canada v. Canadian Assn. of Internet Providers. Canadian Courts have worked toward promoting public internet freedom such as the Supreme Court of Canada ruling in 2012 that companies supplying internet access services are not subject to the federal Broadcasting Act which would enable the government to control content on the internet as in Reference Re Broadcasting Act.

From a legal perspective, Canada regards technology with a principle of neutrality. This means that the providers that run the internet do not discriminate or censor against the sites that they provide access toward. For these reasons, the legal framework for the Metaverse will likely be free, transparent, and open in Canada. Western democracies treat the regulation of the internet similarly in general. In contrast, in China, the Metaverse would likely take on another character. The Chinese Communist Party regularly censors stories, bans applications, disables connectivity to external new sources, and imposes criminal sanctions against individuals that do not support the party agenda (*Freedom House, 2021*). At least from the perspective of democratic countries, the Metaverse will remain relatively open, transparent, and free to innovate as a technology unbound by the constraints of legal regulation.

In Canada and within the Western world, privately owned platforms are permitted to govern how individuals use their services despite the absence of strong state control and censorship legislation. Social networks like Twitter, Facebook, and Youtube all rely on algorithms to moderate and police content by automatically identifying unlawful content and, where required, censoring it. While the internet is to a degree decentralized, anonymous, and user-driven, and thus not amendable to censorship, a significant proportion of users are clustered in a few sites (*Cobbe, 2020, p. 750*). The use of these algorithms in censorship is significant because it means that censorship can apply to all communications occurring on a platform (as opposed to only what humans can feasibly review) and that platforms can intervene in a discourse and shape policy by suppressing particular stories or issues (p. 745). Indeed, a recent example of the power of technology companies is the Hunter Biden laptop scandal. In this case, a consortium of sites including Twitter and Facebook made an effort to censor a story concerning embarrassing comprimant detailing President Joe Biden's son's exploits on the basis it was fake (*Reilly,*

2022). However, the story was in fact true and the sites had censored a issue of public concern. Private, commercial censorship is no less concerning than public censorship. Indeed, technology firms have even greater discretion and power in their censorship are they are unbound by public human rights law for free expression such as the US Second 1st amendment and the Canadian Charter of Rights and Freedoms and, moreover, are not as responsive to democratic public interests especially given the particular centralisation of power in video hosting from YouTube or search in Google, and the fact that these companies operate with a commercial and corporate motivation that lends toward the sanitisation of platforms for advertising purposes (*Cobbe, 2020, p. 761*). These considerations have led recently to Elon Musk's bid to purchase Twitter privately and reduce the extent of censorship occurring on the platform. The present state of the deal is uncertain due to complications in the warranties and representations made by Twitter concerning the extent to which their user-base are made of bots. Policies enabling censorship are problematic because they can grow over time in a form of censorship creep wherein ambiguous terminology enables a company to start by censoring content promoting terror and real harm to then policing news it deems to be disinformation or stifle legitimate but dissenting views (*Citron, 2017, p. 1052*).

The main means for the enforcement of these policies are digital contracts known as click through agreements and click wrap licenses. These will be familiar among readers as the non-optional agreements to which one must often click 'I accept', often without reading the agreement in its entirety. These agreements have legal implications for the ownership of content posted on the site, the activities permitted on the site (such as rudeness or inappropriate behavior), exclusions on liability from the platform, and the use and protection of data (*Steingard, 2020*). There are two legal considerations bearing on online user contracts constraining one's use of platforms within the Metaverse. First, the issue of proper disclosure. At law, sites are required to display their moderation policies and seek from the user a signification of their acceptance. Second, the issue of unconscionability and unfairness in contract construction due to the imbalance of power between the parties. At law, a contract can be voided in enforcement if it can be established that (1) proof of an inequality of bargaining power, stemming from some weakness or vulnerability affecting the claimant and (2) proof of an improvident transaction as determined by the Supreme Court in Uber Technologies Inc. v. Heller. The law of unconscionability applies in limited cases wherein the transaction is very unfair, such as where the claimant lacked counsel, where the imbalance in power was extreme, or where the contract or other party takes advantage of that disadvantage. This law comes from a case where the technology company Uber unfairly required that the drivers submit to an expensive dispute resolution process. In addition, tort actions in the law of defamation, Jones v Tsige, 2012 ONCA 32 (intrusion upon seclusion), and nonconsensual release of intimate information would apply to limit freedom in the Metaverse. The broader issue, however, is that users of digital platforms seldom read these terms of service and privacy policies that comprise the contract for their use of the platform. In one study, it was found that 98 per cent of users missed clauses in a contract purporting to share site use information with National Security Agency or require first-born child as payment for access (*Obar, 2020, p. 129*). It is unlikely this will change so long as the costs for engaging in online platforms are low.

Moreover, while the Metaverse in Canada will probably be highly globalized and diverse, much like the country itself, it is likely to be highly regulated with the terms of service of providers and platforms in addition to the other contracts individuals form in business dealings. Law in the Metaverse will be defined by the legality of intellectual property law in the form of patents, copyrights, trademarks, industrial designs and trade secrets. Copyright law protects the duplication of creative works. Trademark law protects a sign or symbol that indicates the origin or producer of a good, like the Nike swoosh. Trade secrets are commercial expertise that is protected from disclosure and reuse. Patents protect an inventor's work product. These forms of legal protection for technology have existed for a long time and it is beyond present purposes to investigate the details of how they function. In recent years, a new form of digital property protection that is unlike any of these legacy legal models. NFT, or Non-Fungible Tokens, are a form of unique digital property. This technology enables persons to claim ownership of digital collectables, property, trading cards, stamps, images, and artwork. Despite being entirely digital, the trading market for these assets was approximately 4,592, 146, 914 USD in 2021 (*Wang, 2021, p. 2*). The most visceral example of an NFT is a unique and singular work of digital art that would be owned as an individual and displayed in a virtual art gallery. In theory, NFT's should enable persons to resell their assets and use them as they please. However, NFT and digital assets are unique in that intellectual property agreements that circumstances the purposes of which one can use an NFT. This is equivalent to purchasing a book and discovering you can only read it on a particular day of the week (p. 46). Despite these limitations, the demand for NFT is projected to grow 33.9 per cent from 2022 to 2030 (*BusinessWire, 2022*). Moreover, a 69 million dollar NFT was sold by Christie's art auction house in 2021 (*Moscufo, 2021*). NFT are separate but related to the conventional law of intellectual property. A sale of NFT does not affect transfer of any legal rights (*Mukaddam, 2021*). In a sense, an NFT is a signed, authenticated version of a digital asset. For this reason, there are concerns in business about the creation of unauthorized NFT when a creator does not have legal rights to the underlying subject material. For example, Nike is litigating online shoe retailer StockX for selling NFT versions of Nike shoes to consumers

(*Brittain, 2022*). Likewise, luxury fashion brand Hermes is suing a creator for its digital NFT reproductions of the brand's famous Birkin handbag (*Siegler, 2022*). NFT are quickly becoming the standard means by which to register and hold digital property as a lawful owner; however they are distinct from traditional intellectual property law protection regimes for technology assets.

In conclusion, this chapter has sought to set out the large impacts that legal technology will have on private practice. It has described how developing technologies will bear on transaction management, signature digitalisation, contract review and design, due diligence, and discovery. Moreover, this chapter has described and probed the impacts of smart contracts on the practice of law in streamlining conventional areas of legal practice like insurance, corporate governance, and financial services while also potentially forming the basis for the developing of the law of the Metaverse and NFTs. Finally, this chapter described the legal regulation and causes of action applicable to these new technologies and envisioned the future for the metaverse and the private practice of law.

REFERENCES

Automation Replaces About 23 Percent of Lawyer's Work. (2017, March 27). FindLaw. https://www.findlaw.com/legalblogs/technologist/automation-replaces-about-23-percent-of-lawyers-work/

ArtificialLawyer. (2020, October 8). *AXA Scraps Fizzy Insurance Smart Contract...But Still Interested in the Tech.* Artificial Lawyer. https://www.artificiallawyer.com/2020/10/08/axa-scraps-fizzy-insurance-smart-contract-but-still-interested-in-the-tech/

BitMix.Biz. (2021, January 12). *Achieving Bitcoin Anonymity Through Mixers.* Bitcoin Magazine. https://bitcoinmagazine.com/culture/achieving-bitcoin-anonymity-through-mixers

Brittain, B. (2022, May 11). Nike ramps up sneaker NFT lawsuit with StockX counterfeiting claim. *Reuters.* https://www.reuters.com/legal/legalindustry/nike-ramps-up-sneaker-nft-lawsuit-with-stockx-counterfeiting-claim-2022-05-11/

BusinessWire. (2022, May 24). *Global Non-fungible Token (NFT) Market Report 2022-2030: Growing Demand for Digital Art and Growing Use of Cryptocurrency Globally Drives Market Demand - ResearchAndMarkets. com.* www.businesswire.com. https://www.businesswire.com/news/home/20220524005651/en/Global-Non-fungible-Token-NFT-Market-Report-2022-2030-Growing-Demand-for-Digital-Art-and-Growing-Use-of-Cryptocurrency-Globally-Drives-Market-Demand---ResearchAndMarkets.com

Candaş, A. B., & Tokdemir, O. B. (2022). Automated Identification of Vagueness in the FIDIC Silver Book Conditions of Contract. *Journal of Construction Engineering and Management, 148*(4). https://doi.org/10.1061/(asce)co.1943-7862.0002254

Catterwell, R. (2020). Automation in contract interpretation. *Law, Innovation and Technology, 12*(1), 81–112. https://doi.org/10.1080/175 79961.2020.1727068

Citron, D. K. (2017). Extremist speech, compelled conformity, and censorship creep. *Notre Dame L. Rev., 93,* 1035.

Cobbe, J. (2020). Algorithmic Censorship by Social Platforms: Power and Resistance. *Philosophy & Technology, 34*(4), 739–766. https://doi. org/10.1007/s13347-020-00429-0

Dahlqvist, F., Patel, M., Rajko, A., & Shulman, J. (2019). *Growing opportunities in the Internet of Things.* McKinsey & Company. https:// www.mckinsey.com/industries/private-equity-and-principal-investors/ our-insights/growing-opportunities-in-the-internet-of-things

Davis, K. E. (2006). The demand for immutable contracts: Another look at the law and economics of contracts modifications. *NYUL Rev., 81,* 487.

Deloitte. (2017). *Objections overruled: The case for disruptive technology in the legal profession.*

Freedom House. (2021). *China: Freedom on the Net 2021 Country Report.* Freedom House. https://freedomhouse.org/country/china/ freedom-net/2021

Garon, J. (2022). Legal implications of a ubiquitous metaverse and a Web3 future. *Available at SSRN 4002551.*

Gerding, E. F. (2013). Contract as pattern language. *Wash. L. Rev., 88,* 1323.

Hinkes, D. (2016, April 21). *A Legal Analysis of the DAO Exploit and Possible Investor Rights.* Bitcoin Magazine: Bitcoin News, Articles, Charts, and Guides. https://bitcoinmagazine.com/culture/a-legal-analysis-of-the-dao-exploit-and-possible-investor-rights-1466524659

Joshi, S. (2022, March 15). *The Metaverse, Explained for People Who Still Don't Get It.* www.vice.com. https://www.vice.com/en/article/93bmyv/what-is-the-metaverse-internet-technology-vr

JP Morgan COIN: A Bank's Side Project Spells Disruption for the Legal Industry. (2013, November 13). Technology and Operations Management. https://digital.hbs.edu/platform-rctom/submission/jp-morgan-coin-a-banks-side-project-spells-disruption-for-the-legal-industry/

Kolber, A. J. (2018). Not-so-smart blockchain contracts and artificial responsibility. *Stan. Tech. L. Rev., 21,* 198.

Kosinski, M., Stillwell, D., & Graepel, T. (2013). Private traits and attributes are predictable from digital records of human behavior. *Proceedings of the national academy of sciences, 110*(15), 5802-5805.

Luminance.. (n.d.). *Luminance.* Luminance. https://www.luminance.com/technology.html

Marchant, G. E. (2017). Artificial intelligence and the future of legal practice. *ABA SciTech Law, 14*(1).

McGinnis, J. O., & Pearce, R. G. (2019). The great disruption: How machine intelligence will transform the role of lawyers in the delivery of legal services. *Actual Probs. Econ. & L.,* 1230.

Meegan, X., & Koens, T. (2021). Lessons Learned from Decentralised Finance (DeFi). *ING. URL: https://new. ingwb. com/binaries/content/ assets/insights/themes/distributed-ledger-technology/defi_white_paper_ v2. 0. pdf.*

Metinko, C. (2021, September 23). *Legal Tech Makes Its Case With Venture Capitalists, Tops $1B In Funding This Year.* Crunchbase News. https://news.crunchbase.com/venture/legal-tech-venture-investment/

Middleton, R. (2018, July 5). *Why bankers and lawyers need to understand blockchain and smart contracts.* Www.dentons.com. https:// www.dentons.com/en/insights/articles/2018/july/5/why-bankers-and-lawyers-need-to-understand-blockchain-and-smart-contracts

Millman, R. (2020, December 1). *What is Ethereum 2.0 and Why Does It Matter?* Decrypt. https://decrypt.co/resources/what-is-ethereum-2-0

Monrat, A. A., Schelen, O., & Andersson, K. (2019). A Survey of Blockchain From the Perspectives of Applications, Challenges, and Opportunities. *IEEE Access, 7,* 117134–117151. https://doi.org/10.1109/ access.2019.2936094

Moscufo, M. (2021, March 11). *Digital artwork sells for record $69 million at Christie's first NFT auction.* NBC News. https://www.nbcnews. com/business/business-news/digital-artwork-sells-record-60-million-christie-s-first-nft-n1260544

Mukaddam, F. (2021, October). *NFTs and Intellectual Property Rights.* https://Www.nortonrosefulbright.com/En/Knowledge/ Publications/2021. https://www.nortonrosefulbright.com/en/knowledge/ publications/1a1abb9f/nfts-and-intellectual-property-rights#section4

Norton, S. (2017). *Law Firm Hogan Lovells Learns to Grapple with Blockchain Contracts.*

Obar, J. A., & Oeldorf-Hirsch, A. (2020). The biggest lie on the internet: Ignoring the privacy policies and terms of service policies of social networking services. *Information, Communication & Society, 23*(1), 128-147.

Organisation for Economic Co-operation and Development. (2021, January 19). *Why Decentralised Finance (DeFi) Matters and the Policy Implications - OECD.* Www.oecd.org. https://www.oecd.org/finance/why-decentralised-finance-defi-matters-and-the-policy-implications.htm

Ortolani, P. (2015). Self-Enforcing Online Dispute Resolution: Lessons from Bitcoin. *Oxford Journal of Legal Studies, 36*(3), 595–629. https://doi.org/10.1093/ojls/gqv036

Reilly, P. (2022, May 1). *"You failed": Bill Maher blasts Twitter for censoring Post after bombshell report on Hunter Biden's laptop.* New York Post. https://nypost.com/2022/04/30/bill-maher-says-twitter-failed-for-censoring-posts-report-on-hunter-biden-laptop/

Scholz, L. H. (2019). Algorithms and Contract Law. *Cambridge Handbook of the Law of Algorithms.*

Siegler, M. (2022, January 21). *Hermès suing artist over Birkin bag NFTs.* Page Six. https://pagesix.com/2022/01/20/hermes-suing-artist-over-birkin-bag-nfts/

Skolnik, S. (2021, August 6). *Canada Joins U.S. in Nonlawyer*

Legal Service Ownership Tests. News.bloomberglaw.com. https://news.bloomberglaw.com/business-and-practice/canada-joins-u-s-in-nonlawyer-legal-service-ownership-tests

Steingard, J. (2020, March 1). *Social Media Terms of Use: I agree? - LawNow Magazine.* www.lawnow.org. https://www.lawnow.org/youth-the-law-social-media-terms-of-use-i-agree/#:~:text=Each%20platform

Vlastelica, R. (2017, December). *Why bitcoin won't displace Visa or Mastercard soon.* MarketWatch. https://www.marketwatch.com/story/why-bitcoin-wont-displace-visa-or-mastercard-soon-2017-12-15

Vujičić, D., Jagodić, D., & Ranđić, S. (2018). *Blockchain Technology, Bitcoin, and Ethereum: A Brief Overview.*

Wang, Q., Li, R., Wang, Q., & Chen, S. (2021). Non-fungible token (NFT): Overview, evaluation, opportunities and challenges. *arXiv preprint arXiv:2105.07447.*

Wieshofer, M. (2022). Data Privacy Is Not Meta: Why Facebook's Foray Into the Metaverse Could Be Flawed From the Start.

Woebbeking, Maren K. & The impact of smart contracts on traditional concepts of contract law. & *J. Intell. Prop. Info. Tech. & Elec. Com. L.* 10 (2019): 105.

CHAPTER 7 - JAILS, INCARCERATION, & THE USE OF TECH TO REHABILITATE

"It is by presence of mind in untried emergencies that the native metal of man is tested."

- James Lowell

Body Imaging Technologies in Prison

Considering the advancements of modern weapons, high security locations must take all possible precautions to protect people. When looking into the importance of technology in jails and prisons, one must understand the importance of protecting inmates, staff and visitors from contraband items. Similarly observed in airports, prisons rely heavily on metal detectors and x-rays as a source of contraband detection (*Sheen et al., 1996*). Furthermore, a more modern use of technology lies in body scanning devices, so as to provide a view of an entire body, beneath the clothes (*MW1000AA Body Inspection Device, n.d.*). Finally, technology development is leading itself into the possibility of detecting concealed items from within the body cavity while still maintaining an element of privacy for the individual undergoing scanning. Not only do these technologies inhibit the likelihood of offenders due the physical nature of discovery but a physiological effect has been noted as well (*Sheen et al., 1996*).

Metal Detectors

Metal detectors can be used as an "effective situational intervention" tool when it comes to security (*Hsu & Apel, 2015, p. 34*). Looking deeper into the workings of a general metal detector, the technology that is behind the machine is a very low frequency (VLF) transmitter and receiver (*Rowan & Lahr, 2002*). The transmitter is made of a coil of wires that, when an electric current is run through, creates an electromagnetic field (*Rowan & Lahr, 2002*). This electromagnetic field has a transmit frequency that pulses the current flow from clockwise to counterclockwise thousands of times per second so that when a metallic object is within range, the opposite polarity is detected (*Rowan & Lahr, 2002*). Similarly, the receiver portion of the metal detector is an electro-charged coil of wires that creates a transmitting field that cancels out that of the transmitter, allowing for the detection and signaling of magnetic fields within range (*Rowan & Lahr, 2002*). The unbiasedness of the metal detector creates an ideal instrument as there is a large range of contraband that can be detected from within the prison system.

With the understanding of the physical workings of a metal detector, one may explore the benefits that this technology might provide in prisons and jails. Metal detectors are not only limited to a stationary machine. Technological advancements in 2017 allowed prisons in Maryland, USA to use a mobile 161 Cellsense metal detectors that can be "moved around facilities and can detect small pieces of metal inside a person's body and even through a wall" (State officials show off new contraband detectors for prisons, 2017, para. 4). The use of metal detectors as a form of intervention aids in both deterrence and discouragement (*Weisburd et al., 2006*). Clarke & Weisburd (1994) continue that, even though offenders are no longer under an increased threat of detection and arrest, many of them continue to believe that they may be and desist from offending due to their perception of increased cost of crime.

Furthermore, the deterrent reach of situational interventions may be overestimated by potential offenders who believe they are under a greater threat of apprehension than is the case because they do not know how extensive the risk is (p. 169).

Breaking this information down, there is a strong implying tone that deterrence is not only found because of the physical machine, but that by having added security measures in a facility.

X-rays/Radiographs

X-rays are similar to metal detectors in the way that they depend on electromagnetism but generate radiation through its electromagnet (*National Institute of Biomedical Imaging and Bioengineering [NIH], n.d.*). By using an x-ray machine, waves of x-rays are sent through the body from x-ray source to detector and as a result a photographic film or radiograph is generated (*NIH, n.d.*). The basics of a radiograph interpretation depends on the ability to recognize visual differences between densities in the shadows, the most common being "gas, fat, water and mineral" (*Hook, 2000, p.1*). Doctors, technicians and trained individuals are immersed in practical examples to identify these basic densities so they may be able to interpret a radiograph to determine a physical ailment or foreign body in prisoners/visitors.

When considering an x-ray there is always a need to compare benefits against the negatives. Within Canada, an x-ray is justifiable when "practices must produce a positive net benefit to the exposed individuals or to society" (*International Atomic Energy Agency [IAEA], 2014, p.3*). Despite the benefits for security, one must consider the fact that x-rays produce ionizing radiation: a radiation that is potentially harmful to living tissue (*NIH, n.d.*). It is outlined that an individual should limit their exposure to ionizing radiation. According to a 1990 ICRP study, an 'effective dose' is roughly 50 mSv annual exposure with special circumstances with no more than "100 mSv over a five-year period" (*Government of Canada, 2008, Appendix 1C*). For individuals who are exposed to over 1000 mSv of radiation in their lifetime, there is a 5 per cent chance of developing a fatal cancer (*University of California San Francisco, n.d.*). The following case studies will illustrate how prison x-rays and radiation have been used in the incarceration system.

During the Cold War, scientists exposed prisoners in Washington and Oregon to a decade of human trials using x-rays and radiation. The purpose of this testing was to determine how much radiation astronauts could tolerate during space flight and was funded by the federal government through the Atomic Energy Commision (*Hornblum, 1998; Hoffman, 2000*). Focusing on the effects of directed x-rays, under the direction of Dr. C. Alvin Paulsen "reproduction radiation tests" were conducted on 131 prisoners of the Washington State Penitentiary in Walla Walla to "find the dose that would make them sterile" (*1963-1973: High-Dose Radiation Tests on Prisoners' Testicles to Find Sterility Dose, 2014, para.3; Steele, 1994*). Paulsen was not the only offender of such trials; Dr. Carl Heller of Oregon State Penitentiary, also concluded similar experiments on 67 inmates and was funded through the National Aeronautics and Space Administration (NASA) (*1963-1973: High-Dose Radiation Tests on Prisoners' Testicles to Find Sterility Dose, 2014*). Furthermore, it later came out that the inmates were exposed to over 400 rads (4000 mSv) of radiation in 10 minute intervals and were not informed of the risks of such trials (*Anderson, 2000*).

X-ray technology is not only used as a punishment for inmates but there are also case studies where the use of radiographs have helped detect tuberculosis (TB). Prisons in low and middle income countries show an increased rate of TB in inmates compared to the general population (*Sanchez et al., 2013*). Through this study, it was discovered that early stage TB, while less contagious, was more detectable by x-ray compared to smearing, which showed extensive lesions on the lungs (*Sanchez et al., 2013*). Similar studies have been conducted across the world. The World Health Organization (WHO) "recommends systematic screening of prisoners in countries with high TB prevalence, proposing chest x-ray (CXR) as an initial examination" (*Steiner et al., 2015, p.249*). With these findings, it could be argued that x-ray machines are invaluable devices in prisons with internal endemics and have an overwhelming benefit to outweigh the initial costs.

Body Scanners

Unlike an x-ray or metal detector, the use of body scanners allows security officials to "look through clothing to detect weapons, cell phones and nonmetallic objects" (*Bulman, 2009, p.38*). Initially developed for airport Transportation Security Administration (TSA), detention centers have recently started testing the use of body scanners, devices that use millimeter wave imaging technology (MMW) to give an overall picture of an individual. Unlike radio waves, MMW protects individuals from the harmful effects of ionizing radiation as they use non-ionizing instead (*Nuctech™ MW1000AA: Body Inspection Device, 2019*). These body scanning devices, also referred to as backscatters, can be used both actively or passively to complete its radar interrogation (*Gilchrist, 2015*). As DMRC breaks down the definition, passive MMW "directly detect[s] the natural radiation from the objects" where active MMW "first illuminate[s] the objects and subsequently detect[s] the the reflected [MMW]" (*Millimeter-wave Imaging and Sensors, n.d., para.4*).

One controversial aspect that has arisen with this technology is that the imaging created is similar to that of a nude photograph (*Bulman, 2009*). This brings an individual's privacy into question. Actions have been taken in both airport and prison securities to negate the problem of privacy. For TSA, they have commited to "immediately deleting the images" whereas Graterford State Correctional Institution in Pennsylvania has "used a privacy screen that cuts out the most explicit views" while leaving the image still discernible (*Bulman, 2009, p.39*). These were only temporary privacy attempts while in testing and since 2013, it has been mandated that all backscatters use software technology such as Automatic Target Recognition to display a generic body outline to protect individuals' privacy (*Ahlers, 2013*). Despite these attempts to implement software privacy protections, backscatters have been removed from airports at TSA's request, with no indication of current status of such technology in penitentiaries (*Ahlers, 2013*).

With privacy concerns being so important it was necessary to find another means of detecting non-permissible, concealed items from those who frequent a high security institution. Stepping away from traditional stationary machines that require the individual to walk through for examinations, the Weapons and Non-Permitted Devices Detector (WANDD) was created by Luna Innovations Inc., and has proved exceptionally helpful in correctional institutions (*Bulman, 2009*). The WANDD relies on sound waves similar to sonar that "includes an ultrasonic wave transmitter and an acoustic receiver" (*Bulman, 2009, p.40*). Individual privacy is thus protected as an auditory signal is projected as the device listens to reflected sound waves (*Bulman, 2009*). In "the Virginia Peninsula Regional Jail in Williamsburg ...The WANDD prototype successfully detected objects such as cell phones, plastic knives, guns and credit cards" (*Bulman, 2009, p.40*). By using technological advancements, it is possible to achieve maximum security standards while maintaining the dignity and privacy of individuals all while completing searches in a timely manner.

Ultrasound technology

Ultrasounds are used to capture a real-time image/video of internal happenings. An ultrasound is typically a small hand-held device called a transducer which creates images via soundwaves when touching the body (*Ultrasound, n.d.*). The transducer is most commonly used outside the body in order to complete an examination with little to no pain (*Ultrasound, n.d.*). In Brazil's Hospital Centre of the Penitentiary System, the Obstetrics ward relies heavily on ultrasound images (*Andrade et al., 2017*). This Brazilian institution, through ultrasound, was able to complete and publish findings of a five year study where both the condition of the mothers and their fetus were monitored (*Andrade et al., 2017*). It was through the incarceration process that these women were able to contribute to scientific findings while also having regular monitoring during their prison pregnancy.

Ultrasounds are not only used for gynecological purposes but when working in conjunction with other medical technologies, as an in depth image may help reveal health complications. Polish officers examines patients via CT scan and ultrasound to determine that the prisoner suffered from multiple liver abscesses (*Duda et al., 2004*). With the help of available technology in the prison, a diagnosis was made quickly and the patient was administered antibiotics to resolve the issue (*Duda et al., 2004*). Another case of beneficial ultrasounds was used during a hepatology study carried out in Portuguese prisons (*Liberal et al., 2017, p. 599*). Monitoring for symptoms of hepatitis c virus (HVC), hepatitis B virus (HBV) and human immunodeficiency virus (HIV) those who came forward were given the chance to confirm the diagnosis via endoscopic screening and abdominal ultrasound (*Liberal et al., 2017, p. 599*). Once HVC, HBC and/or HIV was confirmed, the inmates were treated over a three month period (*Liberal et al., 2017, p. 599*) . With the ability to safely screen from the correction facility, the inmate was treated much quicker for their ailments.

Human Error with Technology

When thinking about traditional body scanners, there is a high probability that it is a x-ray machine or metal detector that is being considered. This is the case for most penitentiary settings based on the accessibility, the amount of available space and the allowable budget for such technology. Considering the methods already discussed, one must consider the operator of the equipment and therefore the ability to interpret and relay the information being provided through the technologies.

It is a common consensus across the professional community that "all imaging procedures should include an expert radiologist's opinion" (*Brady, 2017*). For cases highlighted in USA news during the height of the COVID-19 pandemic in 2021, it was found that due to the demand of medical professionals in prisons, shortcuts were taken.

Concerns over medical care and the qualifications of those responsible for it — from administrative leaders to staff members who treat patients — are not unique to the federal system. From California to Alabama, news reports and public records show that prisons routinely hire underqualified and even disgraced medical staff (*Blakinger, 2021, para.11*).

Although this report is focused on the shortcomings of the systems in the USA, Canadian jails are also facing a similar frustration. In Nova Scotia the president of the correctional officers union was prompted to come forward to the media because "[n]ot just anybody can read an X-ray" (*Burke, 2018, para.5*). As Burke further points out the difficulty in telling the difference between body anatomy and contraband, "can lead correctional officers to misinterpret a scan and potentially miss contraband bound for the inside of jail" (*Burke, 2018, para.6*). With this in mind, and applying it to the various body scanning technologies, it is appropriate to infer that all scans are not read with confidence or accuracy. This unfortunate lack of training of correctional officers and medical staff alike can be the initial cause of a potentially dangerous situation within a correctional facility.

To combat these errors, it is possible to step away from traditional reading methods and consider the possibility of computerizing the process. In Tanzania, preventative CXRs are completed to "detect asymptomatic cases" of TB but the actions following these screenings is limited based on the availability of experienced radiograph readers in the penitentiary system (*Steiner et al., 2015, p.249*). To combat the shortage of trained staff to interpret CXRs, computer-aided detection (CAD) has been introduced with good margins of success (*Steiner et al., 2015*). Another example of artificial intelligence (AI) being used in technology is through metal detectors. The ADANI System metal detector is at the peak of its operations with the ability to use privacy masking but, more importantly, the ability to highlight and color code the received image. In its successful operation, this machine will allow AI to detect and visualize items by color: green being clothing, blue showing electronic devices, red highlighting dangerous items and/or weapons and finally orange demonstrating other feoreign bodies such as drugs (*Johnson, 2019*). AI will not provide a hundred per cent accuracy rate, but compared to the margin of human error, adopting AI into prison technology could implement a safer environment for all by becoming a second 'set of eyes'.

Biometrics

Biometrics can be defined as the "automated methods of recognizing a person based on physiological or behavioral characteristics" (*Li, 2009, p.233*). Stemming from the Greek language, biometrics can be broken into 'bio' meaning life and 'metrics' meaning to measure (*Mayhew, 2018*). When thinking of the term biometric, face recognition and fingerprinting often come to mind. However, this was not always the known means of biometric identification. In the earliest verbal recolations fingerprints have been used as signatures by Babylonians in 500 B.C. and also in China during the fourteenth century (*Bhatia, 2019; Jain & Kumar, 2010*). Individuals such as "colonial administrator William Herschel, the anthropologist and eugenicist Francis Galton and the detective Alphonse Bertillon" were among the founding fathers of biometric technology (*Maguire, 2009, p.10*). By looking into the biometric methods of each founding father, a comparison of the progress and furthermore a debate of the reliability of these methods can be sparked. Taking these comparisons into account when considering current and future biometric technologies will provide an in depth analysis while also demonstrating the applications in current law.

Founding Fathers

Sir William Herschel (*1833-1918*) is recognized as the first individual to record finger and hand prints (*Bhatia, 2019*). In 1858, Herschel was acquiring materials for road-building on behalf of the East India Company and British administration (*Maguire, 2009*). It was during a transaction that Herschel demanded a local man, Rajyadhar Konai, to sign a contract with a "palm print with the intention of 'frightening' him" (*Maguire, 2009, p.10*). At the time this was not an uncommon practice, but Herschel realized that this natural signature was reproducible and real, giving a direct tie to Konai (*Maguire, 2009*). In

1860, Herschel was appointed Magistrate of Nadia, India, during the Indigo Revolt; it was due to the revolt that Herschel found a need to experiment with identifying individuals by prints (*Ray, 2019*). In his position, Herschel was able to use fingerprinting to "combat fraud in pension claims, where it was rumored that one could hire an elderly 'relative'" and limit deceitful imprisonments (*Maguire, 2009, p.10*). By the time Herschel retired, his method of fingerprinting was not fully embraced and furthermore lacked scientific credibility. It was at this time that Francis Galton, cousin of Darwin, took interest in Herschel's efforts because of an article published in 1880 (*Maguire, 2009*).

Francis Galton (*1822-1911*) came across Herschel's work in 1880 and was able to connect it with his own biometric findings (*Maguire, 2009*). Galton has since been noted as a significant figure in the discovery of eugenics (*Maguire, 2009*). Galton's own studies had been started in the 1870s as he experimented with the "heritable characteristics of 'race'" using individuals across various schools, the army, prisons, asylums and hospitals (*Maguire, 2009, p.11*). Working with photographs of faces, Galton attempted to piece together a map of the human face to find distinguishable characteristic markers (*Galton, 1904*). Using these headshots proved to be difficult due to the ghostly quality of the photographs and for this reason, Galton halted his facial recognition quest and opted for the fingerprinting techniques of Herschel (*Galton, 1904*). Galton was able to create scientific credibility for fingerprint analysis by taking note of the uniqueness of the "arches, loops or whorls", and subsequently created a database to allow for "future identification" (*Maguire, 2009, p.12*). With this discovery, Galton connected with detective Alphonse Bertillon in 1880. Bertillon, similarly to Heschel, was interested in biometrics to increase security measures.

Alphonse Bertillon (1853-1914) was interested in the "practical and administrative side of research" when it came to biometric discovery, experimenting with fingerprinting (*Maguire, 2009, p.12*). The 1860s modernizing of Paris caused Bertillon to be concerned about a dangerous class of people having more access and mobility within the city (*Maguire, 2009*). Being a detective who dealt with the lower class, Bertillon took it upon himself to create a system that would help conclude identities by measuring, photographing and describing all detained individuals (*Vats & Kaur, 2016*). Bertillon published in the English edition of Signaletics that "[e]very human being should be partially signalized…The process of signalment would take place of passports at every frontier…It would then be possible to find any person at once whenever desired" (*Maguire, 2009, p.12*). By 1882 the Bertillonage system consisted of filing detailed cards for prisoners and the general population which created his legacy, not only because of the filing system but the reliability of this information when identifying individuals (*Maguire, 2009*). It is through the triumph of filing, rather than science, that this system was able to gain global recognition, and ultimately became the basis for modern biometrics.

Biometric Traits

As previously mentioned, there are a variety of methods that are classified as biometrics including fingerprinting and facial features. Some of the most common biometric traits include face, fingerprints, iris, palmprint, hand geometry, hand veins, voice, signature and deoxyribonucleic acid (DNA) (*Jain & Kumar, 2010*). When used in combination with one another, these traits can be used in a variety of professions including forensics and security, ultimately allowing law enforcement to deduce reliable identifications.

Face

The face is one trait that most individuals are able to observe, retain and recognize through various lengths of time. Features of the face such as eyes, nose, lips and chin are most commonly distinctive and when combined into computer programming, facial recognition can then take shape. There is a line between what is deemed socially acceptable and intrusive with this technology; iris scanning, though reliable, is considered intrusive where facial recognition is more socially acceptable (*Abate et al., 2007*). There are more ways now than ever to explore facial recognition, be that through photographs, mugshots or video feeds, however there is also a time and place that will help provide better results. It was found that outdoor environments posed challenges that were not present during controlled testing (*Abate et al., 2007*). By testing these facial recognition systems, important data is gathered which can then be used to improve current systems.

The Face Recognition Vendor Test (FRVT) 2002 is an independent test of facial recognition systems (*Phillips et al., 2003*). Consisting of a large pool of "121,589 operational facial images of 37,437 individuals," the test provided a few conclusions: indoor recognition had substantially improved over a two year span, males were easier to identify compared to females and the system had more success with elderly people compared to younger (*Phillips et al., 2003, p.1*). FRVT 2002 also tested the reliability of three new techniques: "three-dimensional morphable models, normalization of similarity scores, and face recognition from video sequences" (*Phillips et al., 2003,p.1*). Three Dimensional Morphable Models (3DMM) is technology that is able to take 2D images and transfer them onto a 3D model, a blank face per say, and provide an hypothesized result for the characteristics not fully provided in the 2D image (*Ploumpis et al., 2020*). Similarity scores refer to the points on one subject's face compared to the other;

the more points that match, the higher the similarity score is. To ensure accurate identification, it is important to normalize the similarity scores so that the technology can find more identifiable aspects (*Phillips et al., 2003*). Finally, facial recognition through video sequencing means that in the time of a video, various frames are taken and then compared to another session, providing insight into facial inflections that may not be provided in a standard static photograph (*Phillips et al., 2003*). The results of the FRVT also provided insight into the differences between an indoor and outdoor setting and through images in the report, it can be concluded that uncontrolled testing posed a challenge as factors such as shadows, wind and sun exposure altered the appearance of individuals when compared directly to a proper headshot (*Phillips et al., 2003*).

Iris

Iris biometrics are more common today than ever before with the use of smartphone security however this technology is more useful in high security settings such as airports and prisons. The iris is the coloured ring that encircles the pupil and under infrared illumination. Images of the iris detail complex textured patterns and provide a unique picture, resulting in reliable identification (*Jain & Kumar, 2010*). Iris scanning is considered to be one of the most reliable methods of biometrics as the iris's texture is stable, distinguishable (even between identical twins) and nearly impossible to surgically manipulate (*Bowyer et al., 2008*). Image acquisition is a very important aspect of iris biometrics and has advanced in the last two decades. Prior to 1996, the standard procedure of capturing the iris was to have the subject pose for a photo, which would then be analyzed (*Bowyer et al., 2008*). In 1996, a project by the name of "Iris on the Move" was put in motion so that the iris image could be accurately captured from a one to three foot distance (*Bowyer et al., 2008, p.281*). By using a "wide field-of-view cameras and a cross-correlation-based stereo algorithm" the camera could focus on a head and use "a narrow field-of-view (NFOV) camera" to confirm the eye placement and capture an image (*Bowyer et al., 2008, p.282*). By using a mobile method to capture the iris, it becomes less invasive and increases its ability to aid in security.

Iris biometrics is strongly based on computer technologies and is mainly used for identity verification and identification (*Bowyer et al., 2008*). In a situation where iris recognition is being used for verification and a known sample is provided and a second image is used to compare against the first (*Bowyer et al., 2008*). The second situation is iris identification where an iris that is not in a database is captured and compared against the others. The closest match is then used as the new identificacion and is updated as more samples are collected (*Bowyer et al., 2008*). Successful identification occurs when a true match is found between iris images (*Bowyer et al., 2008*). In both situations there is a chance of false positives and/or negatives. This proves that technology is not perfect, but these errors can be limited in time as more samples are collected and categorized.

Voice

Speech is made up of many factors and is more suited to verification purposes over the phone, although also not reliable due to sensitivity to background noise and the ability to record (*Jain & Kumar, 2010*). According to Jain and Kumar, the human voice consists of behavioral and physiological features.

The physiological component of voice generation depends on the shape and size of vocal tracts, lips, nasal cavities, and mouth. The movement of lips, jaws, tongue, velum, and larynx constitute the behavioral component of voice which can vary over time due to person's age and medical condition (e.g., common cold). The spectral content of the voice is analyzed to extract its intensity, duration, quality, and pitch information, which is used to build a model (typically the Hidden Markov Model) for speaker recognition (2010).

With this in mind, it is possible to create an identity of one's speech abilities and patterns but it is not the most practical or reliable use of biometrics within the law.

Hand Geometry

Hand geometry refers to the ability to identify the characteristics on an individual's hand while limiting discriminating factors (*Jain & Kumar, 2010*). To limit discrimination in hand images, a low-resolution photo is taken and then used to extract features such as finger length, width, thickness and area (*Štruc & Pavešić, 2009*). This biometric method is best used in low security verification roles and is not commonly integrated into existing security systems due to the equipment's large size (*Jain & Kumar, 2010*).

Hand Veins

Hand veins are another characteristic that has a surprising amount of accuracy within adult populations spanning from 20-50 years old (*Jain & Kumar, 2010*). Similar to iris imaging, the veins in the palm and fingers are identifiable through infrared illumination (*Kumar & Prathyusha, 2009*). It is the patterns and thicknesses of veins that are examined when considering biometrics with a positive touchless application by the user (*Jain & Kumar, 2010*). Factors such as aging, diseases and tumors can affect the results of these particular scans and for this reason, there is a limited window of use per individual.

Palm prints

Palm prints are becoming more common in the forensic world as around thirty per cent of all latent prints lifted are of the palm compared to the fingers (*Dewan, 2003*). Similar to iris recognition, systems used for palm prints use infrared to determine textures in the palm (*Jain & Kumar, 2010*). Within palm prints there are palmar friction ridges and flexion creases that can be captured and compared (*Adler, 2004*). Although there is not a known civilian use for this biometric technology yet, it is most commonly used in forensics, adding to another ever-growing database (*Jain & Kumar, 2010*). In high-security environments, palm prints can be used in conjunction with fingerprints to provide a comprehensive identity.

Signature

Signatures are used as a method of authentication and often used on paper documents to prove identity and accountability. There is not a system that has been successfully developed at this time that has the ability to recognize signatures due to the changes of signatures over time (*Jain & Kuman, 2010*). With this in mind there have been attempts to make more sensitive touchpads that can recognize the pressure, speeds, order and shape of signatures, which in turn may be able to help better identify static signatures (*Jain & Kumar, 2010*).

DNA

DNA is living proof of individuals and their respective physiological characteristics. All DNA is unique from one another except in cases of identical twins (*Jain et al., 2002*). DNA is largely used in forensics and can be collected from various sources including but not limited to hair, fingerprints, fingernails, and body fluids (*Jain & Kumar, 2010*).

DNA sampling is a long tedious process and requires many steps. From isolating samples to creating target sequences which can be matched, the process is challenging due to the combination of manual and automated processes (*Jain & Kumar, 2010*). DNA also has the ability to be contaminated and the results may become skewed if the process is done incorrectly (*Jain & Kumar, 2010*). For these reasons DNA is not the best option for large-scale biometric applications and is most applicable for law enforcement and forensic purposes.

Fingerprints

As previously mentioned, fingerprinting has been around from as early as 500 B.C. and was used by the Babylonian people and Chinese for business purposes (*Bhatia, 2019*). It was realized from an early time that fingerprints were unique, identifiable, and attainable from a variety of situations. In modern science and law, fingerprints are universally recognized and respected when presented as a form of identification. From passports or criminal record checks to identifying an incarcerated individual with forensic evidence, fingerprints are classified as strong irrefutable evidence. A brief look into the characteristics of fingerprint patterns and analysis should provide some insight into the complexities of this method.

Patterns

The texture pattern of a fingerprint consists of ridges and valleys and forms a variation of set patterns. These patterns have distinct markers called minutiae (*Jain & Kumar, 2010*). There are three possible patterns when it comes to fingerprint analysis: arches, loops and whorls, all of which have subcategories (*Bhasin et al., 2016*). Arches are formed when ridges lay above each other and form a general arching pattern and belong to about ten per cent of the population (*Bhasin et al.,*

2016). There are two different subtypes of arches, a simple arch that crosses the finger without recurving and tented which has the ridges meet at a point of interruption (*Bhasin et al., 2016*). Loops are the most common fingerprint with around sixty to seventy per cent of the population having this type of pattern (*Bansal et al., 2014*). Loops are generally characterized by being circular or oval-shaped and can be broken into three subcategories. Radial loops are loops which flow in a "downward slope from the little finger toward the thumb" (*Smart Eye Technology, 2022, para.11*). An ulnar loop is circular and runs from the thumb toward the pinky, opposite of the radial loop (*Smart Eye Technology, 2022*). Double loops are exactly as it states, a fingerprint with two distinctive loops that share an inner pattern ridge (*Smart Eye Technology, 2022*). The last pattern is the whorl which contains three subcategories for classification and belongs to about thirty per cent of the population (*Smart Eye Technology, 2022*). The plain whorl has "concentric circles, with one complete circle and two deltas", the central pocket loop whorl is a loop with a whorl at the end and finally the accidental whorl as implied by the name describes irregular shaped whorls (*Smart Eye Technology, 2022, para.13*).

Collection and analysis. Collecting prints can be done in a variety of ways from ink, inkless or photographic collection. Fingerprints in whatever capacity are extremely valuable. Fingerprints are commonly used in security settings including everyday items such as smartphones. In more secure settings such as travel, countries such as the USA, Japan and the United Kingdom (UK) request that ten fingerprints be submitted to a national security database (*Sperry et al., 2017*).

Due to the modernization of fingerprinting technology, the method of inking and rolling for a fingerprint is not used as commonly. Prior to such sophisticated technology, inking fingerprints was the method used for collection and often occurred during 'booking' process in prison or for criminal background checks as it was cheap and provided instant results (*Bhasin et al., 2016; Team, 2015*). Although still used today for certain applications, the main reason for phasing out the inking method was due to prints becoming smudged or not accurately capture all the ridges making the prints unusable (*Team, 2015*). These faults could be slightly mitigated by moisturizing before printing which would reduce the unevenness of dry skin but ultimately a decision was made to find a more reliable method (*Team, 2015*).

The inkless method produces prints using "latent-print powder and transparent vinyl adhesive sheets" (*Bhasin et al., 2016, p.4*). The advantages to such a method include the flexibility of the vinyl 'tape' allowing for a fingerprint to be lifted off an uneven surface paired with the quick and clear result it provides (*Bhasin et al., 2016*). Although this method is reliable, there are still disadvantages to the technique as training is required, prints created are not durable and the individual who is being printed may be sensitive to the latent powder (*Bhasin et al., 2016*). As explained, this method involves having the individual in question in person; however, this method is often used at crime scenes to lift prints that were left behind.

Similar to the inkless method, the photographic method provides a clean feel for the individual while using the methods of the inking technique. Photographic paper is used to capture fingerprints using a working solution that will develop on the paper (*Bhasin et al., 2016*). In the likeness of traditional photo washing, the prints must be washed and processed in a dark room (*Arthur, 1972*). For this reason, the challenges of this method, including training, slow process time and difficulty, outweigh the benefits of portability and durability (*Bhasin et al., 2016*).

The most common and least invasive method of collection is electronic fingerprinting. This method allows an individual to roll their fingerprints across a high quality scanner which captures the textured images of the fingerprint and holds them in a database for future reference (*Jain & Kumar, 2010*). This method of fingerprinting minimally invasive and creates highly accurate and instant images while being relatively low cost (*Advantages and Disadvantage of Fingerprint Recognition, 2021*). Although electronic fingerprinting is accessible, it poses challenges when it comes to system failures that may happen with power outages, and due to its software it is unable to match prints from the same individual that may have slightly changed with age or injury (*Advantages and Disadvantage of Fingerprint Recognition, 2021*). For this reason, it is important to consider AI technologies to help identify and validate fingerprints in the twenty-first century.

Integrated Automatic Fingerprint Identification System.

Recognized and used almost globally, most forensic and law enforcement agencies use the Integrated Automatic Fingerprint Identification System (*IAFIS*) to verify or identify individuals (*Jain & Kumar, 2010*). The IAFIS was revolutionary as it eliminated the paper trail that previously existed when documenting profiles (*Moses et al., 2011*). This system is "composed of two interdependent subsystems: the tenprint [(TP)] (i.e., criminal identification) subsystem and the latent [(LP)] (i.e., criminal investigation) subsystem" (*Moses et al., 2011, p.6-9*). As a law enforcement officer it is expected that the IAFIS be protected and maintained with integrity to ensure the utmost protection (*Moses et al., 2011*). In short the IAFIS will acquire the data by scanning the fingerprint, extracting a machine representation recognizing minutiae and finally be able to deduce if it is a match with any other stored fingerprints and their subsequent profiles (*Jain & Pankanti, 2001, pp. 282*). While running prints, IAFIS has four basic functions: TP-TP which is 99 per cent accurate, LP-TP, LP-LP and TP-LP with the first print representing the available data, and the second print representing the IAFIS data (*Moses et al, 2011*). With this technology, it is possible to accurately run and compare or log fingerprints into a global system, ultimately creating a more complete and reliable database.

Biometrics in Use

To further understand how these biometric methods can be combined and be practically used, we will consider a case study of a USA Navy Brig. The task of tracking prisoners is not easy and is made up of visual identity verification by officers, and with this system and all of its precautions there is still room for error if attention is diverted or prisoners have gone unnoticed (*Miles & Cohn, 2006*). This element of error inspired the National Institute of Justice to test biometrics at the US Naval Consolidated Brig in Charleston, South Carolina, a project that invested $1 million in technology (*Miles & Cohn, 2006*). Within the Charleston Navy Brig, biometrics were previously used to "track the movement of staff, visitors, and prisoners in and out of correctional facilities" and to account for staff in the event of riots or other disturbances (*Miles & Cohn, 2006, para.4*). This experiment, called the Biometrics Inmate Tracking System (BITS), was aimed at tracking the movement of prisoners inside the prison using computer technologies to prove that advanced hardware/software can improve a corrections facility (*Miles & Cohn, 2006*).

Over the three year testing period of the BITS using a combination of "iris, facial, retinal finger and hand geometry, voice and fingerprint[s]" it was found to be only partially effective for a prison setting (*Miles & Cohn, 2006, para.2*). Through the testing period, it was found that voice recognition was the least reliable, facial recognition produced a high number of false positives, and iris recognition was extremely reliable but slow (*Miles & Cohn, 2006*). Charleston Brig found that the most reliable and cost effective method was a combination of fingerprinting and hand geometry biometrics, providing accurate identifications with quick results (*Miles & Cohn, 2006*). This facility also entertained the idea of a tracking card, cards containing prisoner data that had a magnetic strip that would be used to track movements (*Seymore et al., 2001*). The result and current use of the system required that scanners were installed and the system would accurately track prisoner movement by finding a "biometric match, identifi[ng] the individual prisoner, and confirm[ing] that he or she is authorized to go from one part of the brig to another" while also notifying the officer on the other side of the authorized movement (*Miles & Cohn, 2006, para.14*). By using this system there is less need for escorting officers and stacks of paperwork, using prison staff more effectively; furthermore if a prisoner does not show up at their intended location within a five minute window, alarms are sounded to alert staff of the situation (*Miles & Cohn, 2006*). Overall the experiment was successful in integrating BITS into the correction facility and using the system to its fullest potential to protect staff and accurately track prisoner movements.

Inmate Monitoring

Prisoner monitoring is an essential component in correctional facilities. Monitoring can be completed by a variety of means but generally consists of drones, body cameras, global positioning systems (GPS) and radios with the intention of providing safety monitoring for staff. By using video and audio surveillance, data can be stored for later consultation, training and trials while also providing valuable feedback on situations and inmates.

Drones

Drones can be used both to benefit the prison staff or to attempt to smuggle contraband into the facility for the prisoners. Drones can be small, swift and serve many purposes making them versatile in the security work. In Hungary, law enforcement utilizes small unmanned aerial vehicles (UAVs) to capture video and image footage, some even equipped with night vision or thermal cameras (*Petrétei, 2018*). During border patrols UAVs are useful in providing preparation specifically to unmask the terrain; however, drones also lack the ability to be quiet and have the potential to alert criminals to their whereabouts (*Petrétei, 2018*). Not only do drones aid officers in the field but also can be used in prisons to track missing prisoners or provide footage for review (*Petrétei, 2018*). To provide a rounded picture, negatives of drones must also be considered, which includes the noise generated while surveying and the ability for prisoners to also utilize the UAV technology (*Petrétei, 2018*).

"Both in Europe and in the US there have been incidents when contrabands were carried to prisons by drones, or the small UAVs simply made video footage or tool photographs in order to map the structure, degree of security and the applied safety measure of the jails" (*Petrétei, 2018,p.49*). There have been many cases where prisoners have had accomplices outside of the prison take advantage of drones for the benefit of prisoners locked inside. A 2013 Canadian prison found a drone surveying a prison. With further investigation, the pilot, payload and drone could not be traced (*Russon, 2013*). An American prison in 2014 seized a drone which crashed into the fence, overloaded with drugs, cigarettes and phones (*Khaw, 2014*). These examples are not limited to North America but are documented across the world and demonstrate the ability for technologies to be used with both positive and negative intentions within the prison system.

Body Cameras

Body cameras are worn on law enforcement officers to implement accountability and safety. As has already been discussed, technology allows an unbiased view of the situation and for this reason, removes the inconsistencies of witness reports. Stepping out of the prison system is an example from a 2014 Missouri case where an officer, Darren Wilson, was accused of using excessive force resulting in the death of Michael Brown (*Nunes, 2016*). During the court examination, the main highlight of the case was the need and importance of body camera footage. Wilson did not have any recording device and if he had worn one the court would have had access to the events as they unfolded in reality (*Nunes, 2016*). When addressing safety, police departments that had adopted regular use of body cameras noted a 90 per cent decrease in complaints against officer behaviours (*Stross, 2013*). As for accountability, officers who wear body cameras tend to act on their best behaviour as they are aware that recording is in progress allowing a fair interaction between the officer and suspect (*Nunes, 2016*).

Video evidence does present challenges with how it is perceived, only revealing a two-dimensional representation of a three-dimensional event. With relation to distance, a study was completed that depicted two perspectives of the same interrogation, one from the perspective of the officer and one showing the officer in the same frame as the suspect (*Harvard Law Review, 2015*). This study found that juries were more likely to believe the intention of the interrogating officer and the confession from the perspective of the officer compared to the full frame video (*Considering Police Body Cameras, 2015*). Another study completed by the University of Illinois demonstrated "inattentional blindness" where a video was shown to a group that was asked to focus on one aspect; during the video events such a gorilla in the background and character clothing changes took place, following the video, participants were asked a series of questions regarding their focus (*Simons, 2010, p.3*). This revealed that around 50 per cent of the subjects focused purely on the task which they were instructed while the other half took note of some or all of the other background events (*Simons, 2010*). Considering the two studies, it is important to take time and an unpersuaded perspective while examining evidence collected from body cameras to allow for judges and juries alike to formulate unbiased opinions.

Communication Technology for Inmates

It is a key element of incarceration to rehabilitate inmates by allowing outside contact as individuals can choose to make positive connections and communications with friends, family and others. Prisoners have long been encouraged to interact with others in the free world and this started with pen pals. The premise of pen pals was to limit isolation, distract, express identity, create motivation and create the potential to have connections after release (*Hodgson & Horne, 2015*).As technol;ogy quickly evolved, prisons moved from pen and paper to online and digital communication methods. Similar to the restrictions of pen and paper, digital communications are still monitored but when considering the abilities as a whole, a video visit or digital message allow for quick replies and a higher quality of communication.

Video Visits

The introduction of video visitation began in the mid 1990s and was introduced by private companies which has now spread to many prisons (*Fulcher, 2013*). There are two means of video conferencing "(1) onsite video visitation via individual kiosks; or (2) online video visitation outside of the correctional facility" (*Fulcher, 2013, p.92*). Within both methods of video conferencing there are designated kiosks, scheduled times and supervision of the equipment and overall visit.

There are extreme examples of onsite visitation, for example the District of Columbia Department of Corrections (*DCDC*) removed face-to-face interactions in favour of video visits in 2012 (*Online Scheduling for Video Visitation/Scheduling for Face to Face Visitation, n.d.*). In this Washington prison, the videos claimed to "significantly streamline visitor check-in, improve the management of inmate visitation and improve safety and accessibility for family members and friends" (*Ribbon-Cutting Ceremony for Department's New Video Visitation Center, 2012, para.2*). Considering that the inmate and visitor are in the same building during this type of visit, there is no real benefit other than safety to justify the lack of face-to-face and physical communication.

The benefit of online visitation is the ability to allow visitation with people who are not local to the prison. Although the cost of travel is eliminated for the visitor there is often a fee associated with the video feed service (*Fulcher, 2013*). Unfortunately there is no regulation on the online visits and there is a wide range of costs per minute. One prison using Securus as the video platform and monitoring service only makes 45 per cent of the costs as the rest goes to the "county's Director of Detention Services" (*Jones, 2012, para.1*). Despite this fee, within the first two weeks of the pilot program, visitation was up 65 per cent with the only complaints being the impersonal feel of video interaction (*Jones, 2012*). In general the idea of online visitation is successful as it allows families that chance to stay together during the unexpected change brought on with incarceration.

Digital Messaging

Video communication is not the only means of communication with prisoners. Messaging platforms have become more common, replacing the traditional pen and paper methods of letter writing. By introducing digital messaging, there has been a strong decline in contraband, specifically that which would be received through the post (*Arguelles & Ortiz-Luis, 2021*). With the rise of 'smart prisons,' facilities in Sweden are attempting to mitigate social media isolation and have introduced a prison-approved application run on assigned prisoner cell phones to stay connected with friends and family (*Kaun & Stiernstedt, 2020*). Not only are these cell phones used for daily contact with people, but the application also administers health checks, provides digital rehabilitation videos, schedules, online therapy and tracking (*Kaun & Stiernstedt, 2020*). By integrating smart technologies into prisons for communication and more, there is a higher success rate of rehabilitation and transition.

Education and Inmates

Rehabilitation of inmates includes having resources to create outreach programs for education, whether that is taking classes towards finishing highschool or getting a general educational development (GED). Those who chose to participate in the programs have a lower chance of recidivism (*Murphy, 2012*). However, the ability to gain an education while in prison is not available in all situations or countries. Barriers to education while incarcerated include lack of funding, cost of textbooks, limited/no internet access, transfers and short sentences (*Murphy, 2012*). These challenges can create a difficult learning environment but there is a move toward changing to benefit prisoners and allowing/providing means of education.

Looking at current initiatives globally, prisons are finding valid and secure means of providing education to prisoners while working within the means of their limitations. In Tasmania, approximately half the population has minimal education; the Tasmanian Prison Service has partnered with Tasmanian Polytechnic to develop a system for education while in prison (*Koudstaal et al., 2009*). Working around the inability to provide internet access to incarcerated individuals, Polytechnic has developed a secure network to allow communication between students and teachers; this allows teachers to provide digital copies of approved websites in conjunction with standard feedback (*Koudstaal et al., 2009*). For prisons that allow internet access, many firewalls have been put in place to ensure that students are limited to approved sites for the completion of their courses. In a Norway prison, Skien, prisoners were provided computers in both a classroom and their individual cells with the goal being to educate inmates to reduce recidivism; at the end of the study, it was concluded that these factors appeared to correlate but further research was needed (*Denny, 2016*).

This brings up the question of whether education is a solution to repeat offenses or should be considered a privilege. With continued research it is noted that education is more "cost-effective than incarceration, and reduces recidivism at a more significant rate than other forms of crime control" (*Prigg, 2017, para.2*). There is strong correlation between incarceration and undereducated people; furthermore, 85 per cent of juveniles who have gone through the court system are illiterate and 60 per cent of all inmates share this trait (*Prigg, 2017*). When considering the recidivism rate of prisoners who have taken advantage of education while incarcerated, the rate moved from 70 per cent down to 16 per cent, this directly demonstrates the effectiveness of education in prison (*Prigg, 2017*). According to an online poll, 69 per cent of participants believed that education was a basic human right where 31 per cent said it was a privilege (*Zoukis, 2018*). Considering that a majority of people agreed that education was a right, it is important to integrate it into rehabilitation programs, allowing prisoners to shed the stigma of incarceration but also to open avenues for employment after completing their sentence.

REFERENCES

1963-1973: High-Dose Radiation Tests on Prisoners' Testicles to Find Sterility Dose. (2014, Decemeber 29). Alliance for Human Research Protection. https://ahrp.org/1963-1973-high-dose-radiation-tests-on-prisoners-testicles-to-find-dose-that-makes-them-sterile/

Abate, A. F., Nappi, M., Ricco, D., & Sabatino, G. (2007). 2D and 3D Face Recognition: A Survey. *Pattern Recognition Letter, 28*(14), 1885-1906. https://doi.org/10.1016/j.patrec.2006.12.018

Adler, A. (2004). Images can be Reconstructed from Quantized Biometric Match Score Data. *Canadian Conference on Electrical and Computer Engineering, 1*(1), 469-472. https://doi.org/10.1109/CCECE.2004.1345057

Advantages and Disadvantage of Fingerprint Recognition. (2021, November 22). NEC New Zealand. https://www.nec.co.nz/market-leadership/publications-media/advantages-and-disadvantages-of-fingerprint-recognition/#:~:text=Security%20%E2%80%93%20security-wise%2C%20it%20is%20a%20vast%20improvement,user%-20they%20are%20simple%20and%20easy%20to%20use.

Ahlers, M. M. (2013, May 30). *TSA Removes Body Scanners Criticized as too Revealing.* CNN. https://edition.cnn.com/2013/05/29/travel/tsa-backscatter/

Anderson, R. (2000, January 4). *Great Balls of Fire.* Mother Jones. https://www.motherjones.com/politics/2000/01/great-balls-fire/

Andrade, F. M., Andrade, S. G., Gonçalves, T. R., Malavasi, T., & Aldrighi, J. (2017) Obstetric Ultrasound of Patients in Prison. *Obstetrics & Gynecology, 50*(S1), 341-342. https://doi.org/10.1002/uog.18608\

Arguelles, P., & Ortiz-Luis, I. (2021). Bars Behind Bars: Digital Technology in the Prison System. SSRN. http://dx.doi.org/10.2139/ssrn.3812046

Arthur, A. M. (1972). A new Method for Taking Fingerprints Using Photographic Film. *American Jounral of Biological Anthropology, 36*(3), 441-442. https://doi.org/10.1002/ajpa.1330360316

Bandal, H. D., Badiye, A. D., Kapoor, N. S. (2014). Distribution of Fingerprint Patters in an Indian Population. *Malaysian Journal of Forensic Sciences, 5*(2), 18-21. https://www.researchgate.net/profile/Hansi-Bansal/publication/272676488_Distribution_of_Fingerprint_Patterns_in_an_Indian_Population/links/602b8b0b4585158939a95c93/Distribution-of-Fingerprint-Patterns-in-an-Indian-Population.pdf

Best Inmate Dating Sites Reviews of 2022. (n.d.) Inmate Dating Sites. Retrieved June 13, 2022 from https://www.inmatedatingsites.com/

Bhasin, M. T., Bhasin, P., Singh, A., Bhatia, N., Shewale, A. H., & Gambhr, N. (2016). Dermatoglyphics and Maloccusion- A Forensic Link. *British Biotechnology Journal, 13*(1), 1-12. https://doi.org/10.9734/BBJ/2016/24451

Bhatia, S. (2019). Systematic Review of Biometric Advancement and Challenges. *International Journal of Electronics Engineering, 11*(1), 812-821. http://www.csjournals.com/IJEE/PDF11-1/135.%20Sakshi.pdf

Blakinger, K. (2021, July 1). *Disgraced Doctors, Unlicensed Officials: Prisons Face Criticism Over Health Care.* NBC News. https://www.nbcnews.com/news/us-news/disgraced-doctors-unlicensed-officials-prisons-face-criticism-over-health-care-n1272743

Bowyer, K. W., Hollingsworth, K., & Flynn, P. J. (2008). Image Understanding for Iris Boimetrics: A Survey. *Computer Vision and Image Underst, 110*(2), 281-307. https://doi.org/10.1016/j.cviu.2007.08.005

Brady, A. P. (2017). Error and Discrepancy in Radiology: Inevitable or Avoidable?. *Insights into Imaging, 8*(1), 171-182. https://doi.org/10.1007/s13244-016-0534-1

Bulman, P. (2009). Using technology to make prisons and jails safer. *NIJ Journal, 262,* 38-41. http://www.tass.org.mx/estudios/Proyectos_y_programas_carcelarios/Usando%20la%20tecnologia%20para%20hacer%20reclusorios%20mas%20seguros.pdf

Burke, D. (2018, August 23). *Jails get Body Scanners, but Guards say Telling Drugs from Anatomy is a Struggle.* CBC News. https://www.cbc.ca/news/canada/nova-scotia/body-scanners-x-ray-jail-nova-scotia-drugs-detection-1.4794187

Clarke, R. V., & Weisburd, D. (1994). Discussion of Crime Control Benefits: Observations on the Reverse of Displacement. *Crime Prevention Studies 2,* 165-183.

Considering Police Body Cameras. (2015) *Harvard Law Review, 128*(6), 1794-1817. https://harvardlawreview.org/wp-content/uploads/2015/04/Considering-Body-Cameras.pdf

Denny, M. (2016). Norway's Prison System: Investigating Recidivism and Reintegration. *Bridges: A Journal of Student Research, 10*(10), 22-37. https://digitalcommons.coastal.edu/cgi/viewcontent.cgi?article=1032&context=bridges

Dewan, S. K. (2003, November 21). *Elementary Watson: Scan a Palm, Find a Clue.* New York Times. https://www.nytimes.com/2003/11/21/nyregion/elementary-watson-scan-a-palm-find-a-clue.html

Duda, S., Dziedzic, K., Wilburg, J., & Juszczak, K. (2004). Hepatic Abscesses in Surgical Practice of Prison Hospital. *Wiadomosci Lekarskie, 57*(7-8), 381-384. PMID:15631197

Fulcher, P. A. (2013). The Double-Edged Sword of Prison Video Visitation: Claiming to Keep Families Together While Furthering the Aims of the Prison Industial Complex. *Florida A & M University Law Review, 9*(5), 83-112. https://commons.law.famu.edu/cgi/viewcontent.cgi?article=1099&context=famulawreview

Galton, F. (1904). Eugenics: Its Definistion, Scope, and Aims. *American Journal of Sociology, 10*(1), 1-25. https://www.journals.uchicago.edu/doi/pdfplus/10.1086/211280

Gilchrist, T. (2015, February 17). *The Truth About Correctional Facility Backscatter X-ray Body Scanners.* Corrections1. https://www.corrections1.com/contraband/articles/the-truth-about-correctional-facility-backscatter-x-ray-body-scanners-g2NfuCzcbZlTCX2b/

Government of Canada. (2008, September 15). *Safety Requirments and Guidance for Analytical R-ray Equipment - Safety Code 32.* https://www.canada.ca/en/health-canada/services/environmental-workplace-health/reports-publications/radiation/safety-requirements-guidance-analytical-equipment-safety-code-32.html#app1

Hodgson, J., & Horne, J. (2015). Imagining more than just a prisoner: The work of Prisoners' Penfriends. *Warwick School of Law Research Paper,* (2015/12). https://www.prisonlegalnews.org/media/publications/Imagining%20more%20than%20just%20a%20prisoner%20-%20Prisoners%20Penfriends%2C%20Warwick%20Law%20School%2C%202015.pdf

Hoffman, S. (2000). Beneficial and Unusial Punishment: An Argument in Support of Prisoner Participation in Clinical Trials. *Faculty Publications 33*(475), https://scholarlycommons.law.case.edu/cgi/viewcontent.cgi?article=1221&context=faculty_publications

Hook, W. F. (2000). X-ray Film Reading Made Easy. Retrieved May 18, 2022, from http://citeseerx.ist.psu.edu/viewdoc/download?doi=10.1.1.713.8003&rep=rep1&type=pdf

Hornblum, A. M. (1998). *Acres of Skin: Human Experiments at Holmeburg Prison.* Routledge.

Hsu, H. Y., & Apel, R. (2015). A Situational Model of Displacement and Diffusion Following the Introduction of Airport Metal Detectors. *Terrorism and Political Violence, 27*(1), 29-52. https://doi.org/10.1080/09546553.2014.962989

International Atomic Energy Agency [IAEA]. (2014). *IAEA Safety Standards for Protecting People and the Environment: Justification of Practices, Including Non-Medical Human Imaging.*

Jain, A., & Pankanti, S. (2001). Automated fingerprint identification and Imaging System. In Lee, H. C., & Gaensslen, R. E. (Eds.), *Advances in Fingerprint Technology* (pp. 275-326). CRC Press. http://citeseerx.ist.psu.edu/viewdoc/download?doi=10.1.1.21.380&rep=rep1&type=pdf

Jain, A. K., Prabhakar, S., & Pankanti, S. (2002). On the similarity of identical twin fingerprints. *Pattern Recognition, 35*(11), 2653-2663. https://doi.org/10.1016/S0031-3203(01)00218-7

Jain, A. K., & Kumar, A. (2010). Biometrics of Next Generation: An Overview. *Second Generation Biometrics, 12*(1), 2-3. https://www.cse.msu.edu/~rossarun/BiometricsTextBook/Papers/Introduction/JainKumarNextGenBiometrics_BookChap10.pdf

Johnson, B. B. (2019, October 24). *How New Technology Takes the Guesswork out of Inmate Screening.* Corrections1. https://www.corrections1.com/products/facility-products/body-scanners/articles/how-new-technology-takes-the-guesswork-out-of-inmate-screening-sF76p9oqjXkLfqwX/

Jones, Y. (2012, November 26). *County Jail First in State to Debut Video Visitation.* Jail Training. Retrieved on June 5, 2022 from https://jailtraining.org/desoto-county-tn-jail-first-in-state-to-debut-video-visitation/#:~:text=DeSoto%20County%20TN%20Jail%20First%20in%20State%20to,video%20visits%20with%20a%20webcam%20system%20like%20Skype.

Kaun, A., & Stiernstedt, F. (2020). Doing Time, the Smart Way? Temporalities of the Smart Prison. *New Media & Society, 22*(9), 1580-1599. https://doi.org/10.1177/1461444820914865

Khaw, C. (2014, August 1). *Drone Crashes While Smuggling Weed into Maximum Security Prison.* The Verge. Retreived Jun 8, 2022 from https://www.theverge.com/2014/8/1/5958101/drone-contraband-smuggling-south-carolina

Koudstaal, D., Cianchi, J., Knott, M., Koudstaal, M., & Australia, P. W. (2009, August). Creating cooperatively with all stakeholders an advanced and highly secure ICT learning network for all inmates within existing cultural prison practices. *In Proceedings of the ACEA/Reintegrafion Puzzle Conference* (pp.1-21). https://d1wqtxts1xzle7.cloudfront.net/49969800/Koudstaal_2009-with-cover-page-v2pdf?Expires=1655233166&Signature=KubxGy7bhqpqedmZSTKCGNqdsl0zMPtdrrShCyP0VcDu8ajbcvgzWE2QOuOQOMHNWyCdMykQp4Gdz2g2UpGHxa4gTbCvk3N2HrqFFkruBvwOo~Mcq7mTK6HOoaAx6HR~rNbxtcJDFykfgrL7q8LAKaywoF5OzTppwt1mwikYVTrgDlRp~8gIY6qQWIfngjanQY1V3tI~ngNUK0ZpN60VmvWnm1-NEPkQLZABxd5~Vq1NPO6VvFYraNi~k2HmveNHA9T75iWJ5lfLDe4ZKTlgUGIyqHf1joD8SS0kvxQwSQCEyvtnCbK6CfiyGNb7yk28RKv7pSA1WqJmqDf54KIlSA__&Key-Pair-Id=APKAJLOHF5GGSLRBV4ZA

Kumar, A., & Prathyusha, K. V. (2009). Personal Authentication Using Hand Vein Triangulation and Knuckle Shape. *IEEE Trans Image Processing, 38*(9), 2127-2136. https://doi.org/10.1109/TIP.2009.2023153

Li, S. (2009). *Encyclopedia of Biometrics: I-Z (Vol 2).* Springer Science & Business Mcdia. https://books.google.ca/books?id=0bQbOYVULQcC&printsec=frontcover&source=gbs_ge_summary_r&cad=0#v=onepage&q&f=false

Liberal, R., Gaspar, R., Andrade, P., Coelho, R., Tavares, J., Morgado, R., & Macedo, G. (2017). Hepatologists in Jails: A proof of Concept for Tackling Hepatitis C in Prisons. *American Journal of Gastroenterology, 112,* 599-600. https://journals.lww.com/ajg/Fulltext/2017/10001/Hepatologists_in_Jails__A_Proof_of_Concept_for.1100.aspx

Maguire, M. (2009). The Birth of Biometric Security. *Anthropology Today, 25*(2), 9-14. https://doi.org/10.1111/j.1467-8322.2009.00654.x

Mayhew, S. (2018, February 8). *History of Biometrics.* Biometric Update. https://www.biometricupdate.com/201802/history-of-biometrics-2#:~:text=The%20term%2

Millimeter-wave Imaging and Sensors. (n.d.). Mavid MM-Wave Research Center. Retrieved May 18, 2022, from https://www.ece.ucdavis.edu/dmrc/research/mmis/%E2%80%9Cbiometrics%E2%80%9D%20is%20derived%20from%20the%20Greek,significant%20advances%20in%20the%20field%20of%20computer%20processing.

Miles, C. A., & Cohn, J. P. (2006) Tracking Prisoners in Jail with Biometrics: An Experiment in a Navy Brig. *National Institute of Justice Journal, 253*(1), 6-9. https://nij.ojp.gov/topics/articles/tracking-prisoners-jail-biometrics-experiment-navy-brig

Moses, K. R., Higgins, P., McCabe, M., Prabhakar, S., & Swann, S. (2011). Automated Fingerprint Identification System (AFIS). *The fingerprint sourcebook,* 6-10. https://lkouniv.ac.in/site/writereaddata/siteContent/202003241550009003kamyani_vajpayee_Automated_fingerprint_identification.pdf

Murphy, A. (2012, April). Digital innovations in prison education: a review of current initiatives. In *Proceedings of the 9th Symposium of Postgraduate and Early Career Research (PGECR 2012).* University of Southern Queensland.

MW1000AA Body Inspection Device. (n.d.). Nuctech. Retrieved May 17, 2022 from http://www.nuctech.com/en/SitePages/ThDetailPage.aspx?nk=PAS&k=HCGFCI

National Institute of Biomedical Imaging and Bioengineering. (n.d.) *X-rays.* Retrieved May 17, 2022, from https://www.nibib.nih.gov/science-education/science-topics/x-rays

Nuctech™ MW1000AA: Body Inspection Device. (2019). Nuctech. https://secureservercdn.net/198.12.144.107/lxl.338.myftpupload.com/wp-content/uploads/2021/02/MW1000AA-En.pdf

Nunes, I. S. (2016). Hands up, don't shoot: Police misconduct and the need for body cameras. *Florida Law Review, 67*(5), 1811-1843. https://scholarship.law.ufl.edu/cgi/viewcontent.cgi?article=1290&context=flr

Online Scheduling for Video Visitation/Scheduling for Face to Face Visitation. (n.d.). Department of Corrections. Retrieved June 12, 2022 from https://doc.dc.gov/service/online-scheduling-video-visitationscheduling-face-face-visitation

Phillips, P. J., Grother, P. J., Micheals, R. J., Blackburn, D. M., Tabassi, T., & Bone, M. (2003). Face Recognition Vendor Test 2002: Evaluation Report. *National Institute of Standards and Technology.* https://doi.org/10.6028/NIST.IR.6965

Ploumpis, S., Ververas, E., O'Sullivan, E., Moschoglou, S., Wang, H., Pears, N., Smith, W. A. P., Gecer, B., & Zafeiriou, S. (2020). Towards a Complete 3D Morphable Model of the Human Head. *IEEE Transactions on Pattern Analysis and Machine Intelligence, X*(X), 1-18. https://doi.org/10.1109/TPAMI.2020.2991150

Petrétei, S. (2018). Drones and Jails. *De Gruyter Open, XXIII*(45), 43-52. https://sciendo.com/abstract/journals/bsaft/23/1/article-p43.xml?rskey=r2SAXI&result=8

Prigg, C. (2017, January 21). *Education a Solution to Repeat Crime, Not a Privilege.* Prison Resource. Retrieved June 14, 2022 from https://prisonerresource.com/education-a-solution-to-repeat-crime-not-a-privilege/

Ray, T. (2019, October 25). *The Future of Biometrics: Opportunities and Challenges. Observation Research Foundation.* https://www.orfonline.org/research/future-biometrics-opportunities-challenges-57067/

Ribbon-Cutting Ceremony for Department's New Video Visitation Center. (2012, July 19). Department of Corrections. Retrieved June 12, 2022 from https://doc.dc.gov/release/ribbon-cutting-ceremony-department%E2%80%99s-new-video-visitation-center

Rowan, M., & Lahr, W. (2002). *How Metal Detectors Work.* White's Electronics. http://www.treasuresweeper.com/wp-content/uploads/2014/07/How-Metal-Detectors-Work.pdf

Russon, M. (2013, November 29). *Drones are being used to smuggle drugs into Canadian prisons.* Insider. Retreived June 8, 2022 from https://www.businessinsider.com/drones-are-being-used-to-smuggle-drugs-into-canadian-prisons-2013-11

Sanchez, A., Massari, V., Gerardt, G., Espinola, A. B., Siriwardana, M., Camacho, L. A. B., & Larouzé, B. (2013). X ray Screening at Entry and Systematic Screening for the Control of Tuberculosis in a Highly Endemic Prision. *BMC Public Health 13*(983). https://doi.org/10.1186/1471-2458-13-983

Seymour, S., Baker, R., & Besco, M. (2001). Inmate Tracking With Biometric and Smart Card Technology. *Corrections Today, 63*(4), 75-77.

Sheen, D. M., McMakin, D. L., Collins, H. D., Hall, T. E., & Severtsen, R. H. (1996). Concealed explosive detection on personnel using a wideband holographic millimeter-wave imaging system. *Signal Processing, Sensor Fusion, and Target Recognition, V*(2755), 503-513.

Simons, D. J. (2010). Monkeying around with the gorillas in our midst: familiarity with an inattantional-blindness task does not improve the detection of unexpected events. *Iperception, 1*(1), 3-6. https://doi.org/10.1068/i0386

Smart Eye Technology. (2022, January 5). *8 Different Types of Fingerprints - Complete Analysis.* Retrieved May 23, 2022, from https://getsmarteye.com/8-different-types-of-fingerprints-complete-analysis/

Sperry, B. P., Allyse, M., & Sharp, R. R. (2017). Genetic Fingerprints and National Security. *The American Journal of Bioethics, 17*(5), 1-3. https://doi.org/10.1080/15265161.2017.1316627

State officials show off new contraband detectors for prisons. (2017, September 6). Corrections1. https://www.corrections1.com/products/facility-products/body-scanners/press-releases/state-officials-show-off-new-contraband-detectors-for-prisons-L2eUOEcbuemAHrmf/

Steele, K. D. (1994, April 4). *Radiation Experiments Raise Ethical Questions.* HighCountryNews. https://www.hcn.org/issues/8/250

Steiner, A., Mangu, C., Van Den Hombergh, J., Van Deutekom, H., Van Ginneken, B., Clowes, P., Mhimbira, F., Mfinanga, S., Rachow, A., Reither, K., & Hoelscher, M. (2015). Screening for Pulmonary Tuberculosis in a Tanzanian Prison and Computer-aided Interpretation of Chest X-rays. *Public Health Action, 5*(4), 249-254. https://doi.org/10.5588/pha.15.0037

Stross, R. (2013, April 6). *Wearing a Badge and a Video Camera.* New York Times. Retrieved June 6, 2022 from http://www.nytimes.com/2013/04/07/business/wearable-video-cameras-for-police-officers.html

Štruc, V., & Pavešić, N. (2009). Hand-Geometry Device. In: Li, S. Z., & Jain, A. (eds) *Encyclopedia of Biometrics*. Springer. https://doi.org/10.1007/978-0-387-73003-5_14

Team, B. (2015, December 2). *Digital vs. Traditional Ink Fingerprinting*. Barton Associates. https://www.bartonassociates.com/blog/digital-vs-traditional-ink-fingerprinting

Ultrasound. (n.d.) Mayo Clinic. Retreived on May 19, 2022, from https://www.mayoclinic.org/tests-procedures/ultrasound/about/pac-20395177

University of California San Francisco. (n.d.). *How much Radiation?*. Know Your Dose. Retreived on May 18, 2022, from https://knowyourdose.ucsf.edu/how-much-radiation

Vats, S., & Kaur, H. (2016). A Comparative Study of Different Biometric Features. *International Journal of Advanced Research in Computer Science, 7*(6).

Weisburd, D., Wyckoff, L. A., Ready, J., Eck, J. E., Hinkle, J. C., & Gajewski, F. (2006). Does Crime Just Move Around the Corner? A Controlled Study of Spatial Displacemtn and Diffusion of Crime Control Benefits. *Criminolgy 44,* 549-592. http://doi.org/10.111/j.1745-9125.2006.00057.x .

World Health Organization. (2013). *Systematic Screening for Active Tuberculosis: Principles and Recommendations.* https://www.ncbi.nlm.nih.gov/books/NBK294083/pdf/Bookshelf_NBK294083.pdf

Zoukis, C. (2018, July 26). *Prison Education-Is it a Right or a Privilege?*. Prison Resource. Retreived June 14, 2022 from https://prisonerresource.com/prison-education-is-it-a-right-or-a-privilege/

CHAPTER 8 - SURVEILLANCE TECHNOLOGY & LAW

"We are all now connected by the Internet, like neurons in a giant brain."

- Stephen Hawking

Mass surveillance and privacy have emerged as issues of public concern with the advent of the internet, cellular phone, big data, and artificial intelligence (AI). In the last decade, governments across the world have sought to employ technology and legal power to monitor and collect data on citizens. Scholars have identified the key concerns in this respect as the state carrying out arbitrary surveillance, the secrecy and disinformation involved in the process of covert surveillance, and, finally, the potential for violation of human rights (*Michaelsen and Glasius, 2018, p. 3789*). In popular culture and in academia, the phrase used to describe the global growth and development of state surveillance networks is 'Orwellian' in reference to the book Nineteen Eighty-Four by author George Orwell published in 1949. This book famously describes a fictional world defined by the use and abuse of surveillance technology as a tool of state domination. In particular, Nineteen Eighty-Four is famous for describing the 'telescreen' which was a device placed within the home that enabled the state to peer into the activities of a household at any moment (*Banks, 2018*). Today, cell phones operate as a surveillance technology far more capable than Orwell could have ever imagined. They generate vast amounts of geographic and user information, stay with most users 24/7, and their producible data is permanent in the digital record. Orwell's book depicts technology and terror as instruments of state power and tools to ensure the continuity of totalitarian regimes. However, technology and surveillance are not limited to the unfree world where civil liberties like freedom of speech and association are limited by the government. The purpose of this chapter is to explore how the use of technology backed by the force of law has become a primary instrument of state control. In specific, this chapter will look at how liberal democratic governments, like Canada and the United States, are expanding and utilizing their surveillance capabilities. Moreover, it will look at how totalitarian states like China have strengthened and leveraged their surveillance capabilities to exert dominion over individuals. Overall, this chapter serves to survey how technology and the state's underlying legislative power have become a primary instrument of state control.

The United States

In the United States, technology has empowered the state and its security agencies to enhance how it surveils and controls the populations it serves. In 2013, it was revealed by former intelligence contractor Edward Snowden that the National Security Agency has been operating a massive surveillance program codenamed PRISM. This program provided even low ranking intelligence analysts the ability to spy into any and all emails, phone calls, browsing histories, and even Word Documents with unlimited discretion and no need for court or even internal supervisor permission (*Rea, 2013*). These revelations of the state's robust surveillance capabilities and the apparent undermining of privacy rights were so dramatic that they impacted how everyday users search Google. A study found that the PRISM leaks have caused the suppression of searches containing personally-sensitive and government-sensitive content (*Marthews, 2017*). While the PRISM surveillance programme has been scaled back after Snowden leaked its content, American authorities retain the ability to request access to the user data which technology companies possess. Indeed, authorities have been requesting user information in subpoenas, search requests, emergency search orders, and preservations requests at an exponential rate according to Google's Transparency Report (Google). According to the firm TechRobot, no country requests more access to user information than the United States (*Hellerud, 2021*). Technology firms have an incentive to resist states accessing user information as privacy is generally regarded as a right and a valuable feature of any platform. However, corporations are at a disadvantage compared to governments that can leverage law and the coercive power of the state to secure access to privileged and confidential information. The United States Government has broad powers to impose financial sanctions against companies that refuse to comply with demands and requests for information. Additionally, the United States has a particular advantage in the capture and review of surveillance data because of its position as a world economic and technology leader, thus enabling it to have native access to most information on the internet (*Austin, 2015, p. 116*). Finally, the technology market's move toward cloud computing and cloud data storage further empowered the state in accessing the private affairs of individuals because of the ongoing centralisation of user information in a select number of data storage centers which makes state requests for access simpler (*Tréguer, 2018, p. 16*). These powers of digital search and seizure are not limited exclusively to technology companies. In 2021, an American appeal court, considering a case in which an National Aeronautics and Space Administration scientist was forced to unlock his company phone for search at the border, concluded that border agents can demand access to traveler passwords for any reason based on their discretion or otherwise deny traveler entry (*Canadian Press, 2018*). American authorities have great powers to undertake surveillance for public purposes.

In recent years, one form of surveillance technology in particular has emerged at the forefront of public concern: facial recognition technology. Its prominence in the public discourse was increased in 2019 when the Federal Trade Commission, a consumer protection agency, levied a record $5 billion fine on Facebook (now Meta) as part of a settlement for privacy complaints (Federal Trade Commission). American federalism has created a piecemeal system of facial recognition technology. For instance, in 2019 the State of California banned the use of facial recognition among its police force. California did this because of ethical and practical concerns about this new identification technology. Specifically, there were concerns about the accuracy and efficacy of the technology, especially in regard to identifying people of color, and women (*Policing Project, 2019*). However, California's ban was only to occur for three years and is set to lapse in 2022. According to Reuters, many American jurisdictions including California are presently reversing course on their initial bans on facial recognition technology, which may be a response to public pressures resulting from the significant increase in crime across the country that began in 2020 following the COVID Pandemic (*Dave, 2022*). For instance, Vermont was the last state in the union that had a total ban on the use of facial recognition technology. In spite of this, the state recently allowed the technology to be used to investigate child sex crimes (*Dave, 2022*). The fact that Vermont partially lifted its total ban on facial recognition technology is material in two key ways. First, it elucidates the fact that every U.S. state may have a slightly different approach to how it deploys this technology. Second, it indicates that facial recognition technology is now being used, to some extent, by every state in the union and it is likely to continue growing in adoption.

The best representation of the tension between overreaching surveillance technology and reasonable concern for public safety, however, is represented by Apple's highly contested announcement regarding built-in image detection surveillance on iPhones. Apple intended to launch software with IOS 15 into its phones that would scan all of a user's photos with reference to images implicated in child sexual abuse. This software would flag explicit photos for a review by Apple moderators who, pending their content, would report the account users to law enforcement and suspend their account access (*Portnoy and McKinney, 2021*). On the one hand, stopping child exploitation is a laudable goal and children are a vulnerable population especially worthy of protection. On the other hand, it appears adverse to the interests of user privacy to have a private corporation monitoring each and every photo sent by an individual and dangerous to build a technology that could be repurposed for censorship. The concern here is that the underlying technology that enables this type of surveillance could grow to include the monitoring and reporting of any content, that innocent people would be potentially implicated, and, moreover, that private companies' reach can potentially be far greater than countries that are confined by their physical borders. Regardless, the future of facial recognition technology in the United States appears to be one of growth among state agents. The Federal Bureau of Investigation, in 2019, possessed 640 million photos, which it could run through its own facial recognition program without a search warrant (*Guliani, 2019*). Moreover, according to the government accountability office report, 10 U.S. federal agencies plan to expand the use of facial recognition technology by 2023 including those that have no mandate for the prevention of terror and protection of public security. These agencies are Agriculture, Commerce, Defense, Homeland Security, Health and Human Services, Interior, Justice, State, Treasury, and Veterans Affairs (*Harwell and Dou, 2020*). The United States' use of facial as part of surveillance and law enforcement provides a useful comparison against the authoritarian governments in China and Russia for two reasons. First, the framework of the United States' system, which grants the states and the federal government power has created different approaches to facial recognition technology in different parts of the country. Second, the United States is a western liberal democracy, thus, by the nature of the system, the operation of this new technology as part of surveillance is different.

Technology firms and their lawyers' resistance to enabling the state's ability to read private data can be a complex ethical issue. In 2016, the FBI demanded that Apple provide them with the ability to unlock and defeat IOS encryption following the recovery of an iPhone possessed by an individual that carried out a terror attack. The National Security Agency experts had been unable to unlock the phone and it appeared Apple was the only alternative solution. Apple resisted this court order as the company has a policy to never undermine the privacy protection of its products. In the end, the FBI was able to unlock the phone by paying third-party hackers. These events demonstrate that the state can gain access to private data whether or not technology companies comply with judicially-issued access demands. As of 2021, the leading spyware used by governments is the Pegasus Project that is reputed to enable state agents to access passwords, location data, and texts without users even having to open any attachment or visit any webpage (*Amnesty, 2021*). This surveillance technology was behind the leaks of billionaire Amazon founder Jeff Bezos'affair and was utilised by Saudi Arabia in orchestrating the murder of anti-regime journalist Jamal Kashoggi (Priest). However, Apple is an organization unusually interested in protecting its users' privacy and commands sufficient resources as the world's most valuable company to pursue protecting its corporate values. However, competing Silicon Valley organizations have a connection to and support for the military industrial complex. Google ended a contract with the Department of Defense to analyze and improve drone footage after resistance by its staff toward the proposed partnership (*Tréguer, 2018, p. 14*). Likewise, Microsoft entered into a contract to develop a battlefield product holographic lens to improve the ability of soldiers to kill (*CBC, 2019*). Surveillance technology such as PRISM and Pegasus are especially problematic from an ethical perspective because the people under secret observation are unable to contest its validity (*Austin, 2015, p. 108*). Overall, there is a strong market for products and services that enable state agencies to collect and monitor citizen data whether or not US firms embrace cooperating with authorities in a manner that undermines privacy rights.

Canada

In Canada, the law offers relatively strong protections for the rights of online users compared to other jurisdictions like China and Russia. In 2014, the Supreme Court of Canada ruled in R v Spencer that the Charter of Rights and Freedoms grants individuals a reasonable expectation of privacy online that prohibits police from taking possession of subscriber information (such as internet search history), even where it is disclosed legally and voluntarily by an internet Service Provider, without securing a warrant from a competent judicial authority. The decision in Spencer ensures due process and procedural protection in the context of an investigation. Yet, the Supreme Court has not offered an unfettered protection for technology data. In R v Have, the Supreme Court concluded that Canadian authorities could lawfully conduct surveillance on Canadians in foreign jurisdictions without the standard protections of the Charter. Elected Canadian governments, too, have sought to undermine user privacy and expand state power. For example, in 2015 Prime Minister Justin Trudeau's Liberal administration introduced Bill C-51, the Anti-Terrorism Bill, which enabled the Canadian Security Intelligence Service, a version of the Central Intelligence Agency, to violate the Charter and Canadian law in the prosecution and prevention of terror. Similarly, it is reported that the Canada Communications Security Establishment has acted as a corporate intelligence arm for Canada's mining companies in Brazil using state power to gain a competitive advantage in the capture and exploration of natural resources (*Ismi, 2013*). Likewise, Canada Border Services Agency makes requests for internet data from technology companies and data mines airport WiFi to track traveler movements (*Lyon, 2014, p. 2*). States are even collecting sensitive personal data such as facial scans or, alternatively, use private databases of facial images taken from social media and online sites to identify persons of interest using services such as Clearview AI (*Eneman et al, 2022, p. 2*). The recent Cambridge Analytica scandal in which a company secured the data of the profiles of 87 million Facebook users and later used this data in order to influence voting behavior through targeted advertising is an example of the vast amount of data usable not only by governments but by private enterprise as well (*Amnesty, 2019*). States have broad surveillance capabilities in even the most democratic and free nations on the planet that flows from their legislative and legal power.

Furthermore, intrusive technology-based surveillance in free nations like Canada comes from private sources as well as state agents. Technology has enabled law enforcement and private citizens to easily make secret recordings of others' conversations. For example, using a phone to secretly record a conversation with one's co-workers or overhearing a conversation with other parties. Moreover, smart homes and smart cities are increasingly webbed in private surveillance networks that are backed up into servers accessible by state agents. In Alberta, the law of evidence defines what can be admissible in a criminal or civil court proceeding. At law, a digital recording must meet several criteria to be admissible as evidence including being: (1) relevant and material, (2) valid under relevant law and policy (Alberta Rules of Court, Alberta Electronic Evidence Act), and (3) more probative than prejudicial. The Alberta Rules of Court require that evidence raised in a civil proceeding be relevant to the issue being pleaded and material to proving/disproving facts at issue. The Rules also impose a duty on parties to disclose all relevant and material information. The relevance and materiality threshold is not overly strict as it is in the interest of justice for parties to make full and complete inquiries. A phone recording would be classified as electronic evidence under the Act given that it is "recorded or stored on any medium in or by a computer system or other similar device" and that it "can be read or perceived by a person or a computer system" (Electronic Evidence Act). To use it as evidence, a civil plaintiff would bear the burden of proving the authenticity of the recording on balance of probabilities. In the event of a criminal proceeding, the Canada Evidence Act, RSC 1985, c C-5 would apply with similar provisions. In Alberta, the recording of employees by employers is governed by the Personal Information Protection Act, SA 2003, c P-6.5. Despite the foregoing, it should be noted that taking recordings of others can risk criminal liability. In general, it is safe to record a conversation secretly so long as the recording party is the person to whom the oral communications are aware. However, there is risk that one can commit a crime in recording another private conversation. The Criminal Code states that knowingly intercepting a private communication via a recording phone is a crime. Private conversations are those wherein both parties were in Canada and the oral communication was "made under circumstances in which it is reasonable for the originator to expect that it will not be intercepted by any person other than the person intended by the originator to receive it" per Section 183 of the Code. Violating this law can lead to imprisonment for a term of not more than five years) or on summary conviction. However, the state and the police are not subject to these regulations.

Authoritarian Nations

It has been suggested that modern communication technologies, namely the internet, will act as tools for liberation because they have the effect of preventing autocrats from monopolizing control of broadcast media and enable citizens to quickly share information and organize opposition to illiberal practices (*Rød and Weidmann, 2015, p. 340*). From a theoretical perspective, the internet has unique effects as a means of communication in that it lows transaction costs for organizing and communicating, products a homophilous sorting by clustering persons with similar perspectives, and reduces preference falsification as individuals are more likely to perceive that others share their views (*Farrell, 2012, p. 39*). Despite these positive effects of the internet as a technology, it is generally reviewed that technology has a double-edged effect in that it is used for good and evil purposes. For instance, the scholar Jeremy Diamond situated the advent of the internet in the context of the invention of the printing press that led to the downfall of the Catholic orthodoxy but at the same time created a more centralized state and created a movement toward censorship (*Diamond, 2015, p. 71*). He believes that channeled information can lead to liberation movements against state governments that have a positive impact as a force for social change. Indeed, there is quantitative data supporting this conclusion. A study profiling 152 countries from the years 1994 to 2003 concluded that increases in internet use meaningfully predicted democratic regimes (*Groshek, 2009, p. 28*). Another study looked at 170 countries with annual or biannual data from 1996 to 2010 and concluded that the countries with higher degrees of internet use were more stable regardless of whether they were democratic or not (*Khazaeli and Stockemer, 2013, p. 474*). It cannot be denied that there is a connection between technology, legality, and democracy.

Around the world, government calls for increased public security and the computing effects of a news media profiting from striking up fear and agitation can lead to the erosion of the legal core of the Western constitutional tradition including the presumption of innocence, the right to privacy, and the right to a fair trial (*Lyon, 2014, p. 9*). Given their interest in security and public safety, citizens are generally accepting of far reaching state powers to surveil for the purposes of managing crime (*Ziller, 2020, p. 1003*). However, the problem is that these powers nominally justified for the prevention of serious crimes like the 9/11 Attack can be expanded unreasonably based on political whim or administrative discretion. For example, Canada used anti-terror legislation to freeze the assets of hundreds of protesters that rejected its vaccination and public health lockdown mandates in 2022 (*Zimonjic, 2022*). This occurrence highlighted the concern among individuals interested in personal privacy and civil liberties that there is creeping surveillance in free and democratic nations will render them increasingly illiberal. These threats to privacy and personal autonomy exist in greater depth in the unfree world. Authoritarian regimes have sought to leverage technology to filter the information received by their populations, expand and enhance surveillance, carry out cyberattacks, and promote state-propaganda disinformation to enhance their power (*Michaelsen and Glasius, 2018, p. 3788*).

States will engage in repression when their ability to manage legislative, executive, and judicial power is threatened or there is competition to their control or monopolization on the use of force (*Dragu and Lupu, 2017, p. 1047*). Just as the internet shapes political incentives and pressures, so too does the internet impact public policy and governance. It has been found in a survey of 13 countries that states possessing centralized control over the internet have reduced speed and proliferation of online connectivity (*Milner, 2006, p. 178*). From a legal and political perspective, regimes occasionally block the development of internet technologies as they can erode a controlling elite's power. However, elites are unlikely to block the development of a technology when there is a high level of competition among them (meaning another party could leverage it against them) or they are highly secure in their power (and thus do not fear replacement) (*Acemoglu and Robinson, 2006, p. 129*). Russia and China are both highly stable and durable autocratic nations ruled by particular individuals, President Vladimir

Putin and President Xi Jinping, who exercise extraordinary discretionary power. These regimes both use technology and law synergistically to extend their power including in the collection of citizen data, the censorship of online content averse to party interests, the monitoring of citizens using CCTV networks, and police power (*Wheelehan, 2019, p. 43*). Autocratic nations are more likely than democratic nations to be able to pass legislation restricting technology and internet diffusion on the basis of protecting the public from dangerous ideas or preventing threats to national security (*Milner, 2006, p. 183*). However, the challenge from autocratic governments is that, on one hand, technology can destabilize their rule but that, on the other, it is essential to their economic development and prosperity on which they depend for popular support (*p. 184*).

Russia

Russia as a regime has similar interests to China in undertaking surveillance in order to secure its power. An example of Russia's efforts includes Safe City, a state surveillance system that was launched in 2015. Safe City utilizes facial recognition technology for the Russian state to identify and track persons of interest (*Polyakova and Meserole, 2019, p. 8*). The core feature of this surveillance programme is that there are approximately 105,000 cameras in Russia's capital that possess facial recognition technology (8). Russia reports that the surveillance is highly capable. In 2020, Moscow's Mayor claimed that facial recognition technology aided the Russian police force in 70 per cent of investigations (*Dixon, 2021*). It is difficult to verify these claims and regimes like Russia have an interest in exaggerating the power of their capabilities in order to inspire deference and fear among citizens. The Russia-Ukraine war also gives a potential insight into how facial recognition technology could be used in future conflicts as both sides have utilized the technology. The Russians, according to some human rights advocates, have asserted that they are using facial recognition to silence critics of the state that speak out against the conflict (*Orecchio-Egresitz, 2022*). As evidence for this claim, it is relevant that on March 15, 2022 the Russian government mandated that its citizens could not wear masks on its public transportation system given that they obscure the facial features on which cameras rely (*Orecchio-Egresitz*). Facial recognition technology has also been deployed by Ukrainians in their resistance against Russian aggression. An American company, Clearview, has sold its technology to the Ukrainians. According to Clearview CEO, the technology can be used to help identify potential Russian spies posing as Ukrainian as well as being used to identify fallen soldiers. The Russian Ukraine war provides a perfect contrast to how facial recognition surveillance technology is a tool without an inherent ethics that is colored by the legal framework in which it subsists. That is, on one side you have the state deploying the surveillance technology as a sword to crush its critics. On the other side, surveillance technology can be utilized as a shield to help identify potential threats and return deceased soldiers back to their families. Russia's use of surveillance technology, however, is outpaced by that of the Chinese government.

China

The Chinese state has robust state surveillance policies. China has no intention of hiding its ability to deploy facial recognition technology which is a source of pride for the state. In 2018 a state-sponsored media outlet boasted that it could scan the faces of some 1.4 billion Chinese citizens in a second (*Davies, 2021*). It should be noted that there is no way to verify the capability of the Chinese state to do this, however, the state's warm embrace of this new technology has the potential to dawn a new age of state surveillance wherein authorities neither require the consent nor even the knowledge that it has occurred. It is unsurprising, then, that between China, Germany, the United Kingdom, and the United States, Chinese citizens were most supportive of the use of facial recognition technology (*Kostka et al., 2021, p. 686*). This may be because China has a weaker tradition of civil liberty and individual privacy compared with Western nations (*Zheng, 2020, p. 1450*). The result, however, is that an absence of public resistance to technological surveillance coupled with the fact that avoiding detection from facial recognition systems is limited to covering the cameras, covering the faces, or corrupting the available data online means a potentially unlimited ability for the state to surveil (*Wenger, 2021, p. 6*).

China's state surveillance policies and projects are expansive and it is impossible to verify their claims as China is a secretive and closed society that is ruled strictly by a small governing party. However, one publicly disclosed program is called "sharp eyes". The phrase sharp eyes is a reference to the founder of the Community People's Party, Mao Zedong, who stated that the Chinese have sharp eyes for their neighbors who fail to live up to the communist ideals (*Gershgorn, 2021*). The goal for Sharp Eyes in 2016 was for complete coverage of China's public spaces (*Gershgorn, 2021*). This goal is near to fulfillment according to sources. Is claimed that the whole of China's capital city of Beijing is entirely covered with closed circuit television (CCTV) footage in a surveillance network comprised of over 450 million individual cameras (*Wheelehan, 2019, p. 44*). CCTV cameras are effective at influencing behavior. In one study, it was found that CCTV had statistically significant impacts on crime by reducing it 21 per cent in experimental condition compared to similar control zones (*Welsh and Farrington, 2004*). And even if the cameras did not function or the footage was not monitored, the mere presence of the surveillance network itself is sufficient to influence the behavior of citizens as it would be impossible to be certain whether or not the state was observing and recording one's actions. These camera systems are sufficiently developed to monitor the gender, clothing, and height of subjects using algorithms built on vast troves of banked data (*Qiang, 2019, p. 57*). Perhaps the most concerning use of surveillance and facial recognition is when it is deployed against a particular ethnic group. A Washington Post article in December 2020 stated that Huewai was using Facial recognition technology to identify minority Muslim Uyghur population (*Harwell and Dou, 2020*) which are being placed into camps in order that the governing party can work toward 're-educating' them in Mandarin, patriotic values, and anti-religious ideology (*Raza, 2019, p. 498*). China possesses the world's largest and most sophisticated lawful surveillance system.

In terms of censorship, sovereign countries generally control the internet service providers operating within their jurisdictions and thus have the ability to impose rules, monitor traffic, and censor content. The preeminent example of this type of censorship is China's Great Firewall which involves several degrees of regulation. For example, news sites must obtain licenses to appear on the internet, internet service providers only enable access to social media where one's identity is proved, and the state has taken measures to prevent and sanction the use of VPN technology to circumvent its internet regulation (*p. 55*). In this respect, even liberal American technology firms like Apple and Facebook that operate in China must follow the law and heed the requests of China to remove adverse applications from their store or remove particular content from online pages (p. 62). The concern among Western academics is that regimes like China will expand their technology output and that censorship and surveillance will travel with the proliferation of these technologies (p. 61). The principal means by which the state enacts technological suppression of censored content is via intermediary computers filtering content from the general internet known as firewalls, routers filtering out content or IP connections from other nations, installing software to prevent users from accessing certain content, employing internet police/censors to carry out surveillance manually, coercing internet service providers into acting as censors under threat of criminal or financial sanctions, increasing the cost of accessing services so only a regime-friendly regime elite use the internet, or developing a national internal version of the internet with regulated content (*Milner, 2006, p. 187*). However, repression based on fear of sanction is not the only option available to a government intent on censorship and control. It is often more effective for a government to introduce misinformation, disinformation, and social dysfunction (*Dragu and Lupu, 2017, p. 7*). China has a variety of tools it can utilize to ensure its control and curation of the internet.

There is a concern that governments will increasingly expand their reach toward the format of China's social credit rating system. This technology-based system uses data from China's database on citizen characteristics, live CCTV footage leveraging facial recognition, banking data, and browsing patterns, to identify a complete picture of a citizen. It represents the amalgamation of private and public data including the collectively supplied four-hundred datasets from across thirty administrative bodies impacting every aspect of life within China (*Qiang, 2019, p. 59*). The result of such a system is that all daily-life decisions are coloured by the extent to which they support state ideology because a Chinese citizen's ability to secure credit, travel, and lead a life of meaning and fulfillment depend on compliance with official policy goals. In fact, the government is building special living zones for loyal subjects, including prioritization schemes for accessing public services, the optimization of administrative services, and decrease in transaction costs. '(*Liang et al., 2018, p. 433*). China is developing the world's most sophisticated surveillance and control network and the power and precision of this system is projected to increase as the Communist Party invests in the development of artificial intelligence (*Zheng, 2020, p. 1443*). It was supposed that the opening up of China would tend it toward democracy and freedom as capitalism would drive social progress. However, this has not materialized as the Communist Party has created a version of elite dominated capitalism characterized by continued state control, including in arresting China's most famous technology entrepreneur after he called for reductions in the state's system of financial regulation (*Pearson et al., 2021, p. 211*).

In general, there is debate about the impact of technology on authoritarianism. The internet and communications technologies have enabled a mobilization effect wherein acts of repression, however remote, are recognised and broadcasted around the world (*Dragu and Lupu, 2017, p. 6*). The internet has had the effect of enhancing the power of civil society groups that act in the zone between the state and the citizen such as the work of special interest groups, purpose-driven social movements, and global advocacy networks for key causes (*Luyt, 2003, p. 122*). Another study looked at the internet in reference to whether it empowered activists or autocrats and concluded that "the data indicate that movements toward democracy are more frequent in countries with low internet penetration" (*Rød and Weidmann, 2015, p. 339*). This study concluded that totalitarian states concerned about controlling the spread of information within their borders are more likely to work to speed up the extension of internet coverage (p. 348). These effects of communications technology on liberty are highly dependent on the usership of citizens. A study analyzing the effects of social media on perceptions of electoral fraud in the Russian Federation found that there was increases in perceived fraud only on platforms politicized by opposition elites and not in primary channels (*Reuter and Szakonyi, 2015, p. 48*). In summary, technology works in favor of activists at low levels of development but against them when the state is technologically sophisticated (*Dragu and Lupu, 2017, p. 4*). For this reason, it will be challenging for technology alone to inspire a liberation movement within China.

In conclusion, law and legislation have enabled state authorities to undertake projects of mass surveillance of unprecedented scope and size thus energizing a debate on human rights and privacy. This chapter has served to show how technology-based surveillance efforts have adapted with and accommodated for the culture and legal protections that exist in the United States, Canada, Russia, and China. It has moreover described how surveillance and technology are interconnected with private enterprise and the activities of leading technology companies that both provide private individuals with the ability to undertake surveillance as well as provide a primary means for Western democracies to collect and use personal information for their public objectives. This chapter has situated state surveillance within the anti-terror discourse in an effort to show both that technological surveillance will likely increase in effectiveness and societal penetration given that public safety pressures are insatiable and that technology is a tool essential to the maintenance and extension of state power within the free and unfree world.

REFERENCES

Acemoglu, D., & Robinson, J. (2006). Economic Backwardness in Political Perspective. *American Political Science Review, 100*(1), 115–131. https://doi.org/10.1017/s0003055406062046

Amnesty International. (2021, July 18). *Forensic Methodology Report: How to Catch NSO Group's Pegasus.* Www.amnesty.org. https://www.amnesty.org/en/latest/research/2021/07/forensic-methodology-report-how-to-catch-nso-groups-pegasus/

Amnesty International. (2019, July 24). *"The Great Hack": Cambridge Analytica is just the tip of the iceberg.* Amnesty.org. https://www.amnesty.org/en/latest/news/2019/07/the-great-hack-facebook-cambridge-analytica/

Austin, L. M. (2015). Lawful illegality: What Snowden has taught us about the legal infrastructure of the surveillance state. *Law, privacy and surveillance in Canada in the post-Snowden era,* 103-126.

Banks, Thomas. (2018). Nineteen Eighty-Four: A Treatise on Tyranny. Political Science *Undergraduate Review, 3*(1), 82–88. https://doi.org/10.29173/psur53

Canadian Press. (2018, January 19). *U.S. border guards can search your phone: here are some details on how.* CBC. https://www.cbc.ca/news/science/usa-border-phones-search-1.4494371

CBC. (2019, March). *"The military Google industrial complex": How Silicon Valley cashes in on war technology.* CBC. https://www.cbc.ca/radio/day6/jody-wilson-raybould-s-next-move-the-impeach-o-meter-returns-vaccine-skeptics-olympic-breakdancing-and-more-1.5038274/the-military-google-industrial-complex-how-silicon-valley-cashes-in-on-war-technology-1.5038283

Diamond, L. (2015). *Liberation technology 1. In In search of democracy* (pp. 132-146). Routledge.

Davies, D. (2021). *Facial Recognition And Beyond: Journalist Ventures Inside China's 'Surveillance State'.* [online] NPR.org. Available at: https://www.npr.org/2021/01/05/953515627/facial-recognition-and-beyond-journalist-ventures-inside-chinas-surveillance-sta.

Dixon, R. (2021). Russia's surveillance state still doesn't match China. But Putin is racing to catch up. *Washington Post.* [online] 18 Apr. Available at: https://www.washingtonpost.com/world/europe/russia-facial-recognition-surveillance-navalny/2021/04/16/4b97dc80-8c0a-11eb-a33e-da28941cb9ac_story.html.

Dragu, T., & Lupu, Y. (2017). *Does technology undermine authoritarian governments?.* Working Paper. New York University and George Washington University.

Dragu, T., & Lupu, Y. (2017). Collective Action and Constraints on Repression at the Endgame. *Comparative Political Studies, 51*(8), 1042–1073. https://doi.org/10.1177/0010414017730077

Eneman, M., Ljungberg, J., Raviola, E., & Rolandsson, B. (2022). The sensitive nature of facial recognition: Tensions between the Swedish police and regulatory authorities. *Information Polity,* 1–14. https://doi.org/10.3233/ip-211538

Farrell, H. (2012). The Consequences of the Internet for Politics. *Annual Review of Political Science, 15*(1), 35–52. https://doi.org/10.1146/annurev-polisci-030810-110815

Federal Trade Commission (2019). *FTC Imposes $5 Billion Penalty and Sweeping New Privacy Restrictions on Facebook.* [online] Federal Trade Commission. Available at: https://www.ftc.gov/news-events/news/press-releases/2019/07/ftc-imposes-5-billion-penalty-sweeping-new-privacy-restrictions-facebook.

Gershgorn, D. (2021, March 2). *China's "Sharp Eyes" Program Aims to Surveil 100% of Public Space. Center for Security and Emerging Technology.* https://cset.georgetown.edu/article/chinas-sharp-eyes-program-aims-to-surveil-100-of-public-space/

Google. (n.d.). *Google Transparency Report.* Transparencyreport. google.com. Retrieved June 14, 2022, from https://transparencyreport. google.com/user-data/overview?hl=en&user_requests_report_period=series:requests

Groshek, J. (2009). The Democratic Effects of the Internet, 1994—2003. *International Communication Gazette, 71*(3), 115–136. https://doi. org/10.1177/1748048508100909

Guliani, N.. "The FBI Has Access to over 640 Million Photos of US through Its Facial Recognition Database." *American Civil Liberties Union,* American Civil Liberties Union, 10 June 2019, https://www.aclu. org/blog/privacy-technology/surveillance-technologies/fbi-has-access-over-640-million-photos-us-through.

Harwell, D. and Dou, E. (2020). Huawei tested AI software that could recognize Uighur minorities and alert police, report says. *Washington Post*. [online] 8 Dec. Available at: https://www.washingtonpost.com/technology/2020/12/08/huawei-tested-ai-software-that-could-recognize-uighur-minorities-alert-police-report-says/.

Hellerud, A. (2021, September 8). *Which Governments Are Requesting Your Data The Most?* TechRobot. https://techrobot.com/which-governments-requesting-data-the-most/

Ismi, A. (2013, November 1). *Massive Secret Surveillance in Canada.* Canadian Centre for Policy Alternatives. https://policyalternatives.ca/publications/monitor/massive-secret-surveillance-canada

Khazaeli, S., & Stockemer, D. (2013). The Internet: A new route to good governance. *International Political Science Review, 34*(5), 463–482. https://doi.org/10.1177/0192512113494728

Kostka, G., Steinacker, L., & Meckel, M. (2021). Between security and convenience: Facial recognition technology in the eyes of citizens in China, Germany, the United Kingdom, and the United States. *Public Understanding of Science, 30*(6), 096366252110015. https://doi.org/10.1177/09636625211001555

Liang, F., Das, V., Kostyuk, N., & Hussain, M. M. (2018). Constructing a Data-Driven Society: China's Social Credit System as a State Surveillance Infrastructure. *Policy & Internet, 10*(4), 415–453. https://doi.org/10.1002/poi3.183

Luyt, B. (2003). Digital Divide: Civic Engagement, Information Poverty, and the Internet Worldwide. Pippa Norris. Cambridge, UK: Cambridge University Press, 2001. 303 pp. $60.00 (hardback), $20.00 (paperback). *Social Science Computer Review, 21*(1), 120–123. https://doi.org/10.1177/0894439302238974

Lyon, D. (2014). Surveillance, Snowden, and big data: Capacities, consequences, critique. *Big data & society, 1*(2), 2053951714541861

Marthews, Alex, and Catherine E. Tucker. "Government surveillance and internet search behavior." *Available at SSRN 2412564* (2017).

Michaelsen, M., & Glasius, M. (2018). Authoritarian practices in the digital age—Introduction. *International Journal of Communication, 12,* 7.

Milner, H. V. (2006). The Digital Divide. *Comparative Political Studies, 39*(2), 176–199. https://doi.org/10.1177/0010414005282983

Moscufo, M. (2021, March 11). *Digital artwork sells for record $69 million at Christie's first NFT auction.* NBC News. https://www.nbcnews.com/business/business-news/digital-artwork-sells-record-60-million-christie-s-first-nft-n1260544

Orecchio-Egresitz, L.I., Haven (2022). *Ukraine and Russia have both weaponized facial recognition — in very different ways.* [online] Business Insider. Available at: https://www.businessinsider.com/ukraine-russia-have-both-weaponized-facial-recognition-2022-3.

Policing Project. "The Growing World of Face Recognition Legislation: Our New Guide to Local and National Regulations." *The Policing Project,* The Policing Project, 17 May 2021, https://www.policingproject. org/news-main/2019/10/10/the-growing-world-of-face-recognition-legislation-our-new-guide-to-local-and-national-regulations.

Pearson, M., Rithmire, M., & Tsai, K. S. (2021). Party-State Capitalism in China. *Current History, 120*(827), 207–213. https://doi.org/10.1525/curh.2021.120.827.207

Polyakova, A., & Meserole, C. (2019, August 26). *Exporting digital authoritarianism.* Brookings; Brookings. https://www.brookings.edu/research/exporting-digital-authoritarianism/

Portnoy, E. and McKinney, I. (2021). *Apple's Plan to 'Think Different' About Encryption Opens a Backdoor to Your Private Life.* [online] Electronic Frontier Foundation. Available at: https://www.eff.org/deeplinks/2021/08/apples-plan-think-different-about-encryption-opens-backdoor-your-private-life.

Priest, D. (n.d.). *A UAE agency put Pegasus spyware on phone of Jamal Khashoggi's wife months before his murder, new forensics show.* Washington Post. https://www.washingtonpost.com/nation/interactive/2021/hanan-elatr-phone-pegasus/

Qiang, X. (2019). The Road to Digital Unfreedom: President XI's Surveillance State. *Journal of Democracy, 30*(1), 53–67. https://doi.org/10.1353/jod.2019.0004

Raza, Z. (2019). China's 'political re-education'camps of Xinjiang's Uyghur Muslims. *Asian Affairs, 50*(4), 488-501.

Rea, K. (2013, July 28). *Glenn Greenwald: Low-Level NSA Analysts Have "Powerful and Invasive" Search Tool.* ABC News. https://abcnews. go.com/blogs/politics/2013/07/glenn-greenwald-low-level-nsa-analysts- have-powerful-and-invasive-search-tool/

Reuter, O. J., & Szakonyi, D. (2015). Online social media and political awareness in authoritarian regimes. *British Journal of Political Science, 45*(1), 29-51.

Rød, E. G., & Weidmann, N. B. (2015). Empowering activists or autocrats? The Internet in authoritarian regimes. *Journal of Peace Research, 52*(3), 338–351. https://doi.org/10.1177/0022343314555782

Tréguer, F. (2018). *US technology companies and state surveillance in the post-Snowden context: Between cooperation and resistance* (Doctoral dissertation, CERI).

Welsh, B. C., & Farrington, D. P. (2004). Evidence-based Crime Prevention: The Effectiveness of CCTV. *Crime Prevention and Community Safety, 6*(2), 21–33. https://doi.org/10.1057/palgrave.cpcs.8140184

Wenger, E., Shan, S., Zheng, H., & Zhao, B. Y. (2021). SoK: Anti-Facial Recognition Technology. *arXiv preprint arXiv:2112.04558.*

Wheelehan, N. M. (2019). Make Orwell Fiction Again: Authoritarian Regimes' Use of Surveillance Technology in China and Russia.

Zeng, J. (2020). Artificial intelligence and China's authoritarian governance. *International Affairs, 96*(6). https://doi.org/10.1093/ia/ iiaa172

Ziller, C., & Helbling, M. (2020). Public Support for State Surveillance. *SSRN Electronic Journal.* https://doi.org/10.2139/ssrn.3556953

Zimonjic, P. (2022, February 22). *Most bank accounts frozen under the Emergencies Act are being released, committee hears.* CBC. https://www.cbc.ca/news/politics/emergency-bank-measures-finance-committee-1.6360769

CHAPTER 9 - LEGAL IMPLICATIONS OF ASSISTED REPRODUCTIVE TECHNOLOGY

"If I have seen further than most, it is because I have stood on the shoulders of giants"

- Isaac Newton

Background on Assisted Reproduction Technologies

The world's first IVF-conceived baby, Louise Brown, was born July 25th, 1978 as a result of the work of collaborating gynecologist Patrick Steptoe and scientist Robert Edwards, who were joined later by nurse Jean Purdy (*Brinsden & Brinsden, 2009*). Edwards and Steptoe began working together in 1968, publishing papers on early human in-vitro fertilization (IVF). In 1976, their first patient to become pregnant from IVF was discovered to have an ectopic pregnancy (a nonviable pregnancy occurring outside the main cavity of the uterus) that had to be terminated. However, success occurred soon after with a natural IVF cycle with one egg (or oocyte) fertilized and implanted as an 8-cell embryo resulting in the conception of who would become the so-called "Baby of the Century," Louise Brown. Edwards and Steptoe presented their work at the Royal College of Obstetricians and Gynecologists in London and the American Fertility Society meeting both in 1978 to reportedly standing ovations. They continued their work through the establishment of the first IVF treatment and research clinic, Bourne Hall, in Cambridge, United Kingdom. Robert Edwards was ultimately awarded the Nobel Prize in Physiology or Medicine in 2010 for his contribution in the development of in vitro fertilization (*"The 2010 Nobel Prize in Physiology or Medicine"*, *n.d.*).

In vitro fertilization with embryo transfer (IVF-ET) involves four main components: the acquisition of enough mature ova (or eggs), fertilization of the ova, culture of created embryos, and lastly, implantation in the gestational mother (which can be the biological mother or a surrogate) (*Biggers, 2012*). Each progress was originally detailed in a paper published by Edwards (and the last in collaboration with Steptoe), in the years 1965, 1969, and 1970. IVF is largely considered to be the most successful assisted reproductive technology with widespread uses depending on the patients or intended parent's needs. The entire cycle usually takes up to three weeks, beginning with the use of various medications for ovarian stimulation, oocyte maturation, and to prevent early ovulation (*"In Vitro Fertilization" n.d.*). Blood tests or ultrasound can be used to evaluate the suitability of eggs for retrieval. During the actual retrieval process the patient is sedated and a thin needle is used with an ultrasound guide into the follicles to extract mature eggs through a suction device connected to the needle. For fertilization, sperm and mature eggs can either be introduced directly and incubated together in conventional insemination or a single sperm can be injected into a mature egg in a process known as intracytoplasmic sperm injection (ICSI). For implantation, a catheter is inserted to reach the uterus. This catheter is attached to a syringe containing one to two embryos suspended in fluid, that is then placed in the uterus to achieve a pregnancy.

Artificial Insemination

Artificial insemination (AI) is a common assistive technology today with either a partner's or donor's semen, commonly used in circumstances of male infertility, same-sex couples capable of carrying a child without the use of a surrogate, single women, and to generally increase gamete density for fertilization purposes (*Ombelet & Van Robays, 2015*). Instances of rudimentary insemination have been told through stories over time, but the first officially reported artificial insemination occurred with a dog under the care of Italian physiologist Lazzaro Spallanzani. John Hunter published the first instance of human artificial insemination in 1790, where Hunter's assistant collected semen released during coitus which was kept warm and placed in a syringe to be injected into the vagina. More developed methods for insemination were worked on by Ilya Ivanovich Ivanoff in the late 1890s and early 1900s, although his work mainly consisted of working with farm animals. Milovanov carried Ivanoff's work forward and ended up publishing a paper on artificial insemination in Russia which inspired AI procedures in animal husbandry in Denmark and other countries.

The first medical reports of using AI in humans came from Guttmacher in 1943, Stoughton in 1948, and Kohlberg in 1953. Today, intrauterine artificial insemination (IUI) is a relatively simple procedure–washed and concentrated sperm is placed inside the uterus around the expected time of ovulation with the goal of achieving fertilization and a resulting pregnancy (*"Intrauterine Insemination", n.d.*). Fertility medications can be used alongside IUI as well to increase the likelihood of pregnancy.

Advances in Cryopreservation

Experimentation in sperm freezing techniques were first documented in the 1950s and 60s with "dry ice" techniques and later use of liquid nitrogen which enabled the widespread use of frozen sperm samples in healthcare (*Rozati et al., 2017*). In 1953, the first birth resulting from insemination with frozen sperm (with semen that had been stored in dry ice for a short time period) was reported. The first commercial cryobanks were established in the 1970s, but modern sperm storage cryobanks use nitrogen vapor for reduced risk of cross-contamination in comparison to previously used substances. In 1984, the first birth from a cryopreserved embryo was achieved, with the embryo having been cryopreserved (with development halted) for two months before implantation (*Zeilmaker et al., 1984*). Two years later, the first birth from a cryopreserved oocyte occurred, with there being added difficulties in the freezing process compared to the freezing of male gametes and actual embryos (*Chen, 1986*). Oocyte preservation was initially achieved through slow freezing (with slow cooling rates to induce dehydration of materials); however, new techniques involving vitrification showed later success (*Brambillasca et al., 2013*). Vitrification involves using extremely quick cooling rates to limit ice crystal formation, providing an advantage over slow freezing methods. The first birth from a vitrified egg was reported in 1999.

Egg Donation

Egg donation exists today because of its potential use in IVF-ET pregnancies, and as a result of the nature of this form of procreation it has a significantly shorter history than sperm donation. As would be done in the typical IVF procedure, a female donor must undergo hormone therapy to stimulate maturation of multiple eggs (*"Reproductive Technologies: Surrogacy, and Egg and Sperm Donation", n.d.*). Eggs are later retrieved vaginally with specific instruments and used for this intended purpose. This process has a greater burden on the donor compared to sperm donation, and embryos have been much easier to store frozen than mature and immature eggs.

The first pregnancy conceived using a donated egg was born in 1984 through the work of the Monash IVF clinic in Australia (*"History of Monash IVF", n.d.*). However, this pregnancy resulted from a process that is no longer in use today—the egg donor underwent artificial insemination and the resulting embryo was flushed out of the womb and implanted in the womb of the mother that later birthed the baby.

Genetic Testing

The first attempt at genetically testing embryos produced through assistive technologies is credited to Alan Handyside, the American embryologist, geneticist, and later professor in 1989 (*"Preimplantation Genetic Diagnosis", n.d.*). He first looked for genetic defects associated with cystic fibrosis (which is carried on the X chromosome). In 1990, Handyside pioneered preimplantation genetic diagnosis (PGD) where one or more cells is removed from the embryo three days after fertilization to be biopsied and genetically analyzed, resulting in the first successful pregnancies following any form of genetic testing (*Handyside et al., 1990*). PGD was originally intended to be used for couples at high risk of transmitting a single-gene disorder to their children, allowing parents to choose an embryo less likely to inherit the disorder for implantation (*"Preimplantation Genetic Diagnosis", n.d.*). This technology is most frequently used for three types of inherited diseases: cystic fibrosis and sickle cell anemia which result from single-gene mutations, hemophilia which is a sex-linked disorder, and down syndrome which is a chromosomal abnormality (*"Preimplantation Genetic Diagnosis", n.d.*).

A few years after the initial work with PGD, in 1995, the first births resulting from embryos screened for aneuploidies were reported by medical researcher Yury Vrelinksy and his team (*Verlinsky et al., 1995*). Aneuploid cells contain an abnormal number of chromosomes, thereby disrupting cellular equilibrium and are commonly believed to be the primary cause of early miscarriage (*Hassold & Hunt, 2001*). In screening for the presence of aneuploidies, the ultimate goal of Verlinksy's research group was to increase the number of live births from assistive technologies. This progress came to be known as preimplantation genetic screening and has been used with so-called "geriatric mothers" over the age of 35, women at high risk for miscarriage, women who have experienced multiple failed IVF transfers, and women with partners having low sperm quality (*Mastenbroek et al., 2011*).

Pregnancy Following Uterus Transplantation

In 2014, a Swedish woman who had undergone a uterine transplant and IVF delivered her first child (*Brännström et al., 2015*). The mother was born with functioning ovaries but no uterus, but following a transplant from a living 61-year-old donor who had already had two children, she was able to become pregnant through assistive technologies. The baby was delivered early at 31 weeks due to the mother developing preeclampsia (a pregnancy complication with high blood pressure and potential for maternal organ damage), but was otherwise healthy. At the point of this successful birth, there had been 11 previous uterine transplants without any live births. Today there are ongoing clinical trials at multiple institutions centering on providing women with uterine infertility with the opportunity to become pregnant–a unique cross section between surgical and fertility research (*Johannesson et al., 2021; Kuehn, 2017*). Most healthcare professionals recommend that a transplanted uterus be removed once the patient has finished having children due to potential health complications and necessary medications which leave one immunocompromised.

Canadian Context

In 1980, the first IVF clinic in Canada was established at the University of Laval Hospital (CHUL) through the work of Dr. Jacques Rioux, who first introduced laparoscopy to the country, and IVF researcher Raymond Lambert (*Yuzpe, 2019*). The second IVF clinic, started at the University of British Columbia under the tubal microsurgeron and laparoscologist Dr. Victor Gomel, clinician Christo Zouves, and laboratory director Young Moon, produced the first IVF baby, both conceived, transferred and ultimately delivered in Canada. The baby was born on December 26th, 1983, and was followed 53 weeks later by the first IVF baby in Ontario, born on New Year's Eve, 1984. With a growing number of clinics and children born in Canada through the use of assistive reproductive technologies, public concern over the regulation of processes like IVF rose significantly in the 1990s. An established Royal Commission on Reproductive Technologies issued a report, Proceed with Care, sharing almost 300 recommendations regarding legislation and government action on these technologies. A key takeaway from this report is the desire of the committee to prevent the commodification of fertility-associated technology–something that largely informed the shaping of Canada's stance on matters such as gamete donation and surrogacy.

Assisted Human Reproduction Act

Although assisted reproduction technologies had gained popularity in Canada with a number of specialized clinics operating across the country, legislation surrounding the practice did not come into place until the royal assent of the Assisted Human Reproduction (AHR) Act on March 29th, 2004 (*"Assisted Human Reproduction", n.d.*). This piece of legislation was designed to protect the health and wellbeing of women and children, ensure the ethical treatment of all parties, and maintain human individuality and diversity. A number of changes have been made to the Act since it first came into force, principally changes associated with Quebec's challenge that portions of the Act were unconstitutional based on the infringement of provincial jurisdiction in healthcare (*"Assisted Human Reproduction Act (2004)"*, n.d.). While the Quebec Court of Appeal argued that sections 8-19, 40-53, 60, 61, and 68 were unconstitutional, the Supreme Court of Canada found that only sections 10, 11, 13, 14-18, 40(2-5), and 22(2-3) to actually be unconstitutional. This included legislation surrounding the manipulation of eggs, sperm, or embryos, and the control of assisted reproduction information, data, and licensing. The Act stands today with the remaining sections and additions in regulations over recent years.

Research Restrictions

Under research restrictions related to assisted reproductive technology and resulting reproductive materials in sections 5(1) and 9 of the AHR Act, it is illegal to purposely create a human clone for both research and reproductive purposes (*"Prohibitions Related to Scientific Research and Clinical Applications"*, n.d.). A human clone is defined in this case as an embryo containing two sets of chromosomes from a single human being, whether coming from a person (alive or deceased), a fetus, or embryo. Section 5(1) states specifically that a human embryo cannot be created from cells derived from an embryo or fetus, in accordance with the belief that any child born through AHR should have two adult biological parents. One research application of human cloning is therapeutic cloning, where stem cells are collected and used to treat a disease or illness in the person who was cloned. While countries such as the United States of America, the United Kingdom, and Australia have all made distinctions between therapeutic and reproductive cloning to legalize therapeutic research applications, in Canada it is illegal to intentionally make a human clone for any purpose (*"Prohibitions Related to Scientific Research and Clinical Applications"*, n.d.).

Chimeras and Hybrids

Further reproductive limitations are placed on the creation of both chimeras and hybrids, with lengthy definitions stated in the AHR Act. A chimera is defined as either "an embryo that consists of cells from more than one embryo, fetus, or human being" or "an embryo into which a cell of any nonhuman life form has been introduced" (*"Prohibitions Related to Scientific Research and Clinical Applications", n.d.*). While it is illegal to artificially create a chimera and to use such an embryo for reproductive purposes (section 5(1)(i)), natural and artificial chimeras actually exist outside the context of assisted human reproduction. A recipient of a tissue or organ transplant is considered an artificial chimera because they now have cells in their body from different zygotes (*Madan, 2020*). Natural chimeras can result from various circumstance but namely if two zygotes fuse together extremely early on in pregnancy (even before the formation of embryos) to result in one person (fusion chimera) or if zygote and maternal cells are exchanged across the placental barrier so that both mother and child become microchimeras. Cases of chimerism vary from person-to-person, and many chimeras remain unaware of their status throughout life. However, some serious medical problems can occur especially in cases of immune rejection to bodily tissues arising from the other zygote. Because of the unknown health consequences and a desire to limit certain experimentation with reproductive material, it is illegal to intentionally create chimeras (*"Prohibitions Related to Scientific Research and Clinical Applications", n.d.*).

Hybrids, as established in the AHR Act, contain some reproductive or cellular material from a non-human life form in addition to reproductive material from a human being (*"Prohibitions Related to Scientific Research and Clinical Applications", n.d.*). Section 5(1)(j) of the Act renders the creation of partially non-human embryos illegal for reproductive purposes. While the successful creation of such an embryo is unlikely given current technologies, it remains illegal to attempt to do so. Any non-human DNA is not permitted to be introduced to human reproductive cells or established embryos with the intention to be used for reproduction (both in humans or animals), though to do so for experimentation purposes is allowed. Hybrids are often used in research to improve assistive technologies and for ease in procuring materials and lessened ethical concerns overall.

Sex-selection

A common concern with the rising use of assistive reproductive technologies is the potential control and manipulation that individuals may be able to exert over the reproductive process and any resulting children. In the media this phenomenon has been termed the "designer baby," as parents are able to theoretically use assistive technologies to make a variety of choices about their offspring. In Canada, it is illegal to use an assisted reproductive technology to influence the sex of one's future child (*"Prohibitions Related to Scientific Research and Clinical Applications", n.d.*). Sex selection is only permitted for medical purposes, such as if a certain disease was identified on one chromosome using genetic screening and the only sustainable pregnancy would result from selecting an embryo of one sex over the other. An example of this is Duchenne muscular dystrophy, an X chromosome linked disorder which leads to weakness in muscles close to the center of the body—in the upper arms, legs, and pelvis (*Yiu & Kornberg, 2015*). Since this condition results from a mutation on the X chromosome it is significantly more likely to impact males, as they do not have another X chromosome that could mitigate the impact of Duchenne muscular dystrophy.

Mitochondrial DNA and the "Three-Parent Baby"

As discussed previously in this chapter, technologies like PGS and PGD are utilized in some cases of IVF to limit the likelihood of a child inheriting a genetic disorder, failure of uterus implantation, and/or miscarriage (*Lu et al., 2016*). While it is illegal to take action to influence the sex of one's artificially produced embryos, it is legal under the AHR act to select viable embryos using results from genetic testing technologies (*"Prohibitions Related to Scientific Research and Clinical Applications", n.d.*). In this testing process, DNA is removed from the embryo to be analyzed but it cannot be altered or altered reintroduced to an embryo as it is impermissible to alter the genome of a human being or an in-vitro embryo under Canadian law. This prohibition further prevents direct manipulation for the purpose of so-called "designer babies" but also prevents the removal of disease -causing genes.

The majority of DNA within human cells is nuclear DNA, however in addition to the nuclear genome there is a mitochondrial genome housed within the abundant chemical energy-generating organelle. The mitochondrial genome is unique in its maternal inheritance, circular vs. linear structure (which is how DNA organized into chromosomes arc described), and small size (with the mitochondrial genome being 16,569 DNA base pairs long compared to the nuclear genome with 3.3 billion DNA base pairs) (*Taylor & Turnbull, 2005*). Mitochondrial DNA mutations are more likely with the mitochondrial genome having a 100-fold higher mutation rate. This higher mutation rate has been credited to the fact that mitochondrial DNA replicates more often than nuclear DNA and damage to the mitochondrial DNA from high amounts of reactive oxygen species (*Lawless et al., 2020*). Defects in mitochondrial DNA have been associated with some serious diseases and disorders. Mitochondrial Myopathy, Encephalopathy, Lactic Acidosis, and Stroke-Like Episodes (MELAS) syndrome is an example of such a condition with mutations in the mtDNA gene MT-TL1 (most frequently, though some other mutations have been associated with the condition) causing childhood stroke-like episodes with temporary muscle weakness (*"MELAS Syndrome"*, *n.d.*). MELAS syndrome, because of how mitochondrial DNA is inherited, can only be passed on through maternal lines. Due to the nature of such disorders, mitochondrial replacement technologies have been allowed in some research settings in other countries. With significant unknowns about long-term effects of such therapies, they remain illegal in Canada (*"Prohibitions Related to Scientific Research and Clinical Applications"*, *n.d.*).

Another alteration in the mitochondrial genome is the possibility of creating embryos with mitochondrial DNA from a third individual who did not contribute a set of chromosomes. This phenomenon is often referred to as a "three-parent baby" with the genetic material of a man and two women being used to produce a child through different assistive technologies (*"Three-Parent Baby"*, *n.d.*). A process called ooplasmic transfer was used in the 1990s and early 200s to create the first three-parent babies, where cytoplasm from a healthy donated egg was injected into the primary mother's egg before being fertilized by the father's sperm. New technologies to achieve a three-parent baby have since replaced ooplasmic transfer in the limited ongoing research. In Canada, it remains that one cannot knowingly create embryos with mitochondrial DNA from a source that did not contribute nuclear DNA to the embryo (*"Prohibitions Related to Scientific Research and Clinical Applications"*, *n.d.*).

Embryonic Research Limitations

Research done using human embryos has been highly controversial in public debate. The AHR act allows the use of human embryos in research provided that the embryo is no longer needed by the intended parents and both any gamete donors and the intended parents provide their consent for its use in research (*"Prohibitions Related to Scientific Research and Clinical Applications", n.d.*). Section 10(3)(b) of the Act generally prohibits "obtaining, storing, transferring, destroying, importing, or exporting" human embryos for any non-research related purpose (*"Prohibitions Related to Scientific Research and Clinical Applications", n.d.*). Lab-generated embryos are allowed to be kept in vitro for 14 days, excluding any time in which the embryo is frozen and development is suspended. This 14 day rule was first established by the Ethics Advisory Board of the US Department of Health, Education and Welfare in a 1979 report, which was a difficult stretch of time to sustain an in vitro embryo given the state of assistive technologies at the time (*Appleby & Bredenoord, 2018*). Terminating the use of embryos at two weeks serves to prevent the use of embryos after a "key point of complexity" (*Subbaraman, 2021*). Previous to this point, all the embryonic cells are pluripotent with the ability to become any human cell type. One argument that has been made in this case is that the growing complexity of the embryo and onset of gastrulation makes a unique individual with greater potential for personhood—making research past a certain point of development unethical (*Hyun et al., 2016*). Counter-arguments have been made that embryos used in the research process are not intended to be used in reproduction and thereby have no claim to personhood (*Appleby & Bredenoord, 2018*). Regardless of current debate amongst scientists in the field, Canada maintains a 14 day rule for experimentation and research on human embryos (*"Prohibitions Related to Scientific Research and Clinical Applications", n.d.*).

Limits on the Sale and Purchase of Reproductive Material

The trade of reproductive material and human embryos largely falls under section 7 of the AHR Act. No one in Canada may buy, offer to buy, or advertise their intention to buy donor sperm, eggs, in vitro embryos, or human cells or genes (*"Prohibitions Related to Purchasing Reproductive Material and Purchasing or Selling In Vitro Embryos"*, *n.d.*). In this, no sperm or egg donor may receive payment for their donation and must instead elect to donate their gametes for altruistic reasons. Donors who provide reproductive materials for the sake of research also cannot be paid for their donation. The only monetary provision associated with donating reproductive materials is recovering out-of-pocket costs directly associated with their donation. The AHR Act allows the sale of gametes as long as the seller is not acting on behalf of the original donor, enabling Canadian fertility clinics and sperm banks to charge for various services they provide.

Consent

Free and informed consent is required in advance of any assisted reproductive technology being employed, whether coming from a donor or an intended parent (*"Consent to Use Human Reproductive Material and In Vitro Embryos"*, *n.d.*). Consent, as outlined in the AHR Act, relies on a person being fully competent and able to agree to the circumstances without convincing or promised reward and with adequate information to make their decision. Written consent is required from any sperm or egg donor, while surrogacy requires legal contracts between intended parents and the surrogate mother. Despite giving written consent, donors may choose to overturn their decision and refuse the use of their donated reproductive material if they meet specific time requirements.

Under section 8 of the AHR Act, it was made illegal to collect reproductive material from a deceased person for reproductive use in Canada (*"Consent to Use Human Reproductive Material and In Vitro Embryos"*, *n.d.*). If the deceased person had, previous to their demise, provided written consent for the removal of their reproductive material and its use in reproductive use of one's spouse or common law partner then it would be allowable.

Surrogacy

Surrogacy, the practice where a woman carries and delivers a baby to be raised by another parent(s), can be part of the assisted reproduction process for women unable to sustain a pregnancy, infertile couples, same-sex couples, and others (*Nakash & Herdiman, 2007*). Internationally, two types of surrogacy have been recognized: traditional surrogacy where the surrogates own eggs are fertilized with the selected sperm, typically through artificial insemination, and gestational surrogacy where an IVF-conceived embryo is implanted in the surrogate's uterus.

Surrogacy is covered under section 6 of the AHR act, with it being illegal to pay or offer to pay a woman to be a surrogate mother as well as persuading a person to become one (*"Prohibitions Related to Surrogacy", n.d.*). In this, the intention of the Canadian Government is to ensure that women become surrogates for altruistic reasons rather than coercion or for offered compensation. Like with the regulation of the use of donor eggs and sperm, there has been a demonstrated effort to ensure that people are not taken advantage of for their reproductive material or capabilities. However, the restrictions on surrogacy do not prevent reparations for out-of-pocket expenses associated with a pregnancy nor do they criminalize persons who choose to act as a surrogate mother (*"Prohibitions Related to Surrogacy", n.d.*). Any indirect or disguised payments associated with the agreement between parent(s) and surrogate are illegal and all written contracts must follow national and provincial laws. Another effort to limit any abuse of the reproductive capabilities of women is by increasing the age limit to act as a surrogate to 21 years of age. This differs from the limit of 18 years of age to donate one's gametes for research or reproductive use as established in section 9 of the AHR act (*"Consent to Use Human Reproductive Material and In Vitro Embryos", n.d.*).

Additional regulations regarding the reimbursement of donors and surrogates became law when section 12 came into force on June 9th, 2020 (*"Assisted Human Reproduction", n.d.*). Under this section, surrogates are allowed to be reimbursed for specific expenses outlined in the regulations as well as a guidance document that is not part of the law, granted a receipt is provided. However, it is stated in the guidance document that there is no obligation of the parent(s) to reimburse the surrogate mother (*"Guidance Document: Reimbursement Related to Assisted Human Reproduction Regulations", n.d.*).

Difference in Assisted Reproduction Technology Legislation in the United States

The status of assisted reproduction technologies in the United States of America differs significantly from its northern neighbor, Canada. In summary, there is no comprehensive law pertaining to assisted reproduction in the US but instead a number of governmental agencies that maintain restrictions on medical procedures, the use of specific drugs and therapeutics, and the donation of human cells in accordance with pre-existing laws. Specific legislation focusing on the specifics of assistive reproduction are tasked to individual states and consequently vary in legality, the views of legal parents, and if monetary compensation is allowable. With this variation, several key states have enabled the fertility and reproduction industry to take off in the US– allowing for the controversial commodification of human reproduction.

The Centers for Disease Control and Prevention (CDC)

The Centers for Disease Control and Prevention is a federal agency, first formed in 1946 and focussing today on the threat of infectious diseases, environmental health, and occupational health and safety among other issues in public health (*Parascandola, 1996*). In the context of assisted reproduction in the United States, the CDC collects data from over 440 clinics and uses the information to calculate standardized success rates at each location and provide assisted reproduction users with more knowledge about the clinics (*"National ART Surveillance", n.d.*). It was the Fertility Clinic Success Rate and Certification Act that made it mandatory for each assisted reproduction cycle to be reported to the CDC. The National ART Surveillance System (NASS) established in 2006 collects patient demographics, the medical and obstetric patient history, if there is an official infertility diagnosis and what that diagnosis is, details of the specific assisted reproduction procedure, and the outcome of the cycle. Clinics who do not share their ART data with the CDC are listed in annual reports as "non-reporters" and it is also important to note that multiple cycles for the same patient are unlinked in the final reports. An updated reporting system, NASS 2.0 was launched by the CDC in 2016 to improve upon the quality of data and how it is shared.

The Food and Drug Administration (FDA)

The United States Food and Drug Administration is responsible for protecting public health through monitoring and regulating food products, nutritional supplements, medications, certain medical devices and various biologics. In this, the FDA also controls the approved use of drugs, biological products (such as human gametes), and medical devices relating to assisted reproduction and the screening and testing of any reproductive materials (Adamson, 2002). Included in FDA regulations are strict requirements for gamete donors to have their medical history taken and documented, for there to be identification controls, and for any donated gametes to be free of infectious diseases. Additionally, the FDA mandates inspections of facilities that handle human reproductive tissues.

The Centers for Medicaid Services (CMS)

The Centers for Medicare and Medicaid Services is a federal agency that runs the Medicare program and facilitates Medicaid and multiple health insurance programs in partnership with individual states. The CMS also upholds the Clinical Laboratory Improvement Act which regulates laboratory testing and requires clinical laboratories to meet certain standards before they can proceed with using human tissues in any diagnostic capacity ("Clinical Laboratory Improvement Amendments (CLIA)", n.d.). The CMS details specific CLIA rules and regulations, conducts inspections, and actually issues laboratory certificates while the CDC evaluates laboratory quality improvement through studies, creates technical standards for lab work, and manages the advisory committee to the CLIA.

SART and ASRM

The American Society for Reproductive Medicine (ASRM) is a nonprofit organization that looks at the advancement and practice of reproductive medicine, including assisted reproductive medicine which is overseen by the Society for Assisted Reproductive Technology (SART). With the College of American Pathologists, ASRM provides a laboratory accreditation program for embryology labs, ensuring high quality of standards in such spaces (*"Oversight of Assisted Reproductive Technology", n.d.*). SART monitors member clinics and ensures that they follow ASRM guidelines, properly train staff, and submit their data to the CDC.

Surrogacy Laws by State

The regulation of surrogacy, with no national legislation to act as a guidance, is left to individual states. Because of this divisive regulation, the status of the legality of commercial surrogacy varies significantly across the country from states like California which welcome international clients in addition to California residents to Virginia where altruistic surrogacy is tightly regulated and Louisiana where commercial surrogacy is a criminal offense (*"Commercial Surrogacy in the United States", n.d.*). California law allows for commercial gestational surrogacy contracts with no residency requirement and no limitations on who can act as a surrogate. Pre-birth parentage orders are able to be had in the state, meaning that the intended parents become the legal parents once the child is born. The Assisted Reproduction Law was introduced in 2016 to ensure parental protections regardless of marital status, biologic relation, or sexual orientation of the intended parents and to extend protections further to families using at-home insemination methods (*"California Statutory Forms for Assisted Reproduction", n.d.*). Under California law a person is considered to be a sperm donor if they provided a fertility clinic or sperm bank with a sperm sample, had signed a written contract prior to conception, or if the intended parent(s) have clear and compelling proof that an oral agreement had been made prior to conception–further clarification that favours the role of the intended parents as legal parents. Another reproductive matter that the state of California has tried to account for is ovum sharing, where one partner's eggs are harvested and fertilized before being implanted in the womb of the second partner who carries their partner's biological child. For both parents to be considered the legal parents of the resulting child, the court finds satisfactory evidence that both parents intended the provider of the egg to be a legal parent of the child.

In Virginia, the gestational mother is the legal mother by default and the spouse of the gestational mother is considered the other parent, unless an intended parent is the genetic parent (*"Surrogacy Contracts Permissible", n.d.*). Pre-birth orders are not obtainable in the state and instead intended parents must complete a birth certificate amendment process for their names to be listed on the birth certificate. The surrogate completes the necessary forms, including one relinquishing her parental rights and a statement from the physician involved in the assisted reproduction procedure three days after the birth (*"Surrogacy in Virginia for Surrogates and Parents", n.d.*). Altruistic surrogacy is allowed in Virginia with the surrogate being able to be reimbursed for medical expenses or costs directly related to the surrogacy.

In Louisiana, gestational surrogacy contracts are upheld for intended parents who are married and whose gametes were used via IVF to result in the surrogate pregnancy (*"HB1102", n.d.*). This means that the state will recognize the biological, intended parents as the legal parents of the child and no adoption process is needed following the birth. A surrogacy contract must be signed by the surrogate, her spouse if she is married, and the intended parents and be approved by a Louisiana court before embryo transfer occurs. Louisiana has one of the strictest laws regarding surrogacy in the country, as commercial surrogacy and providing any monetary compensation is illegal and no contact may mandate an abortion in the case of disability, a medical disability, gender discrimination, or to reduce the number of fetuses in the case of multiple pregnancy. The state also places restrictions on who can become a surrogate, unlike California. A surrogate must be between the ages of 25 and 35 and have given birth at least once. In addition, a surrogate is required to undergo two counseling sessions before signing the contract and at least one following the birth.

Legal Issues Arising from Assisted Reproduction Technologies

In discussing assisted human reproduction and established limitations in Canada and guiding organizations and agencies in the United States, there are many legal issues arising from assisted reproduction that have not been discussed. Although this part in the chapter is by no means a complete discussion on legal issues with these technologies, the highlighted examples have been included to provide additional insight into how regulations have changed over time and what issues continue to be debated by policy makers.

The Case of Baby M

Before the advent of IVF and consequent rise of gestational surrogacy, traditional surrogacy occurred with high controversy in the public and legal spheres. One of the best known cases of this in the U.S. is the case of Baby M where William Stern entered into a contract in 1985 with Mary Beth Whitehead where she would be inseminated, carry the resulting child to term, and then terminate her parental rights for $10,000 (*"What the Baby M Case Is Really All About,"* 2017). William Stern's wife, Elizabeth, had mild multiple sclerosis and feared how pregnancy may worsen her condition but the pair wished to be parents and it was important to Mr. Stern to have a biological child because of the losses his family experienced in the Holocaust (*Haberman, 2014*). The arrangement turned incredibly complicated after the birth of a baby girl and the decision of Ms. Whitehead to go against the original contract and attempt to keep the child. The child was issued a birth certificate at the hospital under the name of Sara Elizabeth Whitehead, with the father being listed as Ms. Whitehead's husband (*"First Surrogacy Case - In Re Baby M, 537 A.2d 1227, 109 N.J. 396 (N.J. 02/03/1988)"*, n.d.). Despite her reluctance to part with the child and her claim to having a strong emotional bond, Ms. Whitehead gave the baby to the Sterns who took her home and gave her the name Melissa. Shortly thereafter, Ms. Whitehead went to the Sterns and spoke of her severe mental distress and said that she could not live without the baby– frightened of what the woman might do to herself, the Sterns agreed that Ms. Whitehead could spend a few more days with the child before she surrendered the child wholly to them. However, Ms. Whitehead and her husband instead took the child to Florida alongside their two children. The Sterns sued for enforcement of the surrogacy contract, igniting a legal battle that was the first of its kind in regards to surrogacy in New Jersey and the United States.

Baby M was returned to the custody of the Sterns throughout the legal proceedings with Mrs. Whitehead being granted limited visitations. The first trial was 32 days long, with Judge Sorkow finding that the surrogacy contract was permissible and even protected under the constitution and that in regards to custody, what was in the best interest of the child was her remaining with the Sterns (*"What the Baby M Case Is Really All About", 2017*). However, the Supreme Court of New Jersey disagreed on the state of the contract, stating that the Legislation and corresponding laws were not intended to pertain to surrogacy contracts and that such a contract goes against other public policy (namely related to the compensation for providing a child), making Mr. Stern and Ms. Whitehead's contract invalid in the state (*"First Surrogacy Case - In Re Baby M, 537 A.2d 1227, 109 N.J. 396 (N.J. 02/03/1988)"*, n.d.). Ultimately, the biological parents were deemed the legal parents of Baby M or Melissa Stern, with custody being granted to the more affluent Stern family. Melissa Stern elected to terminate the parental rights of Ms. Whitehead once she reached the age of maturity, and was formally adopted by the mother who raised her, Elizabeth Stern (*NJ Monthly, n.d.*). While the nature of surrogacy and related legal contracts has changed since the 1980s, parental rights remains an issue especially in the context of a parent not being biologically related to their intended child, or cross-border reproductive care because the legislation regarding this assistive technology varies so much across states and between countries.

Cross Border Reproductive Care

With extreme differences in the legality of assisted reproduction internationally, cross-border reproductive care has been a hot button issue since processes like surrogacy became possible through the advent of in-vitro fertilization and has remained an issue with changes in national regulation and navigating differences in countries' legal systems in regards to parentage and citizenship. Although transnational surrogacy is possible, seeking legal recognition of parentage in the intended parent's country of origin is not always possible or a simple process.

Surrogacy was first made legal in India in 2002 under the National Guidelines for the Accreditation, Supervision, and Regulation of ART Clinics, and with relatively minimal restrictions, lower costs, and a seemingly large population of willing women, the country soon became a surrogacy hub for international intended parents (*Bhatia, 2021*). Reports from this surrogacy boom share that many women become surrogates because of the monetary provision which was often equivalent to up to 20 years of labour for lower class women, despite the cost to parents being significantly less than in the U.S. (*Saravanan, 2013*). Furthermore, the lives of many surrogates were disrupted with some living in surrogate group housing, being expected to take extreme caution as to not "cause a miscarriage", and where some surrogates continued to care for the child after birth acting as a nurse and nanny by the intended parent's wishes. With cases of exploitation in the surrogacy industry coming out and issues with some surrogate-born children being unable to travel home with their intended parents (such as the case of Baby Manji Yamada v. the Union of India, where the child remained in India for 3 months before the Japanese government issued a visa on humanitarian grounds), the Indian government made attempts from 2008 to 2014 to pass legislation regulating the practice without any success (*Suresh, 2020; Bhatia, 2021.*). The Surrogacy (Regulation) Bill was introduced by the lower house of Indian Parliament in 2016, and reintroduced in 2019. Under this proposed piece of legislation, surrogacy is only permittable for infertile women who cannot carry a baby to term (requiring a "certificate of essentiality" as proof) and these eligible women must be in a heterosexual marriage for 5 years before pursuing surrogacy (*Sharma, 2014*). Only altruistic surrogacy would be legal for these infertile Indian couples and it is expected that the surrogate would be a "close relative" of the intended parents, between the ages of 25-35, and may only act as a surrogate once (*Gupta & Chaturvedi, 2020*). Parents that attempt to pay a surrogate beyond covering necessary pregnancy-related expenses could face up to 10 years of imprisonment; however, the bill is still controversial for lack of provisions to ensure that women are not exploited. The Bill was officially passed on December 17th, 2021.

Contrary to how surrogacy law has evolved in India, many European countries have yet to approve any type of surrogacy. In Sweden, surrogacy continues to fall under the rules of assisted reproduction under chapters 6 and 7 of the Genetic Integrity Act. While intended parents can seek surrogacy abroad, these agreements made outside the country lack legality in Sweden. By default, under Swedish law the person who gave birth to the child is the legal mother with the mother's spouse sharing in parental responsibilities. The genetic father is seen as the legal father, though a court order may be required, and a partner of the father may apply to adopt the child in a process that usually takes 6-8 months. It is now in place that any child born to a Swedish parent is eligible for citizenship, though paternity needs to be established in cases where the father is a Swedish citizen. In regards to the state of surrogacy in the country, the Swedish National Council on Medical Ethics (SMER) in 2013 found altruistic surrogacy to be an ethical process for reproduction. A 2016 governmental report had the opposite finding–that even altruistic surrogacy arrangements should not be made within the Swedish healthcare system and that foreign determinations of legal parentage should not be recognized.

The Right to Know

One way in which Sweden sets itself apart on the topic of surrogacy and assisted reproduction is its acknowledgement of children's right to know the circumstances of their conception and birth. Under the previously mentioned Genetic Integrity Act, children conceived with the use of donor material have the right to obtain information on the donor once they reach the age of maturity. While gamete donors cannot be anonymous, they are usually unknown to the intended parents and they have no responsibility towards any resulting children.

With growing numbers of children born through assisted human reproduction, the idea of a "right to know" has sparked global conversations and has been considered by some policy makers in select countries. In the U.S., the longstanding standard of anonymity and respect to the donor's autonomy over anything in the child's interest has prevented comprehensive and highly regulated documentation of donors across all 50 states (*Sabatello, 2015*). ASRM can only recommend that a donor's information is collected and kept, and there is minimal incentive for clinics to ensure that donor-provided information is accurate. Conversely, in Australia it has been required that gamete donors consent to being contacted in the future by any resulting children since 2006 (*Hammarberg et al., 2011*). However, with limitations in the ability of clinics to find current contact information for donors the original intention was met with unequal access to donor information across the country. In 2016 Narelle's law was passed, enabling all donor conceived persons to receive information about their donor (*Pennings, 2012*). The legislation's namesake, Narelle Grech, passed from heritable bladder cancer after searching for her donor for 15 years without success. Narelle's law is the first piece of legislation in the world to grant donor-conceived children with information on their genetic parentage, not only going forward in time but retroactively as well. Although the ability to grant information retroactively is limited based on available records, donor-conceived persons now have a right to any information that is known. A notation on donor-conceived children's birth certificates can also alert them to additional information being available if desired.

The "right to know" concept has emerged as people have started to consider the impact of assisted reproduction on the end product, the actual children who grow up to become normal people in society. One's genetic background impacts them in many ways from their sense of identity and culture, to potential family had in half siblings and the family of their genetic parent, to relevant medical history that could allow one to make informed decisions on their care (such as what Narelle Grech was unable to do) (*Pennings, 2012*). There is also concern for the possibility of consanguineous relationships unknowingly occurring, if biological half-siblings are unaware of their relation and if children resulted from such a relationship there could be additional impacts on their health and wellbeing. One approach to eliminating this possibility is restricting the number of families that use reproductive material from a single donor, but there has been no significant effort to limit this in Australia nor many other countries.

Fertility Fraud

Before IVF, artificial insemination was already being widely used to help couples conceive. While patients consented to the use of either an intended parent's sperm or donor sperm for inseminations, there have been cases throughout the world of fertility doctors utilizing their own sperm to impregnate their patients. Before large scale cryobanks were founded and access to frozen sperm samples became widespread, many doctors relied on "fresh" sperm samples which were often from medical students working in adjacent hospitals (*Mroz, 2022*). A lack of regulation and proper donation collection methods, in addition to the initial environment of secrecy surrounding sperm donation enabled many doctors to cross the line in using their own samples.

With the increasing use of direct-to-consumer DNA tests, many children conceived by the use of doctor's sperm or so-called deceived donor children have discovered their genetic origin through related family members also using DNA kits. In May 2015, it became publicly known that the physician Donald Cline from Indianapolis fathered children from inseminations in his clinic during the 70s and 80s–the realization that started with one of his genetic children, Maggie, using 23andMe to find family members (*Madeira, 2020*). Maggie's parents, like many other patients, had been told that either the intended father or a medical student who resembled him would be used to create a child. Instead, almost 100 children have been proven to be biological offspring of Cline's. Cline has since had his medical license revoked, pled guilty to two counts of felony obstruction of justice, and was fined $500.

In Canada, a similar case occurred with Norman Barwin doing wrong in his Ottawa-based practice. Barwin was sued in 1995, 2004, 2006, and 2010 for using an unintended, and therefore unconsented to, sperm sample (*Madeira, 2020*). In 2016 another case was raised against him by Davina and Daniel Dixon and their daughter Rebecca who was found to not be Daniel's biological daughter but instead the child of Norman Barwin. Barwin had his medical license revoked in 2019 and was initially ordered a fine of $10,730 (*Pfeffer, 2021*). A $13 million dollar settlement has since been reached, to be distributed according to "categories of harm" and to cover legal fees for patients of Barwin and their children affected by his medical wrongdoing and create a fund for a DNA database for other patients of his that wish to use it. The first child in each affected family is entitled to $40,000, with each additional child able to receive $10,000. Patients whose sperm samples were entrusted for storage purposes but were actually used to conceive a child are entitled to $25,000 and any resulting children eligible up to $40,000.

Fertility fraud has been met with great upset in the public and especially in affected families. In any healthcare setting, personal autonomy is a primary bioethical principle guiding how we go about treating people. In the infamous Mohr v. Williams case, Dr. Williams operated on Mrs. Mohr's left ear instead of the right ear which she had consented to because he found it to be more diseased than he originally thought (*Madeira, 2020*). When Mrs. Mohr sued Dr. Williams, the Minnesota Supreme Court ruled in favour of Mrs. Mohr, as unconsented actions against her constituted assault and battery. The same principle of autonomy is at play when a doctor uses a different sperm sample, whether that be his own or some other donor's, than what was approved of by the intended parents and especially the women undergoing artificial insemination.

Many states have since introduced specific legislation regarding the consequences for medical staff who knowingly use the wrong sperm sample in insemination, ensuring protections for families impacted by fertility fraud. States such as Indiana, Florida, Texas, Arizona, California, Colorado, Utah, and Arkansas have laws in place against fertility fraud (*Mroz, 2022*). Ohio is one state currently with a proposed bill, House Bill 64, which would make fraudulent assisted reproduction a crime in the state (*"House Bill 64", n.d.*). However, specific legislation on fertility fraud is still lacking in many states with gaps in existing American laws not allowing for the criminal prosecution of at fault doctors. As the insemination process was itself consented to, neither rape nor sexual assault applies. It could also not be considered fraud in the factum, because patients entered into the procedure understanding general risks. Instead, fertility fraud falls under the term fraud of inducement–where consent is given based on false information. Ultimately, patients have a right to not be deceived and their consent is dependent on their access to all the available information in truth.

REFERENCES

Adamson, D. (2002). Regulation of assisted reproductive technologies in the United States. *Fertility and Sterility, 78*(5), 932–942. https://doi.org/10.1016/S0015-0282(02)04199-7

Appleby, J. B., & Bredenoord, A. L. (2018). Should the 14-day rule for embryo research become the 28-day rule? *EMBO Molecular Medicine, 10*(9). https://doi.org/10.15252/emmm.201809437

Assisted human reproduction - Canada.ca. (n.d.). Retrieved May 9, 2022, from https://www.canada.ca/en/health-canada/services/drugs-health-products/biologics-radiopharmaceuticals-genetic-therapies/legislation-guidelines/assisted-human-reproduction.html

Assisted Human Reproduction Act (2004) | The Embryo Project Encyclopedia. (n.d.). Retrieved May 10, 2022, from https://embryo.asu.edu/pages/assisted-human-reproduction-act-2004

Bhatia, S. (2021). *India's new Surrogacy Regulation Bill falls short of protecting bodily autonomy and guaranteeing reproductive liberty | LSE Human Rights.* Retrieved May 18, 2022, from https://blogs.lse.ac.uk/humanrights/2021/04/21/indias-new-surrogacy-regulation-bill-falls-short-of-protecting-bodily-autonomy-and-guaranteeing-reproductive-liberty/F

Biggers, J. D. (2012). IVF and embryo transfer: historical origin and development. *Reproductive Biomedicine Online, 25*(2), 118–127. https://doi.org/10.1016/j.rbmo.2012.04.011

Brambillasca, F., Guglielmo, M. C., Coticchio, G., Mignini Renzini, M., Dal Canto, M., & Fadini, R. (2013). The current challenges to efficient immature oocyte cryopreservation. *Journal of Assisted Reproduction and Genetics, 30*(12), 1531–1539. https://doi.org/10.1007/s10815-013-0112-0

Brännström, M., Johannesson, L., Bokström, H., Kvarnström, N., Mölne, J., Dahm-Kähler, P., Enskog, A., Milenkovic, M., Ekberg, J., Diaz-Garcia, C., Gäbel, M., Hanafy, A., Hagberg, H., Olausson, M., & Nilsson, L. (2015). Livebirth after uterus transplantation. *The Lancet, 385*(9968), 607–616. https://doi.org/10.1016/S0140-6736(14)61728-1

Brinsden, P. R., & Brinsden, P. R. (2009). Thirty years of IVF: the legacy of Patrick Steptoe and Robert Edwards. *Human Fertility (Cambridge, England), 12*(3), 137–143. https://doi.org/10.1080/14647270903176773

California Statutory Forms for Assisted Reproduction (AB 960) - National Center for Lesbian Rights. (n.d.). Retrieved May 17, 2022, from https://www.nclrights.org/get-help/resource/california-statutory-forms-for-assisted-reproduction/

Chen, C. (1986). Pregnancy after human oocyte cryopreservation. *The Lancet, 1*(8486), 884–886. https://doi.org/10.1016/s0140-6736(86)90989-x

Clinical Laboratory Improvement Amendments (CLIA) | FDA. (n.d.). Retrieved May 16, 2022, from https://www.fda.gov/medical-devices/ivd-regulatory-assistance/clinical-laboratory-improvement-amendments-clia

Commercial Surrogacy in the United States | Georgetown Journal of Gender and the Law | Georgetown Law. (n.d.). Retrieved May 17, 2022, from https://www.law.georgetown.edu/gender-journal/commercial-surrogacy-in-the-united-states/

Consent to Use Human Reproductive Material and In Vitro Embryos - Canada.ca. (n.d.). Retrieved May 9, 2022, from https://www.canada.ca/en/health-canada/services/drugs-health-products/biologics-radiopharmaceuticals-genetic-therapies/legislation-guidelines/assisted-human-reproduction/consent-human-reproductive-material-vitro-embryos.html

First Surrogacy Case - In re Baby M, 537 A.2d 1227, 109 N.J. 396 (N.J. 02/03/1988). (n.d.). Retrieved May 17, 2022, from https://biotech.law.lsu.edu/cases/cloning/baby_m.htm

Guidance document: Reimbursement related to Assisted Human Reproduction Regulations - Canada.ca. (n.d.). Retrieved May 9, 2022, from https://www.canada.ca/en/health-canada/programs/consultation-reimbursement-assisted-human-reproduction/document.html

Gupta, A. and Chaturvedi, V. (2020). *The Indian Ban on Commercial Surrogacy - Gender Policy Journal.* Retrieved May 19, 2022, from https://gpj.hkspublications.org/2020/06/19/the-indian-ban-on-commercial-surrogacy/

Haberman, C. (2014). *Baby M and the Question of Surrogate Motherhood - The New York Times.* Retrieved May 17, 2022, from https://www.nytimes.com/2014/03/24/us/baby-m-and-the-question-of-surrogate-motherhood.html

Hammarberg, K., Johnson, L., & Petrillo, T. (2011). Gamete and embryo donation and surrogacy in australia: the social context and regulatory framework. *International Journal of Fertility & Sterility, 4*(4), 176–183.

Handyside, A. H., Kontogianni, E. H., Hardy, K., & Winston, R. M. (1990). Pregnancies from biopsied human preimplantation embryos sexed by Y-specific DNA amplification. *Nature, 344*(6268), 768–770. https://doi.org/10.1038/344768a0

Hassold, T., & Hunt, P. (2001). To err (meiotically) is human: the genesis of human aneuploidy. *Nature Reviews. Genetics, 2*(4), 280–291. https://doi.org/10.1038/35066065

HB1102. (n.d.). Retrieved May 18, 2022, from https://www.legis.la.gov/legis/BillInfo.aspx?s=16RS&b=HB1102&sbi=y

History of Monash IVF | Life Starts Here | Monash IVF. (n.d.). Retrieved May 13, 2022, from https://monashivf.com/why-monash-ivf/history/

House Bill 64 | 134th General Assembly | Ohio House of Representatives. (n.d.). Retrieved May 19, 2022, from https://ohiohouse.gov/legislation/134/hb64

Hyun, I., Wilkerson, A., & Johnston, J. (2016). Embryology policy: Revisit the 14-day rule. *Nature, 533*(7602), 169–171. https://doi.org/10.1038/533169a

Intrauterine insemination (IUI) - Mayo Clinic. (n.d.). Retrieved May 13, 2022, from https://www.mayoclinic.org/tests-procedures/intrauterine-insemination/about/pac-20384722

In vitro fertilization (IVF) - Mayo Clinic. (n.d.). Retrieved March 27, 2022, from https://www.mayoclinic.org/tests-procedures/in-vitro-fertilization/about/pac-20384716

Johannesson, L., Testa, G., Putman, J. M., McKenna, G. J., Koon, E. C., York, J. R., Bayer, J., Zhang, L., Rubeo, Z. S., Gunby, R. T., & Gregg, A. R. (2021). Twelve live births after uterus transplantation in the dallas uterus transplant study. *Obstetrics and Gynecology, 137*(2), 241–249. https://doi.org/10.1097/AOG.0000000000004244

Kuehn, B. M. (2017). US uterus transplant trials under way. *JAMA, 317*(10), 1005. https://doi.org/10.1001/jama.2016.20735

Lawless, C., Greaves, L., Reeve, A. K., Turnbull, D. M., & Vincent, A. E. (2020). The rise and rise of mitochondrial DNA mutations. *Open Biology, 10*(5), 200061. https://doi.org/10.1098/rsob.200061

Lu, L., Lv, B., Huang, K., Xue, Z., Zhu, X., & Fan, G. (2016). Recent advances in preimplantation genetic diagnosis and screening. *Journal of Assisted Reproduction and Genetics, 33*(9), 1129–1134. https://doi. org/10.1007/s10815-016-0750-0

Madan, K. (2020). Natural human chimeras: A review. *European Journal of Medical Genetics, 63*(9), 103971. https://doi.org/10.1016/j. ejmg.2020.103971

Madeira, J. L. (2020). *Understanding Illicit Insemination and Fertility Fraud, from Patient Experience to Legal Reform. 39,* 110.

Mastenbroek, S., Twisk, M., van der Veen, F., & Repping, S. (2011). Preimplantation genetic screening: a systematic review and meta-analysis of RCTs. *Human Reproduction Update, 17*(4), 454–466. https://doi. org/10.1093/humupd/dmr003

MELAS Syndrome - NORD (National Organization for Rare Disorders). (n.d.). Retrieved June 13, 2022, from https://rarediseases.org/rare-diseases/melas-syndrome/

Mroz, J. (2022). *When an Ancestry Search Reveals Fertility Fraud - The New York Times.* Retrieved May 19, 2022, from https://www.nytimes.com/2022/02/28/health/fertility-doctors-fraud-rochester.html

Nakash, A., & Herdiman, J. (2007). Surrogacy. *Journal of Obstetrics and Gynaecology, 27*(3), 246–251. https://doi.org/10.1080/01443610701194788

National ART Surveillance | CDC. (n.d.). Retrieved May 16, 2022, from https://www.cdc.gov/art/nass/index.html

NJ Monthly. (n.d.). Retrieved May 17, 2022, from https://web.archive.org/web/20070526004403/http://www.njmonthly.com/issues/2007/03-Mar/babym.htm

Ombelet, W., & Van Robays, J. (2015). Artificial insemination history: hurdles and milestones. *Facts, Views & Vision in ObGyn, 7*(2), 137–143.

OVERSIGHT OF ASSISTED REPRODUCTIVE TECHNOLOG. (n.d.).

Parascandola, J. (1996). From MCWA to CDC--origins of the Centers for Disease Control and Prevention. *Public Health Reports (Washington, D.C. : 1974), 111*(6), 549–551.

Pennings, G. (2012). How to kill gamete donation: retrospective legislation and donor anonymity. *Human Reproduction, 27*(10), 2881–2885. https://doi.org/10.1093/humrep/des218

Pfeffer, A. (2021). *Disgraced fertility doctor agrees to $13M settlement with families, including 17 "Barwin babies" | CBC News.* Retrieved May 19, 2022, from https://www.cbc.ca/news/canada/ottawa/disgraced-fertility-doctor-agrees-to-13m-settlement-with-families-including-17-barwin-babies-1.6119754

Preimplantation genetic diagnosis | medicine | Britannica. (n.d.). Retrieved May 13, 2022, from https://www.britannica.com/science/preimplantation-genetic-diagnosis

Preimplantation Genetic Diagnosis | The Embryo Project Encyclopedia. (n.d.). Retrieved May 13, 2022, from https://embryo.asu.edu/pages/preimplantation-genetic-diagnosis

Prohibitions related to Purchasing Reproductive Material and Purchasing or Selling In Vitro Embryos - Canada.ca. (n.d.). Retrieved May 10, 2022, from https://www.canada.ca/en/health-canada/services/drugs-health-products/biologics-radiopharmaceuticals-genetic-therapies/legislation-guidelines/assisted-human-reproduction/prohibitions-purchasing-reproductive-material-selling-vitro-embryos.html

Prohibitions related to scientific research and clinical applications - Canada.ca. (n.d.). Retrieved May 10, 2022, from https://www.canada.ca/en/health-canada/services/drugs-health-products/biologics-radiopharmaceuticals-genetic-therapies/legislation-guidelines/assisted-human-reproduction/prohibitions-scientific-research-clinical-applications.html

Prohibitions related to Surrogacy - Canada.ca. (n.d.). Retrieved May 9, 2022, from https://www.canada.ca/en/health-canada/services/drugs-health-products/biologics-radiopharmaceuticals-genetic-therapies/legislation-guidelines/assisted-human-reproduction/prohibitions-related-surrogacy.html

Reproductive Technologies: Surrogacy, and Egg and Sperm Donation (PRB 00-35E). (n.d.). Retrieved May 13, 2022, from https://publications.gc.ca/Collection-R/LoPBdP/BP/prb0035-e.html

Rozati, H., Handley, T., & Jayasena, C. N. (2017). Process and pitfalls of sperm cryopreservation. *Journal of Clinical Medicine, 6*(9). https://doi.org/10.3390/jcm6090089

Sabatello, M. (2015). Regulating gamete donation in the U.S.: ethical, legal and social implications. *Laws, 4*(3), 352–376. https://doi.org/10.3390/laws4030352

Saravanan, S. (2013). An ethnomethodological approach to examine exploitation in the context of capacity, trust and experience of commercial surrogacy in India. *Philosophy, Ethics, and Humanities in Medicine : PEHM, 8,* 10. https://doi.org/10.1186/1747-5341-8-10

Sharma, R. S. (2014). Social, ethical, medical & legal aspects of surrogacy: an Indian scenario. *The Indian Journal of Medical Research, 140 Suppl,* S13-6.

Subbaraman, N. (2021). Limit on lab-grown human embryos dropped by stem-cell body. *Nature, 594*(7861), 18–19. https://doi.org/10.1038/d41586-021-01423-y

Suresh, S. (2020). *Baby Manji Case Analysis and Surrogacy in India - Ex Gratia Law Journal.* Retrieved May 19, 2022, from https://exgratialawjournal.com/blawg/women-and-law/baby-manji-case-analysis-and-surrogacy-in-india/

Surrogacy contracts permissible. (n.d.). Retrieved May 17, 2022, from https://law.lis.virginia.gov/vacode/title20/chapter9/section20-159/

Surrogacy in Virginia for Surrogates and Parents | Circle Surrogacy and Egg Donation. (n.d.). Retrieved May 17, 2022, from https://www.circlesurrogacy.com/surrogacy/surrogacy-by-state/surrogacy-in-virginia

Taylor, R. W., & Turnbull, D. M. (2005). Mitochondrial DNA mutations in human disease. *Nature Reviews. Genetics, 6*(5), 389–402. https://doi.org/10.1038/nrg1606

The 2010 Nobel Prize in Physiology or Medicine - Press release - NobelPrize.org. (n.d.). Retrieved May 11, 2022, from https://www.nobelprize.org/prizes/medicine/2010/press-release/

Three-parent baby | Definition, Process, History, & Facts | Britannica. (n.d.). Retrieved May 10, 2022, from https://www.britannica.com/science/three-parent-baby

Verlinsky, Y., Cieslak, J., Freidine, M., Ivakhnenko, V., Wolf, G., Kovalinskaya, L., White, M., Lifchez, A., Kaplan, B., & Moise, J. (1995). Pregnancies following pre-conception diagnosis of common aneuploidies by fluorescent in-situ hybridization. *Human Reproduction, 10*(7), 1923–1927. https://doi.org/10.1093/oxfordjournals.humrep.a136207

What the Baby M Case Is Really All About. (2017). *Minnesota Journal of Law, 6*(2), 75.

Yiu, E. M., & Kornberg, A. J. (2015). Duchenne muscular dystrophy. *Journal of Paediatrics and Child Health, 51*(8), 759–764. https://doi.org/10.1111/jpc.12868

Yuzpe, A. A. (2019). A brief overview of the history of in vitro fertilization in canada. *Journal of Obstetrics and Gynaecology Canada, 41 Suppl 2,* S334–S336. https://doi.org/10.1016/j.jogc.2019.08.020

Zeilmaker, G. H., Alberda, A. T., van Gent, I., Rijkmans, C. M., & Drogendijk, A. C. (1984). Two pregnancies following transfer of intact frozen-thawed embryos. *Fertility and Sterility, 42*(2), 293–296. https://doi.org/10.1016/s0015-0282(16)48029-5

CHAPTER 10 - PERSONHOOD, ABORTIONS, & EUTHANASIA

"The definition of legal personhood [...] asks us to identify the capabilities of a creature, not its genetic makeup. When we look at the fringes of humanity—such as fetal life, infant life, and the permanently comatose—and the abilities of higher mammals, we see how the definition of legal personhood is not easily mapped directly onto the category of humanity."

- Alexis Dyschkant

Background on Abortion Services

Modern Abortion Technology & Methods

Today, the method for each abortion largely depends on how far along the pregnancy is. The medication abortion method can be used early on in pregnancy, up to 7-9 weeks gestation (*"Methods of Abortion", n.d.*). The most commonly used medications for abortion include oral Mifepristone, which blocks progesterone resulting in the thinning of the uterine lining, and oral Misoprostol, which causes uterine contractions and expulsion of the embryo (*"Medical Abortion", n.d.*). Suction curettage (aspiration), where a tube attached to a suction machine is inserted into the uterus and used to empty the contents of the pregnancy, can be employed from 6-14 weeks gestation (*"Methods of Abortion", n.d.*). This abortion method may also include the prescription of antibiotics to avoid infection of the uterus. The dilation and evacuation method is similar to the suction aspiration process, but some tools are used in addition to suction to remove the contents of the uterus. This method can be used from 12-24 weeks of gestation, and requires additional effort to open the cervix prior to removing uterine contents (this can be done with a natural sponge called laminaria that causes the cervix to stretch as it expands). In advanced pregnancies, labour can be induced as an abortion method. Medications like prostaglandin or oxytocin can trigger contractions and the start of labour, and additional chemicals can be injected into the uterus to ensure that the fetus will not survive delivery. Most women who are induced end up delivering in 10-20 hours, and the likelihood of the fetus surviving increases with the length of gestation.

Abortion in the United States

Up until the mid-19th century, abortion law in most states followed the pre-exisiting English common law–with early abortions being allowable until the point of the "quickening" or when the mother began to feel the movement of the fetus (*Reagan, 1997*). The state of Connecticut was the first to pass any official abortion law in 1821, which criminalized the action of providing noxious substances with the intention of ending a pregnancy, effectively banning medical abortions past the quickening (*Brockell, 2019*). This law came to be because of a scandal arising from the relationship of a minister, Ammi Rogers, and a female congregant, Asenath Smith. When Smith became pregnant, Rogers refused to marry her as he would face judgement in the religious community. Rogers tried both a medication and mechanical form of terminating Smith's pregnancy which both failed before Smith delivered a stillborn child. This case became challenging to handle in Connecticut as there was no statute on abortion–only the common law that did little in practice to regulate abortion. Rogers was eventually charged with sexual assault, spending two years in prison, and the abortion law that arose in the state prosecuted abortion providers and not women who had an abortion.

Laws like these were also seen as "poison-control" laws, as medicines used to trigger miscarriages were often fatal to women in large doses.

New York delivered legislation in 1828 that criminalized many abortions, with termination before the quickening being labelled as a misdemeanor and termination after the quickening being considered second-degree manslaughter (*"Jane ROE, et al., Appellants, v. Henry WADE.", n.d.*). However, the state did allow for "therapeutic" abortions in cases where physcians recommended abortion for the preservation of the life of the mother. By the mid to late-19th century, state abortion laws became more serious with penalties for abortion increasing and mention of the "quickening" process disappearing. By the late 1950s, most jurisdictions banned abortion or only allowed therapeutic ones (with Alabama and the District of Columbia also permitting abortion to "preserve a woman's health" which has broader interpretations than the typical therapeutic abortion).

The American Medical Association

The American Medical Association (AMA), a prestigious organization and lobbying group comprised of physicians and medical students in the United States, first took a negative stance on abortion. For 120 years, the AMA considered abortions unethical and argued against having physicians perform them (*Lyons, 1970*). There was a change in stance in the 1970s, with the AMA recognizing the choice to have an abortion as a decision to be made between a woman and her doctor (*Rovner, 2019*). Controversially in 1997, the AMA endorsed a Republican bill to ban "partial birth abortions" or the dilation and extraction abortion method. Though this method will be discussed later in the chapter, in auditing AMA leadership at the time of that decision, it was found to violate AMA's own policy.

Changes in Select States

Hawaii was the first state to legalize abortion prior to 20 weeks, making it available to women upon request, on March 13th, 1970 (*Smith et al., 1971*). The state required any abortions to be performed by licensed doctors at accredited hospitals, and was allowable to any woman who was living in Hawaii for at least 90 days. In the first year following the legalization of abortion in Hawaii, 3643 women underwent an abortion across the 15 hospital providers (*Diamond et al., 1973*). New York, Alaska, and Washington also repealed their abortion laws in the same year, allowing abortions to be performed under certain time limits. South Carolina and Virginia both repealed their abortion laws in 1971, and Florida changed their abortion law in 1972.

Roe v. Wade

The now iconic Roe v. Wade case started when Norma McCorvey, under the fake name Jane Roe for her own privacy, started federal action against the district attorney, Henry Wade, of her home county in Dallas, Texas. (*"Roe v. Wade", n.d.*). Roe, both unmarried and pregnant, wished to terminate her pregnancy with the aid of a competent physician and argued for her right to have such a procedure in the state of Texas. Feminist lawyers Sarah Weddington and Linda Coffee represented Roe, and two other clients in their own abortion-related cases, at the U.S. District Court for the Northern District of Texas. The District Court ruled in favour of Jane Roe, but against James Hubert Hallford, a licensed physician with two state abortion prosecutions pending against him, and John and Mary Doe, a childless couple that wished to remain so given Mary's "neural chemical" disorder to the point of securing an abortion should she become pregnant (*"Jane ROE, et al., Appellants, v. Henry WADE.", n.d.*). Weddington and Coffee brought the case to the U.S. Supreme Court, as Wade also brought his own appeal to a partial loss to the court. In 1973, the Supreme Court ruled in a 7-2 decision that under the Fourteenth Amendment–that no state shall deny a person's right to life, liberty, and property–a woman is entitled to a right to privacy that includes her choice to have an abortion (*"Fourteenth Amendment"*, n.d.; *"Jane ROE, et al., Appellants, v. Henry WADE."*, n.d.).

Further Case Law on Abortion and State Regulation

In regulating abortion further, several examples of case law have been impactful. Firstly, there is the case of Belotti v. Baird in 1979 where the U.S. Supreme Court ruled that minors do not need the consent of their parents to have an abortion (*"Bellotti v. Baird , 443 U.S. 622 (1979)"* , n.d.). However, parental permission was not waived for minors and the default remains that minors need parental permisson to have a non-emergent abortion, with multiple Justices citing the unique vulnerability of children and their developing critical thinking skills. If a state explicitly requires parental consent for a minor to have an abortion, there must be other processes in place for the minor to gain access to an abortion (for example, by convincing a judge of their ability to make this decision and the need for an abortion, called a judicial waiver option). In the wake of 1988 and 1989 abortion statues in the state of Pennslyvannia, the case of Planned Parenthood v. Casey had the Supreme Court focusing on the concept of "undue burden" (*"Planned Parenthood of Southeastern Pennsylvania v. Casey"*, n.d.). Governor Robert Casey had led the enactment of these new abortion laws which required parental consent for minors seeking an abortion with the aforementioned judicical waiver option included, that abortion clinics provide certain information in advance of women having abortions, that anyone seeking an abortion wait 24 hours before having one, and that married women inform their husbands of their intention to have an abortion. The Court had to scrutinize whether aspects of the law placed undue burden on women seeking an abortion, that is, if the intention was to primarily deter women or complicate the process for them to have an abortion. The result in this case was that the Court upheld all provisions of the statute, excluding the need for a married woman to inform her husband. Many cases relating to undue burden have since arose, particularly in Texas, where lawmakers have tried to limit abortion clinics with strict requirements of their facilities. In Whole Women's Health v. Hellerstedt in 2016, the Supreme Court struck down two provisions of new Texas laws which required that abortion providers have admitting privileges at a hospital near the clinic they operated out of and that clinics have the same standards as surgicial centres (*"Planned Parenthood of Southeastern Pennsylvania v. Casey"*, *n.d.*). Both provisions were found to cause undue burden on patients and abortion providers, and were deemed unconstitutional.

The Texas Heartbeat Act, enacted on May 19th, 2021, and taken effect on September 1st, 2021, is the most limiting abortion ban in place since before Roe V. Wade (*"Bill Text: TX SB8"*, *n.d.*). As its name suggests, the Act bans abortion after cardiac activity of the fetus has been detected via ultrasound, which is usually around six weeks of pregnancy. Although abortion providers in Texas had taken to the Supreme Court for emergency relief before the Heartbeat Act came into effect, the Court denied their request. The Act remains highly controversial in the state and throughout the country, with the term fetal heartbeat not being commonly used in the medical field (*Simmons-Duffin & Feibel, 2022*). An adult heartbeat is heard because of the opening and closing of valves in the heart, but at six weeks gestation, the fetal heart does not yet have these same valves. Some electrical activity is recognized as this "fetal heartbeat" and many are divided on if that is substantive enough to meet the claims in the Act that it is a signal of a viable pregnancy.

Leaked Supreme Court Decision on Roe v. Wade

On May 2nd, 2022, the American news site Politico published a leaked draft of a Supreme Court decision to overturn Roe v. Wade and Planned Parenthood v. Casey (*"Read Justice Alito's Initial Draft Abortion Opinion Which Would Overturn Roe v. Wade"*, *2022*). Written by Justice Samuel Alito, this draft slates the decision of Roe v. Wade to be unconstitutional with no mention of a right to abortion in the American constitution. Overturning Roe v. Wade would allow states without protections in place to take liberties with abortion laws, and many conservative-leaning states are expected to impose strict abortion bans (*Gerstein & Ward, 2022*). Alito also challenges the viability measure as established in Roe v. Wade, which has changed from 24 weeks to 22 weeks under modern debates, discusses the historical disproportional use of abortion in the United States, and attempts to establish that historical abortion laws equated the human fetus as persons. Women of lower socioeconomic status and racialized women have had higher abortion rates than well-off white women in the U.S. (*Dehlendorf et al., 2013*). In the leaked Supreme Court document, Alito argues that the legalization of abortion had a demographic effect on the United States because of the amount of racialized women who have abortions compared to white women in the country. Alito also echoes Justice Amy Coney Barrett's belief that abortion has been made less necessary by new attitudes and widespread social acceptance of pregnancy outside of marriage and a greater demand or desire for adoption (*Gerstein & Ward, 2022*). This leaked Supreme Court majority decision was met with public outcry and a slurry of news publications both within the U.S. and internationally. The decision has brought many self-proclaimed "pro-choice" individuals and organizations to protest across the country and through online platforms though the state of abortion remains uncertain in the U.S. (*"'We Will Not Go Back': Thousands Rally for Abortion Rights across the US"*, *2022*). On June 24th, 2022, the Supreme Court struck down Roe v. Wade, officially ending the constitutional right to abortion (*"Roe v Wade: US Supreme Court ends constitutional right to abortion", 2022*). With this decision, many abortion clinics stopped their services in line with so-called trigger laws, legislation that comes into place immediately after this Supreme Court Decision.

Abortion Services in Canada

Prior to 1969, Canada had much more extreme prohibitions on receiving and providing abortions than its southern neighbour and changes made by the Liberal government in that year only granted abortion access to women experiencing medical complications (*"History of Abortion in Canada", n.d.*). The abortion had to be deemed necessary by committee of doctors, vouching that continuing the pregnancy would risk the mother's life. The following year, a group of Vancouver women started a large-scale protest caravan, driving from the West Coast to Ottawa to protest for the decriminalization of abortion (*Gray, 2020*). The Vancouver women managed to organize a group of around 400-500 women to march on Parliament Hill. Protestors accumulated at 24 Sussex Drive, demonstrating on the front lawn of the Prime Minister's residence. Days later, 40 women made their way into the House of Commons and chained themselves to seats, disrupting activities for the day. Despite the abortion caravan's protest, Canadian abortion laws did not change until 1988.

In 1982, the Canadian Charter of Rights and Freedoms was enacted, establishing and guaranteeing democratic, mobility, equality, and legal rights of all Canadian citizens (*"THE CONSTITUTION ACTS, 1867 to 1982", n.d.*). Under section 7 of the Charter, all persons are said to have a "right to life, liberty, and security" which both acknowledges the importance of human lives and grants individuals respect to their own autonomy (*Section 7 of The Canadian Charter of Rights and*

Freedoms - Pyzer Criminal Lawyers, n.d.). Section 7 has had broad
applications and has touched upon challenges to national policy, such as
in the case of R. v. Morgentaler, which found Canada's abortion law to
be unconstitutional (*"1988 R. v Morgentaler Supreme Court Decision
Moments That Matter: Canadian History Since 1867", n.d.*). Dr. Henry
Morgentaler was a Holocaust survivor and physician who immigrated
to Canada and had become an abortion rights advocate, performing
medically safe, but illegal, abortions for 20 years before bringing his
case to the Supreme Court. Dr. Morgentaler was joined by Dr. Leslie
Frank Smoling and Dr. Robert Scott, who had both helped provide
clinical abortions at Morgentaler's Toronto clinic (where thay were all
charged with violating section 251 of the Criminal Code in 1983). These
doctors all advocated for the ability of women to procure an abortion for
reasons outside their own medical complications, performing abortions
at their own personal risk, and Morgentaler was even previously
sentenced to a year and a half in jail for his failure to comply with
abortion laws in 1975.

In the Supreme Court ruling, all three majority judgements agreed that
the restrictions on medical abortion breached the right of the "security
of the person" under section 7 of the Charter (*"1988 R. v Morgentaler
Supreme Court Decision Moments That Matter: Canadian History Since
1867", n.d.*). Justice Wilson believed that it also violated one's right to
liberty and freedom of conscience and that women held a Charter right
to an abortion, though she was the only judge to believe so. While the
Supreme Court abolished Canada's abortion law in a 5-2 ruling, they did
not establish a right to abortion for women and they did not discuss the
length of protection granted to any fetuses.

With the Supreme Court decision making therapeutic abortions legal,
a case arose in 1989 regarding the state of the rights of the fetus
and in turn the rights of the father of the unborn child (*"Tremblay v.*

Daigle - SCC Cases", n.d.). Chantal Daigle and Jean-Guy Tremblay, both residents of Quebec, were in a sexual relationship from 1988 to 1989 that resulted in Daigle's pregnancy in 1989. Their relationship ended after a physical altercation where Tremblay beat Daigle despite being aware of her pregnancy, and she consequently sought to have an abortion for her own psychological wellbeing and to raise a child in a peaceful environment separate from Tremblay. Tremblay proceeded to try and get an injunction (an equitable judicial remedy such as an order that prevents another person from doing some action) to prevent Daigle from having an abortion, on the grounds that the fetus was a person with a right to life (*"Tremblay v. Daigle - SCC Cases", n.d.*). Daigle eventually left the country to have an abortion performed in the United States, but the Supreme Court continued with a decision despite the fact that the case could have no real effect, or the Canadian legal concept of "mootness," since the abortion had already been had (*"Tremblay v. Daigle - SCC Cases", n.d.*). While Tremblay's argument for the rights of the fetus was grounded in the Canadian and Quebec Charters of Rights and Freedoms and the Civil Code of Quebec, the Court found that the general language used in the Quebec legislation did not grant fetal rights and that there was no case law to base Tremblay's rights over his potential future child.

A new abortion law was proposed in late 1989, intended to come to a parliamentary compromise and resolve the abortion arguement at the federal level (*"Abortion: Constitutional and Legal Developments (89-10E)", n.d.*). However, this proposed law, Bill C-43, would have made abortion a criminal offense again unless it was performed by a medical doctor deeming the woman's health to be threatened. Any self-performed or underground abortions would be made punishable by two years of jailtime. Health in this piece of legislation was said to include physical, mental, and psychological health–creating a potential loophole or space for interpretation of what constituted a threat to a woman's mental or psychological health. While the law was passed in the House of Commons, there was a tie in the Senate resulting in the termination of the bill and its automatic defeat.

Legalization of Medical Abortions

The abortion pill combination of Mifepristone and Misoprostol, considered to be the "gold standard" of medical abortions and has been used in both France and the United States since around the early 2000s, was not approved in Canada until 2015 (*"FAQ: The Abortion Pill Mifegymiso", n.d.*). It is now marketed under the name Mifegymiso® and as of 2017, many provinces cover the cost of Mifegymiso® under existing provincial and territorial health insurance plans (excluding Nunavut). Without any insurance, the cost varies from $300-450 per package. It can be prescribed for up to nine weeks gestation in Canada. While the pill initially needed to be prescribed and administered by a specially-trained physician, this changed in November 2017 when pharmacies were granted the ability to dispense the prescription (*Boynton, 2022*). From the time of this change in regulating the abortion pill to March 2020, 31.4 per cent of all abortions in Ontario were medical abortions (*Schummers et al., 2022*). In a UBC study looking at all the abortions had in Ontario, they found the abortion pill to be a safe and effective prescription with minimal complications–justifying the 2017 changes to how the abortion pill is used in Canada.

Protections Surrounding Abortion Clinics

With the majority of abortions being performed in clinics and not hospital settings throughout both Canada and the United States, protests outside clinics have become increasingly common. The earliest response in the form of passing laws to regulate spaces surrounding abortion clinics came with the 1995 Access to Abortion Services Act in British

Columbia (*"Access to Abortion Services Act"*, *n.d.*). The Act prohibited protest and "sidewalk" interference, covering any attempts of a person to dissuade another from having an abortion or providing concerning information to a person wanting an abortion. In 2018, the Ontario Safe Access to Abortion Services Act came into effect, to protect the "safety, security, health and privacy of persons" seeking to access an abortion or who work in that clinical setting (*"Safe Access to Abortion Services Act"*, *n.d.*). This act established safe access zones surrounding clinics that provide abortion services, as well as the offices and homes of abortion providers. In these zones around clinics, persons cannot attempt to persuade a person against accessing an abortion, attempt to provide information on abortion (including through written word or graphic images), physically interfere with a person accessing the facility or intimidate them or take any photos or videos. Access zones for clinics include the property that the clinic is on and a surrounding area of 50 metres (or up to 150 metres but no more than that). For a first offence of harassment in an access zone, a person can face a fine of up to $5,000 or six months imprisonment.

In the same year in Alberta, the Protecting Choice for Women Accessing Healthcare Act came into effect, which also establishes boundaries for protesters surrounding healthcare facilities that provide abortions (*"Protecting Choice for Women Accessing Health Care Act"*, *n.d.*). It is an offense to carry out forms of harassment or intimidation of a patient or abortion provider, or take photos or video without their consent in established safe zones. In 2020, Nova Scotia's equivalent law, the Protecting Access to Reproductive Health Care Act, came into effect. This law prohibits protesting within a defined zone surrounding healthcare centres and pharmacies and doctors' offices providing medical abortions (*"Nova Scotia Legislature - Bill 242 - Protecting Access to Reproductive Health Care Act"*, *n.d.*).

The Argument of Personhood

At the heart of the case of abortion is a question of the state of the embryo, fetus, and eventually baby. At what point are human offspring considered actual persons? At what point are they entitled to the legal protections awarded to all persons? Varying answers to these questions direct different opinions on whether abortion is permissible, and if it is, under what circumstances and at what points in the pregnancy it remains so. If an embryo is considered a person, then the act of storing them, doing embryonic research, or destroying embryos from research or assisted reproduction becomes unethical. If a fetus is considered a person, then questions arise as to if any mother has the right to end the life of another person and if parental support should begin at conception rather than after a person is born. If birth is the act that marks the transition to personhood, then we are left without guidance on how to treat fetuses and viable fetuses, even those with very high probabilities of survival, do not hold any rights until they are out in the world. If personhood falls at any time other than conception or birth, it becomes difficult to judge a universal start to personhood and all that is included with that status. And if we fail to consider human beings as persons until they are old enough to have substantive reasoning and critical thinking, associating personhood with intellect, then many human beings with disabilities would fail to be considered persons. Ultimately, the personhood argument has implications beyond just abortion–it shapes how we view people in society, how we treat legal matters, and other issues in healthcare.

Viewing the Fetus As Part of the Mother: The Quickening & Other Examples

Whilst the United States remained under British Common Law, the fetus was considered a person after the quickening when the mother first begins to feel the child moving inside her (*Peterfy, 1995*).

Before the quickening, the fetus was seen as part of the mother, not an independent being, so abortions were allowable. The quickening was a developmental measure that was first known by the mother, as movement could only be felt by others placing a hand on her belly later on. In how this process was seen to happen, the mother was considered the best judge of what was happening in her body.

Today, many "pro-life" arguments centre on establishing the fetus as a unique individual with a valuable future like ours. The fetus often differs from the mother in blood type, its own genome that shares 50 per cent of the mother's genetic code, and potentially biological sex if the fetus is male. When the embryo implants into the uterine wall, a process is triggered to halt a key pathway for immune action against foreign bodies, preventing immune cells from harming the fetus (*Nancy et al., 2012*). That this immune feature is needed in pregnancy provides further argumentation that the fetus is not simply part of the mother. Also, one may perish with the other surviving (depending on fetal viability) which establishes separate lives of the child and the mother. Up until the point that a fetus could survive without maternal support, one could argue that the fetus does not have its own self-sustaining life. Judith Jarvis Thomson argued in her well-known article, In Defense of Abortion, that if a kidnapped person was attached to a crtically ill violinist such that their body was keeping the other alive, that the kidnapped person would maintain their right to detach themselves to the detriment of the violinist (*Thomson, 1976*). The case of depending on another for survival raises many more questions, because even if a fetus is granted personhood, does that make another person have to maintain the pregnancy so that the fetus may reach a point of their own independence from the mother? Does the mother have a right to act against the fetus or does this person need to be protected?

Criminal Law Applications of Personhood

Despite there being no complete and formal decision on if a fetus is considered a person, they are often considered to be a person capable of being a victim of various crimes. In the United States, the Unborn Victims of Violence Act made it possible for an embryo or fetus in utero to be considered a legal victim if they are hurt or killed because of any of the 60 listed federal violence crimes (*"H.R. 1997 - 108th Congress (2003-2004)*: Unborn Victims of Violence Act of 2004", n.d.). President George W. Bush signed the act into law on April 1st, 2004, saying that, "any time an expectant mother is a victim of violence, two lives are in the balance, each deserving protection, and each deserving justice. If the crime is murder and the unborn child's life ends, justice demands a full accounting under the law." ("President Bush Signs Unborn Victims of Violence Act of 2004", 2004). Senator John Kerry, the Democrat who ran against Bush in the 2004 election, opposed the bill on the grounds that recognizing the fetus as a human being in this case whilst allowing other women to choose to end their pregnancy created differences in how a fetus is considered (*"Text of an E-Mail from Sen. John Kerry (D-Ma.) on the Unborn Victims of Violence Act"*, 2003). The distinction in this act is that pregnant women, abortion providers, and emergency medical staff are exempt from any prosecution.

Under the Canadian Criminal Code, a child becomes a human being when it has "completely proceeded" from the mother's body regardless of if it has breathed, if it has independent circulation, or if the umbilical cord is cut or not (*"Criminal Code"*, n.d.). It is only considered homicide when a person has caused harm to a child before or during its birth, resulting in its death once it is considered a "human being"— or has been born. Ultimately, this law in Canada leaves certain gaps in legal prosecution for crimes committed against pregnant women. In 2017, Nicholas Baig, a man from Pickering, Ontario, stabbed his separated wife, Arianna Goberdhan, 17 times (*Urback, 2019*). Goberdhan was in her third trimester of pregnancy when she was killed, only 20 days away from her baby's expected arrival. While the baby was considered viable, she was not considered a legal person under Canadian law and consequently her father was only charged for her mother's death. Had the baby lived for any time outside her mother's body, Baig would have been charged with a double homicide rather than serving a sentence for killing one person. While there are numerous other cases in Canada of pregnant women being killed alongside their unborn children, to change the laws would create a new view of personhood that would also shape our perspective on abortion.

Most recently, Bill C-225 or the Protection of Pregnant Women and Their Preborn Children Act was proposed by Cathay Wagantall as a private member's bill in February 2016 (*"Bill C-225 (Historical)"*, n.d.). Although the bill was ultimately defeated in 2019, it was designed to amend the Criminal Code to make it an offense to cause harm or death to an unborn child while attempting to cause harm or death to the mother. It would have also added pregnancy as an aggravating circumstance to a crime for the purpose of impacting the sentencing. The Abortion Rights Coalition of Canada published a position paper against the bill when it was first proposed, as it would establish some fetal rights and was believed to have a potential impact on women's abortion rights (*"ARCC Cannot Support Bill C-225"*, n.d.). The Coalition also cited a need to consider that most pregnant women are killed in cases of domestic violence and that by focusing on charges related to domestic violence, lawmakers could have a greater impact than by focussing on one potential victim of the circumstance.

Live Births and "Partial Birth" Abortions

When the fetus becomes advanced enough in age and development that
suction method abortions are unable to be safely performed, dilation
and extraction methods are instead employed. In Canada, if the fetus is
more than 20 weeks gestation it will be documented as a stillbirth but
if it is less than 20 weeks gestation then it will be considered bodily
discharge (*Hopper, 2013*). If any evidence of life, such as a beating heart
or the movement of voluntary muscles, both a birth and death certificate
must be issued. However, the matter of a live birth from the dilation and
extraction method is a complicated matter in the country, as the fetus
gains personhood status once it lives outside its mother (*"Criminal
Code", n.d.*). Medical staff then have a responsibility to ensure that the
infant is kept comfortable and free of pain until a natural death. To avoid
legal complication, lethal injection can be administered to the fetus prior
to the abortion.

In the United States, laws banning partial birth abortion were passed
by Congress in 1995 and 1997 before being vetoed by then-President
Bill Clinton (*"CQ Almanac Online Edition", n.d.*). The Partial-Birth
Abortion Act was enacted in late 2003, banning late-term dilation and
extraction abortions (*"S.3 - 108th Congress (2003-2004)*: Partial-Birth
Abortion Ban Act of 2003", n.d.). Under this Act, any physician who
performs this type of abortion resulting in the death of a human fetus
can face a fine and/or two years of imprisonment. The term partial birth
abortion is controversial, having been coined by a member of a pro-life
organziation and not being a medically-used term (*Rovner, 2006*). Partial
birth abortion is defined in the Act as an abortion where the fetus is
intentionally delivered vaginally, at least partially, with the intention of
the death of the fetus.

The Case of Euthanasia

Euthanasia, coming from the Greek words "eu" meaning good and "thanatos" meaning death, is the process of ending a person's life to alleviate their suffering (*"Euthanasia", n.d.*). Although typically considered today in the context of bringing about a patient's inevitable death earlier to avoid additional harm to their wellbeing, euthanasia can also encompass passive processes like withdrawing life-supporting devices, and can be self-administered or mediated through the actions of a healthcare provider. Some ethicists even include "mercy killings," where someone kills another without their consent based out of sympathy for their suffering, under the term euthanasia. Ultimately, in a day and age where persons are able to survive longer due to technological and medical advancements, a growing number of people are electing to end their life early despite being able to live longer. While the practice of euthanasia and its legalization is a reflection of the value of autonomy in healthcare, it raises questions as to what restrictions should be placed on the access to euthanasia? What lives still need protecting from the state, in not allowing them euthanasia? And how are healthcare providers able to judge the condition and amount of suffering that makes it permissible to end a human life?

Canada's Medical Assistance in Dying

In February 2015, the Supreme Court deemed sections of the Criminal Code unconstitutional in the Carter v. Canada case as the sections prevented the action of physicians in facilitating the consensual death of another person (*"Medical Assistance in Dying", n.d.*). The sections of the Criminal Code became invalid and the Supreme Court tasked the federal government with creating a new law to regulate euthanasia by June of the following year. Euthanasia came to be legally referred to as Medical Assistance in Dying (MAiD) in Canada with Bill C-14, allowing both physician-administered euthanasia and physician-assisted suicide for eligible adults. Eligible adults included persons over the age of 18 who are capable of making their own medical decisions, who have a "grievous" or "irremediable medical condition," and have made a voluntary request for MAiD free from outside influence and have given their full informed consent to the procedure (*Konder & Christie, 2019*). MAiD is only available to Canadian residents with Canadian healthcare coverage to avoid issues of medical tourism. Advanced directives, a type of formal document that states a patient's desire for medical treatment should they not be able to communicate their wishes themselves, is not legal for use in consenting to MAiD prior to one's decline in condition or cognition. Bill C-7 was introduced in October 2020 before receiving Royal Assent in March 2021, allowing people to receive MAiD even if their death is not "reasonably foreseeable." While only having a mental illness is not currently considered cause enough to have MAiD and will remain so until March 17th, 2023, it will later become available to adults whose primary affliction is depression, bipolar disorder, any personality disorder, schizophrenia, post-traumatic stress disorder or any other mental illness (*Kirkey, 2022*). This decision remains controversial, even among Canadian physicians, as judging when a mental illness will be irremediable is incredibly difficult and there is no scientific evidence that current healthcare providers can reliably determine this point.

Medications Used in Medical Assistance in Dying

Most Canadian MAiD protocols employ kits with fixed amounts of select medications, including an anesthetic (which induces a loss of sensation) and a paralytic, and a secondary kit if needed and the variable inclusion of anxiolytics (which reduce anxiety), analgesics (which provide relief from pain), and cardiotoxic medications (which cause damage to the heart) (*Stukalin et al., 2022*). The Canadian Association of Medical Assistance in Dying Providers and Assessors recommend using 10 mg midazolam (an anxiolytic), 1000 mg propofol (an anesthetic which induces a coma) and either 200 mg rocuronium or 40 mg cisatracurium (which are neuromuscular blockers which prevent respiration). A recent study from January 2022 looking at MAiD deaths in Canada found that the average time from administration of MAiD to legal death was 9 minutes, with times ranging from 1 to 127 minutes. How the medication is delivered is up to the discretion of regulatory bodies in each province or territory and the medical professionals, as it has not been regulated or restricted by the federal government. Bill C-14 made both intravenous-delivered assisted death and oral self-administered MAiD legal, although IV-delivery is most common (*Harty et al., 2019*).

United States

Euthanasia is illegal in most states, while the states of Oregon, Washington D.C., Hawaii, Washington, Maine, Colorado, New Jersey, California, and Vermont all allow physician-assisted suicide in some capacity (*"Euthanasia", n.d.*). Oregon is an especially interesting case with the 1997 Death with Dignity Act allowing palliating persons to choose to self-administer lethal medications (that have been prescribed by a licensed physician) (*"Oregon Health Authority : Oregon's Death with Dignity Act ", n.d.*). By the nature of how assisted-suicide is carried out in the state, persons can choose where they would like to die and when.

Belgium

Euthanasia was legalized in Belgium in 2002, becoming one of a handful of countries to allow assisted dying but behind the Netherlands which was the first official country to do so in 2001 (*Raus et al., 2021; Wise, 2001*). The Belgian Euthanasia Law has been amended twice: once in 2005 to offer legal protection to pharmacists who fill the prescriptions for the lethal medication used by physicians carrying out euthanasia and again in 2014 to make euthanasia available to minors who have a "capacity for discernment", which had been in discussion since 2001 talks of regulating euthanasia (*Raus, 2016; Raus et al., 2021*). The amendment made any minor who requested euthanasia and who was deemed to be conpetant to consent to the act, to be euthanized if they had a "medically futile condition of constant and unbearable physical suffering that cannot be alleviated and that will, within a short period of time, result in death, and results from a serious and incurable disorder caused by illness or accident" (*Raus, 2016*). While euthanasia is allowed in Belgium for adults experiencing extreme physical or psychological suffering, for minors, only physical illness can be reason for considering euthansia (such as having terminal cancer or an incurable physical disability that signifigantly impairs a kid's quality of life). The first child to receive euthanasia in Belgium did so in 2016, having suffered from an incurable disease (*Narayan, 2016*) . No personal details surrounding the child or their condition were made public knowledge. Though only used in a handful of cases, child euthanasia remains controversial around the globe while being generally accepted of by Belgian physicians (*Reingard & Mora, 2020*).

In requesting euthanasia, the adult, emancipated minor, or child with a "capacity for discernment" must make a voluntary decision (free from outside influence) on multiple occasions (*Raus et al., 2021*). They must experience a medical condition with no foreseen likelihood of improvement, experience constant and unbearable suffering that cannot be lessened, and their experience of suffering must be related to an accident or illness. Two physicans must evaluate the euthanasia request separately, and if the cause is of a psychological nature or the person is not facing a terminal condition, the second physician must be a psychiatrist or an expert in their condition. For adults and emancipated minors, euthanasia can also be granted based on advanced directives prepared for if one loses conciousness permanently or lives in a vegetative state (*Raus, 2016*). This is an extremely rare case in Belgium and is not available to other minors. Reports of euthanasia cases occurs after death in Belgium, and is anonymous unless legal doubts are had in reviewing the report provided by the person's primary physician (the second consulted physician does not directly write any component of the report) (*Raus et al., 2021*).

Assisted Suicide in the Context of the Personhood Debate

The legalization of euthanasia and its acceptance in healthcare aligns with trends of respecting patient autonomy over other principles in bioethics. The complications in relation to personhood arise when we look to evaluate the conditions and requirements for receiving medical assistance in dying. For what reasons should a person be allowed to end their life early? Should both physical and mental illnesses justify an early death? Being unable to compare certain experiences and pain felt by individuals further complicates how we look at specific health conditions and consequently if we view them as being eligible for euthanasia. In Canada, only a person themselves can request medical assistance in dying at a point where they have the mental capacity and awareness to consent to the procedure. Allowing others to consent on behalf of the person could create additional ethical issues as it would be allowing someone to choose when another dies which could create potential for abuse by family members or decision makers. Ultimately, a large concern with euthanasia is what the act of deciding to die says about the value of life. However, since it is most commonly used for persons with terminal conditions and who are advanced in age, many trust in euthanasia for it providing people with a "dignified" death on their own terms.

It will be interesting to see how the practice continues to be regulated in the future, alongside advances in healthcare technology and our understanding of human life.

REFERENCES

1988 R. v Morgentaler Supreme Court Decision Moments That Matter: Canadian History Since 1867. (n.d.). Retrieved May 25, 2022, from https://blogs.mcgill.ca/hist203momentsthatmatter/2018/04/179

Abortion: constitutional and legal developments (89-10E). (n.d.). Retrieved May 26, 2022, from https://publications.gc.ca/Collection-R/LoPBdP/CIR/8910-e.htm

Access to Abortion Services Act. (n.d.). Retrieved May 26, 2022, from https://www.bclaws.gov.bc.ca/civix/document/id/lc/statreg/96001_01

ARCC Cannot Support Bill C-225 | Abortion Rights Coalition of Canada. (n.d.). Retrieved June 2, 2022, from https://www.arcc-cdac.ca/arcc-cannot-support-bill-c-225/

Bellotti v. Baird :: 443 U.S. 622 (1979) :: Justia US Supreme Court Center. (n.d.). Retrieved June 1, 2022, from https://supreme.justia.com/cases/federal/us/443/622/

Bill C-225 (Historical) | openparliament.ca. (n.d.). Retrieved June 2, 2022, from https://openparliament.ca/bills/42-1/C-225/

Bill Text: TX SB8 | 2021-2022 | 87th Legislature | Enrolled | LegiScan. (n.d.). Retrieved June 1, 2022, from https://legiscan.com/TX/text/SB8/id/2395961

Boynton, S. (2022). *Abortion pills can be hard to get in Canada. Demand from the U.S. could make it harder - National | Globalnews.ca.* Retrieved May 26, 2022, from https://globalnews.ca/news/8813838/canada-us-abortion-pill-roe-v-wade/

Brockell, G. (2019). *Abortion laws: How a sex scandal led to the first abortion law in Connecticut in 1821 - The Washington Post.* Retrieved May 30, 2022, from https://www.washingtonpost.com/history/2019/05/16/how-sensational-sex-scandal-led-nations-first-abortion-law-years-ago/

CQ Almanac Online Edition. (n.d.). Retrieved June 2, 2022, from https://library.cqpress.com/cqalmanac/document.php?id=cqal97-0000181133

Criminal Code. (n.d.). Retrieved June 2, 2022, from https://laws-lois.justice.gc.ca/eng/acts/C-46/section-223.html

Dehlendorf, C., Harris, L. H., & Weitz, T. A. (2013). Disparities in abortion rates: a public health approach. *American Journal of Public Health, 103*(10), 1772–1779. https://doi.org/10.2105/AJPH.2013.301339

Diamond, M., Palmore, J. A., Smith, R. G., & Steinhoff, P. G. (1973). Abortion in Hawaii. *Family Planning Perspectives, 5*(1), 54–60.

Euthanasia - MU School of Medicine. (n.d.). Retrieved June 6, 2022, from https://medicine.missouri.edu/centers-institutes-labs/health-ethics/faq/euthanasia

Euthanasia | Wex | US Law | LII / Legal Information Institute. (n.d.). Retrieved June 6, 2022, from https://www.law.cornell.edu/wex/euthanasia

FAQ: The Abortion Pill Mifegymiso | Action Canada for Sexual Health and Rights. (n.d.). Retrieved May 26, 2022, from https://www.actioncanadashr.org/resources/factsheets-guidelines/2019-04-06-faq-abortion-pill-mifegymiso

Fourteenth Amendment | Browse | Constitution Annotated | Congress.gov | Library of Congress. (n.d.). Retrieved May 30, 2022, from https://constitution.congress.gov/browse/amendment-14/

Gerstein, J. and Ward, A. (2022) *Supreme Court has voted to overturn abortion rights, draft opinion shows - POLITICO.* Retrieved May 30, 2022, from https://www.politico.com/news/2022/05/02/supreme-court-abortion-draft-opinion-00029473

Gray, C. (2020). *The Abortion Caravan - Canada's History.* Retrieved May 25, 2022, from https://www.canadashistory.ca/explore/books/the-abortion-caravan

H.R.1997 - 108th Congress (2003-2004): Unborn Victims of Violence Act of 2004 | Congress.gov | Library of Congress. (n.d.). Retrieved June 2, 2022, from https://www.congress.gov/bill/108th-congress/house-bill/1997

Harty, C., Chaput, A. J., Trouton, K., Buna, D., & Naik, V. N. (2019). Oral medical assistance in dying (MAiD): informing practice to enhance utilization in Canada. *Canadian Journal of Anaesthesia, 66*(9), 1106–1112. https://doi.org/10.1007/s12630-019-01389-6

History of Abortion in Canada - National Abortion Federation Canada. (n.d.). Retrieved May 24, 2022, from https://nafcanada.org/history-abortion-canada/

Hopper, T. (2013). *Live-birth abortions a grey zone in Canada's criminal code | National Post.* Retrieved June 2, 2022, from https://nationalpost.com/news/canada/born-alive-dead-in-moments-grey-zone-of-live-birth-abortions-a-deep-divide-between-mps-and-physicians

Jane ROE, et al., Appellants, v. Henry WADE. | Supreme Court | US Law | LII / Legal Information Institute. (n.d.). Retrieved May 30, 2022, from https://www.law.cornell.edu/supremecourt/text/410/113

Kirkey, S. (2022). *Canada will soon offer doctor-assisted death to the mentally ill. Who should be eligible?* | *National Post.* Retrieved June 6, 2022, from https://nationalpost.com/health/canada-mental-illness-maid-medical-aid-in-dying

Konder, R. M., & Christie, T. (2019). Medical assistance in dying (maid) in canada: A critical analysis of the exclusion of vulnerable populations. *Healthcare Policy = Politiques de Sante, 15*(2), 28–38. https://doi.org/10.12927/hcpol.2019.26073

Lyons, R. (1970). *Social Reasons Accepted - The New York Times.* Retrieved June 5, 2022, from https://www.nytimes.com/1970/06/26/archives/social-reasons-accepted-abortion-rules-relaxed-by-ama.html

Medical abortion - Mayo Clinic. (n.d.). Retrieved May 26, 2022, from https://www.mayoclinic.org/tests-procedures/medical-abortion/about/pac-20394687

Medical assistance in dying - Canada.ca. (n.d.). Retrieved June 6, 2022, from https://www.canada.ca/en/health-canada/services/medical-assistance-dying.html

Methods of Abortion | SCDHEC. (n.d.). Retrieved May 26, 2022, from https://scdhec.gov/methods-abortion

Nancy, P., Tagliani, E., Tay, C.-S., Asp, P., Levy, D. E., & Erlebacher, A. (2012). Chemokine gene silencing in decidual stromal cells limits T cell access to the maternal-fetal interface. *Science, 336*(6086), 1317–1321. https://doi.org/10.1126/science.1220030

Narayan, C. (2016). *Belgium euthanasia: First child dies | CNN.* Retrieved June 6, 2022, from https://www.cnn.com/2016/09/17/health/belgium-minor-euthanasia/index.html

Nova Scotia Legislature - Bill 242 - Protecting Access to Reproductive Health Care Act. (n.d.). Retrieved May 26, 2022, from https://nslegislature. ca/legc/bills/63rd_2nd/1st_read/b242.htm

Oregon Health Authority : Oregon's Death with Dignity Act : Death with Dignity Act : State of Oregon. (n.d.). Retrieved June 6, 2022, from https:// www.oregon.gov/oha/ph/providerpartnerresources/evaluationresearch/ deathwithdignityact/pages/index.aspx

Peterfy, A. (1995). Fetal viability as a threshold to personhood. A legal analysis. *The Journal of Legal Medicine, 16*(4), 607–636. https://doi. org/10.1080/01947649509510995

Planned Parenthood of Southeastern Pennsylvania v. Casey | Summary, Origins, & Influence | Britannica. (n.d.). Retrieved June 1, 2022, from https://www.britannica.com/event/Planned-Parenthood-of-Southeastern-Pennsylvania-v-Casey

President Bush Signs Unborn Victims of Violence Act of 2004. (2004). Retrieved June 2, 2022, from https://georgewbush-whitehouse.archives. gov/news/releases/2004/04/20040401-3.html

Protecting Choice for Women Accessing Health Care Act - Open Government. (n.d.). Retrieved May 26, 2022, from https://open.alberta. ca/dataset/70120717-096d-401f-83bc-3d5905437218

Raus, K., Vanderhaegen, B., & Sterckx, S. (2021). Euthanasia in belgium: shortcomings of the law and its application and of the monitoring of practice. *The Journal of Medicine and Philosophy, 46*(1), 80–107. https:// doi.org/10.1093/jmp/jhaa031

Raus, K. (2016). The extension of belgium's euthanasia law to include competent minors. *Journal of Bioethical Inquiry, 13*(2), 305–315. https://doi.org/10.1007/s11673-016-9705-5

Read Justice Alito's initial draft abortion opinion which would overturn Roe v. Wade - POLITICO. (2022). Retrieved May 30, 2022, from https://www.politico.com/news/2022/05/02/read-justice-alito-initial-abortion-opinion-overturn-roe-v-wade-pdf-00029504

Reagan, L. (1997). *When Abortion Was a Crime.* University of California Press.

Reingard, R. and Mora, L. (2020). *Child Euthanasia in Belgium - O'Neill : O'Neill.* Retrieved June 6, 2022, from https://oneill.law.georgetown.edu/child-euthanasia-in-belgium/

Roe v Wade: US Supreme Court ends constitutional right to abortion - BBC News. (2022). Retrieved June 27, 2022, from https://www.bbc.com/news/world-us-canada-61928898

Roe v. Wade | Summary, Origins, & Influence | Britannica. (n.d.). Retrieved May 30, 2022, from https://www.britannica.com/event/Roe-v-Wade

Rovner, J. (2006). *"Partial-Birth Abortion": Separating Fact From Spin : NPR.* Retrieved June 1, 2022, from https://www.npr.org/2006/02/21/5168163/partial-birth-abortion-separating-fact-from-spin

Rovner, J. (2019). *AMA Wades Into Abortion Debate With Lawsuit : Shots - Health News : NPR.* Retrieved June 5, 2022, from https://www.npr.org/sections/health-shots/2019/07/02/738100166/american-medical-association-wades-into-abortion-debate-with-lawsuit

S.3 - 108th Congress (2003-2004): Partial-Birth Abortion Ban Act of 2003 | Congress.gov | Library of Congress. (n.d.). Retrieved June 2, 2022, from https://www.congress.gov/bill/108th-congress/senate-bill/3

Safe Access to Abortion Services Act, 2017, S.O. 2017, c. 19, Sched. 1. (n.d.). Retrieved May 26, 2022, from https://www.ontario.ca/laws/statute/17s19

Schummers, L., Darling, E. K., Dunn, S., McGrail, K., Gayowsky, A., Law, M. R., Laba, T.-L., Kaczorowski, J., & Norman, W. V. (2022). Abortion Safety and Use with Normally Prescribed Mifepristone in Canada. *The New England Journal of Medicine, 386*(1), 57–67. https://doi.org/10.1056/NEJMsa2109779

Section 7 of The Canadian Charter of Rights and Freedoms - Pyzer Criminal Lawyers. (n.d.). Retrieved May 25, 2022, from https://www.torontodefencelawyers.com/section-7-canadian-charter-rights-freedoms/

Simmons-Duffin, S. and Feibel, C. (2022). *The Texas Abortion Law Cites "Fetal Heartbeat," But It's Medically Inaccurate : Shots - Health News : NPR.* Retrieved June 1, 2022, from https://www.npr.org/sections/health-shots/2021/09/02/1033727679/fetal-heartbeat-isnt-a-medical-term-but-its-still-used-in-laws-on-abortion

Smith, R. G., Steinhoff, P. G., Diamond, M., & Brown, N. (1971). Abortion in Hawaii: the first 124 days. *American Journal of Public Health, 61*(3), 530–542. https://doi.org/10.2105/ajph.61.3.530

Stukalin, I., Olaiya, O. R., Naik, V., Wiebe, E., Kekewich, M., Kelly, M., Wilding, L., Halko, R., & Oczkowski, S. (2022). Medications and dosages used in medical assistance in dying: a cross-sectional study. *CMAJ Open, 10*(1), E19–E26. https://doi.org/10.9778/cmajo.20200268

Text of an E-Mail from Sen. John Kerry (D-Ma.) on the Unborn Victims of Violence Act | National Right to Life. (2003). Retrieved June 2, 2022, from https://www.nrlc.org/federal/unbornvictims/kerryemailuvva/

THE CONSTITUTION ACTS, 1867 to 1982. (n.d.). Retrieved May 25, 2022, from https://laws-lois.justice.gc.ca/eng/const/page-12.html

Thomson, J. J. (1976). A defense of abortion. In J. M. Humber & R. F. Almeder (Eds.), *Biomedical ethics and the law* (pp. 39–54). Springer US. https://doi.org/10.1007/978-1-4684-2223-8_5

Tremblay v. Daigle - SCC Cases. (n.d.). Retrieved May 26, 2022, from https://scc-csc.lexum.com/scc-csc/scc-csc/en/item/515/index.do

Urback, R. (2019). *Without new abortion laws, there's no way to seek justice for fetal homicide victims: Robyn Urback | CBC News.* Retrieved June 2, 2022, from https://www.cbc.ca/news/opinion/arianna-goberdhan-fetus-homicide-1.5122096

'We will not go back': thousands rally for abortion rights across the US | US news | The Guardian. (2022.). Retrieved June 1, 2022, from https://www.theguardian.com/us-news/2022/may/14/abortion-rights-protests-us-roe-v-wade

Wise, J. (2001). Netherlands, first country to legalize euthanasia. *Bulletin of the World Health Organization, 79*(6), 580.

Woods, M. (2022). *Freedom Convoy: MPP Randy Hillier released after arrest | CTV News.* Retrieved June 15, 2022, from https://ottawa.ctvnews.ca/mpp-randy-hillier-surrenders-to-ottawa-police-to-face-freedom-convoy-related-charges-1.5837294

Yan, Y., Pang, Y., Lyu, Z., Wang, R., Wu, X., You, C., Zhao, H., Manickam, S., Lester, E., Wu, T., & Pang, C. H. (2021). The COVID-19 Vaccines: Recent Development, Challenges and Prospects. *Vaccines, 9*(4). https://doi.org/10.3390/vaccines9040349

CONCLUSION

This book has reviewed a variety of subjects. It began by outlining that Legal research first started with the advent of printing technology and the sharing of case law and other legal documents that generally allowed people in the profession to become more knowledgeable. Current day research capitalizes on computer capability to organize research and recognize patterns in data, freeing up more available time for legal professionals to focus on other tasks rather than the extensive organization of legal research.

It then addressed how the COVID-19 pandemic has affected the Canadian legal system like it has impacted other industries, causing shutdowns and serious delays in handling cases in court. The switch to remote legal practice over phone and video conferencing was met with challenges related to technology use, sufficient connectivity, and complications arising from persons joining a virtual court from their home or inappropriate settings. In looking at the impact of the pandemic on our legal system, this chapter also looked at major case law from the time and the legality of pandemic-related restrictions and vaccines mandates.

The book thereafter discussed that digital evidence consists of evidence of a crime that is digitally captured or contained, such as cell phone records, cell-site location data, computer files, and audio recordings. Today, digital technology has expanded to become so vital in much of our lives, and therefore they can hold unprecedented amounts of evidence of our activities or correspondences. The amount of data an individual's digital devices can reveal about their daily lives makes them useful in court, but rife with privacy concerns and exceptions under protections for private property that are also in place. This chapter describes how digital data is collected, the regulations around collecting digital data lawfully, as well as concerns under legal tests such as Carpenter and Katz.

This book then set out how DNA profiling is a scientific process that creates a visual representation of the unique construction of an individual's DNA. These visuals can be used to compare the DNA left at crime scenes (such as blood or hair) with DNA collected from suspects or already stored in a database of past offenders, hopefully retrieving a "match" between two profiles. This chapter also covers landmark historical cases in DNA forensics (from the immigration case of Andrew Sarbah, to violent crimes such as Colin Pitchfork), the different databases of DNA profiles and their regulations, and the controversies and failures of the process.

Furthermore, the book aimed to describe how technology will impact the private practice of law in transaction management, signature digitalisation, contract review and design, due diligence, and discovery. This book addressed the prospect of smart contracts streamlining conventional areas of legal practice like insurance, corporate governance, and financial services while also potentially forming the basis for the developing of the law of the Metaverse and NFTs.

The book then addressed how body scanning technologies are used in a variety of methods to keep both inmates, staff and visitors safe while in prison facilities. Technology has come a long way and has become safer to use, limiting the harmful effects of ionizing radiation in x-rays to using better methods such as backscatters which rely on safer xray methods. Furthermore, soundwaves have been used to gather information while completing scans reducing risks even more. Body scanning is used in medical application for prisons and in third world countries has the ability to detect endemic illness that are more common in crowded cells. Prisoner identification is achieved by using a variety and combination of biometric methods. It has been concluded that the most accurate and cost effective method in most prisons is the use of fingerprint and palmprint analysis. By using minutiae points an accurate identification can be traced through the IAFIS. For more developed prisons, biometric tracking is being explored by using face identification methods to track prisoner whereabouts, limiting the error rate and manpower needed to effectively track inmates. An important aspect of rehabilitation is the ability to communicate with friends and family. The standard face to face communication method is not always the most effective option in certain prisons, and is a more time consuming process to scan each visitor. By removing the face to face aspect, prison guards have seen an decrease in contraband and increase in socialization. With two methods of video communication the options have opened up for those who previously had travel barriers. Digital messaging is also an option that has created fast more responsive communication with the public using texting and email. Education is the last aspect of prisoner rehabilitation that has directly influenced the reduction of repeat offenders. Working around challenges such as cost and internet access, prisons have overcome these challenges to provide education to their inmates. This not only increases existing education of the offender but encourages study, communication and job accessibility following their incarceration.

The book furthermore considered the impact and operations of the state on surveillance projects in United States, Canada, Russia, and China. The chapter moreover described how surveillance and technology are interconnected with private enterprise and the activities of leading technology companies like Google that both provide private individuals with the ability to undertake surveillance as well as provide a primary means for Western democracies to collect and use personal information for their public objectives.

Next, the book addressed that in today's day and age having children in a process that is not isolated from technology, with parents having access to a variety of fertility treatments from artificial insemination to in-vitro fertilization and surrogacy–the most natural process on earth now has technological implications. As with other areas of emerging research, there are ethical and moral considerations that drive legal restrictions and frameworks that regulate assisted human reproduction. In Canada, anyone who chooses to donate reproductive material or aid other parents by serving as a gestational surrogate must decide to do so for altruistic reasons without being compensated beyond costs they may incur related to their donation.

It finally addressed how abortion and euthanasia remain to be highly debated aspects of healthcare in Canada and in other countries. Advancements in medications and procedures have made abortion more safe for women and have allowed euthanasia to be done without pain, and access to both have increased across Canada in recent times. However, there are many implications with consent and the right to life that impact how abortion and euthansia are regulated in Canada. When fundamental questions on what it means to be alive or to suffer having no definite conclusion, lawmakers must consider how existing law and case law direct action.

ABOUT THE AUTHORS

Mya E. George is a third year Health Sciences student specializing in Child Health at McMaster University. Originally from High River, Alberta, she has always had a love for books and has previously co-authored 8 books with the Antarctic Institute of Canada. Aside from books, Mya enjoys hiking in the Rocky Mountains and fencing on the McMaster Varsity team.

Thomas Banks is a writer with the Antarctic Institute of Canada holding a degree in political science and pursuing legal studies. Previously, he has co-authored two books including To Be or Not To Be Happy: Perspectives on Well-being and The History, Practice, and Future of Cheating Death.

Tim Chapman is currently in his first year of a Masters of Education after graduating with a bachelor's degree in history from the University of Alberta in 2021. Tim has co-authored several books through the Antarctic Institute of Canada including The Nature of the Future: Climate Change, What is the North Pole and A Comprehensive Guide to Stratigraphy.

Kelsey Godard is a Professional Communications graduate specializing in fiction editing. She has previously co-authored several other Antarctic Institute of Canada books, such as What in the World are Covid Vaccines? and Astronomy Through the Ages: An In-Depth Examination.